A Guide to MATLAB

for Beginners and Experienced Users

Brian R. Hunt   Ronald L. Lipsman   Jonathan M. Rosenberg

with Kevin R. Coombes, John E. Osborn, and Garrett J. Stuck

CAMBRIDGE
UNIVERSITY PRESS

PUBLISHED BY THE PRESS SYNDICATE OF THE UNIVERSITY OF CAMBRIDGE
The Pitt Building, Trumpington Street, Cambridge, United Kingdom

CAMBRIDGE UNIVERSITY PRESS
The Edinburgh Building, Cambridge CB2 2RU, UK
40 West 20th Street, New York, NY 10011-4211, USA
10 Stamford Road, Oakleigh, VIC 3166, Australia
Ruiz de Alarcón 13, 28014 Madrid, Spain
Dock House, The Waterfront, Cape Town 8001, South Africa

http://www.cambridge.org

First published 2001

Printed in the United States of America

Typefaces Century Schoolbook 10.5/13 pt. and Avant Garde   *System* LaTeX 2_ε [TB]

A catalog record for this book is available from the British Library.

Library of Congress Cataloging in Publication Data
Hunt, Brian R.
    A guide to MATLAB : for beginners and experienced users / Brian R. Hunt,
Ronald L. Lipsman, Jonathan M. Rosenberg with Kevin R. Coombes, John E.
Osborn, Garrett J. Stuck.
        p.   cm.
    Includes bibliographical references and index.
    ISBN 0-521-80380-2 – ISBN 0-521-00859-X (pb.)
    1. MATLAB.   2. Numerical analysis – Data processing.   I. Lipsman, Ronald L.
II. Rosenberg, J. (Jonathan), 1951–   III. Title
QA297 H86   2001
519.4′0285′53042 – dc21   00-068880

ISBN 0521 80380 2 hardback
ISBN 0521 00859 X paperback

Contents at a Glance

v

A Guide to MATLAB

This book is a short, focused introduction to MATLAB, a comprehensive software system for mathematics and technical computing. It will be useful to both beginning and experienced users. It contains concise explanations of essential MATLAB commands, as well as easily understood instructions for using MATLAB's programming features, graphical capabilities, and desktop interface. It also includes an introduction to SIMULINK, a companion to MATLAB for system simulation.

Written for MATLAB 6, this book can also be used with earlier (and later) versions of MATLAB. This book contains worked-out examples of applications of MATLAB to interesting problems in mathematics, engineering, economics, and physics. In addition, it contains explicit instructions for using MATLAB's Microsoft Word interface to produce polished, integrated, interactive documents for reports, presentations, or online publishing.

This book explains everything you need to know to begin using MATLAB to do all these things and more. Intermediate and advanced users will find useful information here, especially if they are making the switch to MATLAB 6 from an earlier version.

Brian R. Hunt is an Associate Professor of Mathematics at the University of Maryland. Professor Hunt has coauthored four books on mathematical software and more than 30 journal articles. He is currently involved in research on dynamical systems and fractal geometry.

Ronald L. Lipsman is a Professor of Mathematics and Associate Dean of the College of Computer, Mathematical, and Physical Sciences at the University of Maryland. Professor Lipsman has coauthored five books on mathematical software and more than 70 research articles. Professor Lipsman was the recipient of both the NATO and Fulbright Fellowships.

Jonathan M. Rosenberg is a Professor of Mathematics at the University of Maryland. Professor Rosenberg is the author of two books on mathematics (one of them coauthored by R. Lipsman and K. Coombes) and the coeditor of *Novikov Conjectures, Index Theorems, and Rigidity*, a two-volume set from the London Mathematical Society Lecture Note Series (Cambridge University Press, 1995).

Contents

⋆ indicates an advanced chapter or section that can be skipped on a first reading.

Preface

MATLAB is an integrated technical computing environment that combines numeric computation, advanced graphics and visualization, and a high-level programming language.

— www.mathworks.com/products/matlab

That statement encapsulates the view of *The MathWorks, Inc.*, the developer of MATLAB®. MATLAB 6 is an ambitious program. It contains hundreds of commands to do mathematics. You can use it to graph functions, solve equations, perform statistical tests, and do much more. It is a high-level programming language that can communicate with its cousins, e.g., FORTRAN and C. You can produce sound and animate graphics. You can do simulations and modeling (especially if you have access not just to basic MATLAB but also to its accessory SIMULINK®). You can prepare materials for export to the World Wide Web. In addition, you can use MATLAB, in conjunction with the word processing and desktop publishing features of Microsoft Word®, to combine mathematical computations with text and graphics to produce a polished, integrated, and interactive document.

A program this sophisticated contains many features and options. There are literally hundreds of useful commands at your disposal. The MATLAB help documentation contains thousands of entries. The standard references, whether the MathWorks User's Guide for the product, or any of our competitors, contain myriad tables describing an endless stream of commands, options, and features that the user might be expected to learn or access.

MATLAB is more than a fancy calculator; it is an extremely useful and versatile tool. Even if you only know a little about MATLAB, you can use it to accomplish wonderful things. The hard part, however, is figuring out which of the hundreds of commands, scores of help pages, and thousands of items of documentation you need to look at to start using it quickly and effectively.

That's where we come in.

Why We Wrote This Book

The goal of this book is to get you started using MATLAB successfully and quickly. We point out the parts of MATLAB you need to know without overwhelming you with details. We help you avoid the rough spots. We give you examples of real uses of MATLAB that you can refer to when you're doing your own work. And we provide a handy reference to the most useful features of MATLAB. When you're finished reading this book, you will be able to use MATLAB effectively. You'll also be ready to explore more of MATLAB on your own.

You might not be a MATLAB expert when you finish this book, but you will be prepared to become one — if that's what you want. We figure you're probably more interested in being an expert at your own specialty, whether that's finance, physics, psychology, or engineering. You want to use MATLAB the way we do, as a tool. This book is designed to help you become a proficient MATLAB user as quickly as possible, so you can get on with the business at hand.

Who Should Read This Book

This book will be useful to complete novices, occasional users who want to sharpen their skills, intermediate or experienced users who want to learn about the new features of MATLAB 6 or who want to learn how to use SIMULINK, and even experts who want to find out whether we know anything they don't.

You can read through this guide to learn MATLAB on your own. If your employer (or your professor) has plopped you in front of a computer with MATLAB and told you to learn how to use it, then you'll find the book particularly useful. If you are teaching or taking a course in which you want to use MATLAB as a tool to explore another subject — whether in mathematics, science, engineering, business, or statistics — this book will make a perfect supplement.

As mentioned, we wrote this guide for use with MATLAB 6. If you plan to continue using MATLAB 5, however, you can still profit from this book. Virtually all of the material on MATLAB commands in this book applies to both versions. Only a small amount of material on the MATLAB interface, found mainly in Chapters 1, 3, and 8, is exclusive to MATLAB 6.

How This Book Is Organized

In writing, we drew on our experience to provide important information as quickly as possible. The book contains a short, focused introduction to MATLAB. It contains practice problems (with complete solutions) so you can test your knowledge. There are several illuminating sample projects that show you how MATLAB can be used in real-world applications, and there is an entire chapter on troubleshooting.

The core of this book consists of about 75 pages: Chapters 1–4 and the beginning of Chapter 5. Read that much and you'll have a good grasp of the fundamentals of MATLAB. Read the rest — the remainder of the Graphics chapter as well as the chapters on M-Books, Programming, SIMULINK and GUIs, Applications, MATLAB and the Internet, Troubleshooting, and the Glossary — and you'll know enough to do a great deal with MATLAB.

Here is a detailed summary of the contents of the book.

Chapter 1, *Getting Started*, describes how to start MATLAB on different platforms. It tells you how to enter commands, how to access online help, how to recognize the various MATLAB windows you will encounter, and how to exit the application.

Chapter 2, *MATLAB Basics*, shows you how to do elementary mathematics using MATLAB. This chapter contains the most essential MATLAB commands.

Chapter 3, *Interacting with MATLAB*, contains an introduction to the MATLAB Desktop interface. This chapter will introduce you to the basic window features of the application, to the small program files (M-files) that you will use to make most effective use of the software, and to a simple method (diary files) of documenting your MATLAB sessions. After completing this chapter, you'll have a better appreciation of the breadth described in the quote that opens this preface.

Practice Set A, *Algebra and Arithmetic*, contains some simple problems for practicing your newly acquired MATLAB skills. Solutions are presented at the end of the book.

Chapter 4, *Beyond the Basics*, contains an explanation of the finer points that are essential for using MATLAB effectively.

Chapter 5, *MATLAB Graphics*, contains a more detailed look at many of the MATLAB commands for producing graphics.

Practice Set B, *Calculus, Graphics, and Linear Algebra*, gives you another chance to practice what you've just learned. As before, solutions are provided at the end of the book.

Chapter 6, *M-Books*, contains an introduction to the word processing and desktop publishing features available when you combine MATLAB with Microsoft Word.

Chapter 7, *MATLAB Programming*, introduces you to the programming features of MATLAB. This chapter is designed to be useful both to the novice programmer and to the experienced FORTRAN or C programmer.

Chapter 8, *SIMULINK and GUIs*, consists of two parts. The first part describes the MATLAB companion software SIMULINK, a graphically oriented package for modeling, simulating, and analyzing dynamical systems. Many of the calculations that can be done with MATLAB can be done equally well with SIMULINK. If you don't have access to SIMULINK, skip this part of Chapter 8. The second part contains an introduction to the construction and deployment of graphical user interfaces, that is, GUIs, using MATLAB.

Chapter 9, *Applications*, contains examples, from many different fields, of solutions of real-world problems using MATLAB and/or SIMULINK.

Practice Set C, *Developing Your MATLAB Skills*, contains practice problems whose solutions use the methods and techniques you learned in Chapters 6–9.

Chapter 10, *MATLAB and the Internet*, gives tips on how to post MATLAB output on the Web.

Chapter 11, *Troubleshooting*, is the place to turn when anything goes wrong. Many common problems can be resolved by reading (and rereading) the advice in this chapter.

Next, we have *Solutions to the Practice Sets*, which contains solutions to all the problems from the three practice sets. The *Glossary* contains short descriptions (with examples) of many MATLAB commands and objects. Though not a complete reference, it is a handy guide to the most important features of MATLAB. Finally, there is a complete *Index*.

Conventions Used in This Book

We use distinct fonts to distinguish various entities. When new terms are first introduced, they are typeset in an *italic* font. Output from MATLAB is typeset in a `monospaced typewriter` font; commands that you type for interpretation by MATLAB are indicated by a **boldface** version of that font. These commands and responses are often displayed on separate lines as they would be in a MATLAB session, as in the following example:

```
>> x = sqrt(2*pi + 1)

x =

     2.697
```

Selectable menu items (from the menu bars in the MATLAB Desktop, figure windows, etc.) are typeset in a **boldface** font. Submenu items are separated from menu items by a colon, as in **File : Open....** Labels such as the names of windows and buttons are quoted, in a "regular" font. File and folder names, as well as Web addresses, are printed in a `typewriter` font. Finally, names of keys on your computer keyboard are set in a SMALL CAPS font.

We use four special symbols throughout the book. Here they are together with their meanings.

☞ *Paragraphs like this one contain cross-references to other parts of the book or suggestions of where you can skip ahead to another chapter.*

⇨ **Paragraphs like this one contain important notes. Our favorite is "Save your work frequently." Pay careful attention to these paragraphs.**

✓ Paragraphs like this one contain useful tips or point out features of interest in the surrounding landscape. You might not need to think carefully about them on the first reading, but they may draw your attention to some of the finer points of MATLAB if you go back to them later.

Paragraphs like this discuss features of MATLAB's Symbolic Math Toolbox, used for *symbolic* (as opposed to *numerical*) calculations. If you are not using the Symbolic Math Toolbox, you can skip these sections.

Incidentally, if you are a student and you have purchased the MATLAB Student Version, then the Symbolic Math Toolbox and SIMULINK are automatically included with your software, along with basic MATLAB. Caution: *The Student Edition of MATLAB*, a different product, does not come with SIMULINK.

About the Authors

We are mathematics professors at the University of Maryland, College Park. We have used MATLAB in our research, in our mathematics courses, for presentations and demonstrations, for production of graphics for books and for the Web, and even to help our kids do their homework. We hope that you'll find MATLAB as useful as we do and that this book will help you learn to use it quickly and effectively. Finally, we would like to thank our editor, Alan Harvey, for his personal attention and helpful suggestions.

Chapter 1

Getting Started

In this chapter, we will introduce you to the tools you need to begin using MATLAB effectively. These include: some relevant information on computer platforms and software versions; installation and location protocols; how to launch the program, enter commands, use online help, and recover from hangups; a roster of MATLAB's various windows; and finally, how to quit the software. We know you are anxious to get started using MATLAB, so we will keep this chapter brief. After you complete it, you can go immediately to Chapter 2 to find concrete and simple instructions for the use of MATLAB. We describe the MATLAB interface more elaborately in Chapter 3.

Platforms and Versions

It is likely that you will run MATLAB on a PC (running Windows or Linux) or on some form of UNIX operating system. (The developers of MATLAB, *The MathWorks, Inc.*, are no longer supporting Macintosh. Earlier versions of MATLAB were available for Macintosh; if you are running one of those, you should find that our instructions for Windows platforms will suffice for your needs.) Unlike previous versions of MATLAB, version 6 looks virtually identical on Windows and UNIX platforms. For definitiveness, we shall assume the reader is using a PC in a Windows environment. In those very few instances where our instructions must be tailored differently for Linux or UNIX users, we shall point it out clearly.

⇨ **We use the word Windows to refer to all flavors of the Windows operating system, that is, Windows 95, Windows 98, Windows 2000, Windows Millennium Edition, and Windows NT.**

This book is written to be compatible with the current version of MATLAB, namely version 6 (also known as Release 12). The vast majority of the MATLAB commands we describe, as well as many features of the MATLAB interface (M-files, diary files, M-books, etc.), are valid for version 5.3 (Release 11), and even earlier versions in some cases. We also note that the differences between the Professional Version and the Student Version (not the Student Edition) of MATLAB are rather minor and virtually unnoticeable to the new, or even mid-level, user. Again, in the few instances where we describe a MATLAB feature that is only available in the Professional Version, we highlight that fact clearly.

Installation and Location

If you intend to run MATLAB on a PC, especially the Student Version, it is quite possible that you will have to install it yourself. You can easily accomplish this using the product CDs. Follow the installation instructions as you would with any new software you install. At some point in the installation you may be asked which *toolboxes* you wish to include in your installation. Unless you have severe space limitations, we suggest that you install any that seem of interest to you or that you think you might use at some point in the future. We ask only that you be sure to include the *Symbolic Math Toolbox* among those you install. If possible, we also encourage you to install SIMULINK, which is described in Chapter 8.

Depending on your version you may also be asked whether you want to specify certain directory (i.e., folder) locations associated with Microsoft Word. If you do, you will be able to run the *M-book* interface that is described in Chapter 6. If your computer has Microsoft Word, we strongly urge you to include these directory locations during installation.

If you allow the default settings during installation, then MATLAB will likely be found in a directory with a name such as `matlabR12` or `matlab_SR12` or `MATLAB` — you may have to hunt around to find it. The subdirectory `bin\win32`, or perhaps the subdirectory `bin`, will contain the executable file `matlab.exe` that runs the program, while the current working directory will probably be set to `matlabR12\work`.

Starting MATLAB

You start MATLAB as you would any other software application. On a PC you access it via the **Start** menu, in **Programs** under a folder such as **MatlabR12** or **Student MATLAB**. Alternatively, you may have an icon set up that enables you to start MATLAB with a simple double-click. On a UNIX machine, generally you need only type `matlab` in a terminal window, though you may first have to find the `matlab/bin` directory and add it to your path. Or you may have an icon or a special button on your desktop that achieves the task.

⇨ **On UNIX systems, you should not attempt to run MATLAB in the background by typing `matlab &`. This will fail in either the current or older versions.**

However you start MATLAB, you will briefly see a window that displays the MATLAB logo as well as some MATLAB product information, and then a *MATLAB Desktop* window will launch. That window will contain a title bar, a menu bar, a tool bar, and five embedded windows, two of which are hidden. The largest and most important window is the *Command Window* on the right. We will go into more detail in Chapter 3 on the use and manipulation of the other four windows: the *Launch Pad*, the *Workspace browser*, the *Command History* window, and the *Current Directory browser*. For now we concentrate on the Command Window to get you started issuing MATLAB commands as quickly as possible. At the top of the Command Window, you may see some general information about MATLAB, perhaps some special instructions for getting started or accessing help, but most important of all, a line that contains a prompt. The prompt will likely be a double caret (>> or ≫). If the Command Window is "active", its title bar will be dark, and the prompt will be followed by a cursor (a vertical line or box, usually blinking). That is the place where you will enter your MATLAB commands (see Chapter 2). If the Command Window is not active, just click in it anywhere. Figure 1-1 contains an example of a newly launched MATLAB Desktop.

⇨ **In older versions of MATLAB, for example 5.3, there is no integrated Desktop. Only the Command Window appears when you launch the application. (On UNIX systems, the terminal window from which you invoke MATLAB becomes the Command Window.) Commands that we instruct you to enter in the Command Window inside the Desktop for version 6 can be entered directly into the Command Window in version 5.3 and older versions.**

Typing in the Command Window

Click in the Command Window to make it active. When a window becomes active, its titlebar darkens. It is also likely that your cursor will change from

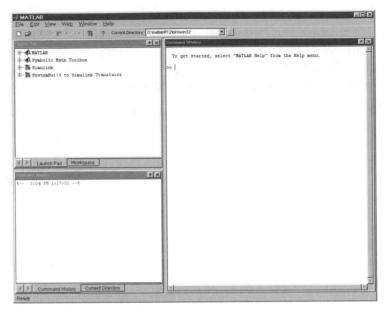

Figure 1-1: A MATLAB Desktop.

outline form to solid, or from light to dark, or it may simply appear. Now you can begin entering commands. Try typing **1+1**; then press ENTER or RETURN. Next try **factor(123456789)**, and finally **sin(10)**. Your MATLAB Desktop should look like Figure 1-2.

Online Help

MATLAB has an extensive online help mechanism. In fact, using only this book and the online help, you should be able to become quite proficient with MATLAB.

You can access the online help in one of several ways. Typing **help** at the command prompt will reveal a long list of topics on which help is available. Just to illustrate, try typing **help general**. Now you see a long list of "general purpose" MATLAB commands. Finally, try **help solve** to learn about the command **solve**. In every instance above, more information than your screen can hold will scroll by. See the *Online Help* section in Chapter 2 for instructions to deal with this.

There is a much more user-friendly way to access the online help, namely via the MATLAB *Help Browser*. You can activate it in several ways; for example, typing either **helpwin** or **helpdesk** at the command prompt brings it up.

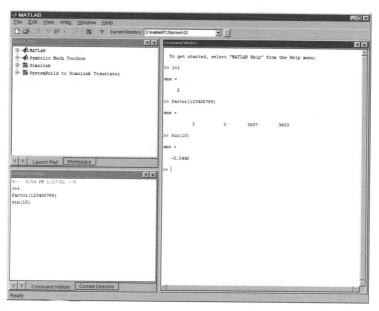

Figure 1-2: Some Simple Commands.

Alternatively, it is available through the menu bar under either **View** or **Help**. Finally, the question mark button on the tool bar will also invoke the Help Browser. We will go into more detail on its features in Chapter 2 — suffice it to say that as in any hypertext browser, you can, by clicking, browse through a host of command and interface information. Figure 1-3 depicts the *MATLAB Help Browser*.

☞ **If you are working with MATLAB version 5.3 or earlier, then typing** `help`, `help general`, **or** `help solve` **at the command prompt will work as indicated above. But the entries** `helpwin` **or** `helpdesk` **call up more primitive, although still quite useful, forms of help windows than the robust** *Help Browser* **available with version 6.**

If you are patient, and not overly anxious to get to Chapter 2, you can type **demo** to try out MATLAB's demonstration program for beginners.

Interrupting Calculations

If MATLAB is hung up in a calculation, or is just taking too long to perform an operation, you can usually abort it by typing CTRL+C (that is, hold down the key labeled CTRL, or CONTROL, and press C).

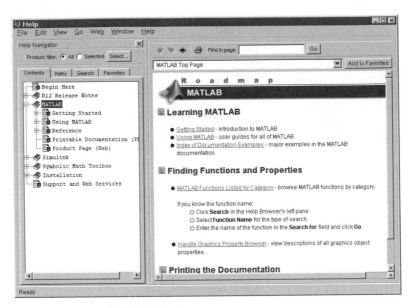

Figure 1-3: The MATLAB Help Browser.

MATLAB Windows

We have already described the MATLAB Command Window and the Help Browser, and have mentioned in passing the Command History window, Current Directory browser, Workspace browser, and Launch Pad. These, and several other windows you will encounter as you work with MATLAB, will allow you to: control files and folders that you and MATLAB will need to access; write and edit the small MATLAB programs (that is, M-files) that you will utilize to run MATLAB most effectively; keep track of the variables and functions that you define as you use MATLAB; and design graphical models to solve problems and simulate processes. Some of these windows launch separately, and some are embedded in the Desktop. You can dock some of those that launch separately inside the Desktop (through the **View**:**Dock** menu button), or you can separate windows inside your MATLAB Desktop out to your computer desktop by clicking on the curved arrow in the upper right.

These features are described more thoroughly in Chapter 3. For now, we want to call your attention to the other main type of window you will encounter; namely graphics windows. Many of the commands you issue will generate graphics or pictures. These will appear in a separate window. MATLAB documentation refers to these as *figure windows*. In this book, we shall also call them graphics windows. In Chapter 5, we will teach you how to generate and manipulate MATLAB graphics windows most effectively.

☞ *See Figure 2-1 in Chapter 2 for a simple example of a graphics window.*

⇨ **Graphics windows cannot be embedded into the MATLAB Desktop.**

Ending a Session

The simplest way to conclude a MATLAB session is to type **quit** at the prompt. You can also click on the special symbol that closes your windows (usually an × in the upper left- or right-hand corner). Either of these may or may not close all the other MATLAB windows (which we talked about in the last section) that are open. You may have to close them separately. Indeed, it is our experience that leaving MATLAB-generated windows around after closing the MATLAB Desktop may be hazardous to your operating system. Still another way to exit is to use the **Exit MATLAB** option from the **File** menu of the Desktop. *Before* you exit MATLAB, you should be sure to save any variables, print any graphics or other files you need, and in general clean up after yourself. Some strategies for doing so are addressed in Chapter 3.

Chapter 2

MATLAB Basics

In this chapter, you will start learning how to use MATLAB to do mathematics. You should read this chapter at your computer, with MATLAB running. Try the commands in a MATLAB Command Window as you go along. Feel free to experiment with variants of the examples we present; the best way to find out how MATLAB responds to a command is to try it.

☞ *For further practice, you can work the problems in* Practice Set A. *The* Glossary *contains a synopsis of many MATLAB operators, constants, functions, commands, and programming instructions.*

Input and Output

You input commands to MATLAB in the MATLAB Command Window. MATLAB returns output in two ways: Typically, text or numerical output is returned in the same Command Window, but graphical output appears in a separate graphics window. A sample screen, with both a MATLAB Desktop and a graphics window, labeled Figure No. 1, is shown in Figure 2–1.

To generate this screen on your computer, first type `1/2 + 1/3`. Then type `ezplot('x^3 - x')`.

✓ While MATLAB is working, it may display a "wait" symbol — for example, an hourglass appears on many operating systems. Or it may give no visual evidence until it is finished with its calculation.

Arithmetic

As we have just seen, you can use MATLAB to do arithmetic as you would a calculator. You can use "**+**" to add, "**-**" to subtract, "*****" to multiply, "**/**" to divide,

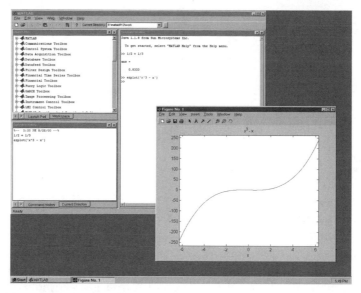

Figure 2-1: MATLAB Output.

and "^" to exponentiate. For example,

```
>> 3^2 - (5 + 4)/2 + 6*3
```

```
ans =
    22.5000
```

MATLAB prints the answer and assigns the value to a *variable* called **ans**. If you want to perform further calculations with the answer, you can use the variable **ans** rather than retype the answer. For example, you can compute the sum of the square and the square root of the previous answer as follows:

```
>> ans^2 + sqrt(ans)
```

```
ans =
    510.9934
```

Observe that MATLAB assigns a new value to **ans** with each calculation. To do more complex calculations, you can assign computed values to variables of your choosing. For example,

```
>> u = cos(10)
```

```
u =
    -0.8391
```

```
>> v = sin(10)

v =
    -0.5440

>> u^2 + v^2

ans =
     1
```

MATLAB uses double-precision floating point arithmetic, which is accurate to approximately 15 digits; however, MATLAB displays only 5 digits by default. To display more digits, type **format long**. Then all subsequent numerical output will have 15 digits displayed. Type **format short** to return to 5-digit display.

MATLAB differs from a calculator in that it can do *exact* arithmetic. For example, it can add the fractions 1/2 and 1/3 symbolically to obtain the correct fraction 5/6. We discuss how to do this in the section *Symbolic Expressions, Variable Precision, and Exact Arithmetic* on the next page.

Algebra

Using MATLAB's Symbolic Math Toolbox, you can carry out algebraic or symbolic calculations such as factoring polynomials or solving algebraic equations. Type **help symbolic** to make sure that the Symbolic Math Toolbox is installed on your system.

To perform symbolic computations, you must use **syms** to declare the variables you plan to use to be symbolic variables. Consider the following series of commands:

```
>> syms x y
>> (x - y)*(x - y)^2

ans =
(x-y)^3
>> expand(ans)
```

```
ans =
x^3-3*x^2*y+3*x*y^2-y^3
>> factor(ans)

ans =
(x-y)^3
```

✓ Notice that symbolic output is left-justified, while numeric output is indented. This feature is often useful in distinguishing symbolic output from numerical output.

Although MATLAB makes minor simplifications to the expressions you type, it does not make major changes unless you tell it to. The command **expand** told MATLAB to multiply out the expression, and **factor** forced MATLAB to restore it to factored form.

MATLAB has a command called **simplify**, which you can sometimes use to express a formula as simply as possible. For example,

```
>> simplify((x^3 - y^3)/(x - y))

ans =
x^2+x*y+y^2
```

✓ MATLAB has a more robust command, called **simple**, that sometimes does a better job than **simplify**. Try both commands on the trigonometric expression **sin(x)*cos(y) + cos(x)*sin(y)** to compare — you'll have to read the online help for **simple** to completely understand the answer.

Symbolic Expressions, Variable Precision, and Exact Arithmetic

As we have noted, MATLAB uses floating point arithmetic for its calculations. Using the Symbolic Math Toolbox, you can also do exact arithmetic with symbolic expressions. Consider the following example:

```
>> cos(pi/2)

ans =
    6.1232e-17
```

The answer is written in floating point format and means 6.1232×10^{-17}. However, we know that $\cos(\pi/2)$ is really equal to 0. The inaccuracy is due to the fact that typing **pi** in MATLAB gives an approximation to π accurate to about 15 digits, not its exact value. To compute an exact answer, instead of an approximate answer, we must create an exact *symbolic* representation of $\pi/2$ by typing **sym('pi/2')**. Now let's take the cosine of the symbolic representation of $\pi/2$:

```
>> cos(sym('pi/2'))

ans =
0
```

This is the expected answer.

The quotes around **pi/2** in **sym('pi/2')** create a *string* consisting of the characters **pi/2** and prevent MATLAB from evaluating **pi/2** as a floating point number. The command **sym** converts the string to a symbolic expression.

The commands **sym** and **syms** are closely related. In fact, **syms x** is equivalent to **x = sym('x')**. The command **syms** has a lasting effect on its argument (it declares it to be symbolic from now on), while **sym** has only a temporary effect unless you assign the output to a variable, as in **x = sym('x')**.

Here is how to add 1/2 and 1/3 symbolically:

```
>> sym('1/2') + sym('1/3')

ans =
5/6
```

Finally, you can also do *variable-precision arithmetic* with **vpa**. For example, to print 50 digits of $\sqrt{2}$, type

```
>> vpa('sqrt(2)', 50)

ans =
1.4142135623730950488016887242096980785696718753769
```

⇒ **You should be wary of using sym or vpa on an expression that MATLAB must evaluate before applying variable-precision arithmetic. To illustrate, enter the expressions 3^45, vpa(3^45), and vpa('3^45'). The first gives a floating point approximation to the answer, the second — because MATLAB only carries 16-digit precision in its floating point evaluation of the exponentiation — gives an answer that is correct only in its first 16 digits, and the third gives the exact answer.**

☞ *See the section* Symbolic and Floating Point Numbers *in Chapter 4 for details about how MATLAB converts between symbolic and floating point numbers.*

Managing Variables

We have now encountered three different classes of MATLAB data: floating point numbers, strings, and symbolic expressions. In a long MATLAB session it may be hard to remember the names and classes of all the variables you have defined. You can type **whos** to see a summary of the names and types of your currently defined variables. Here's the output of **whos** for the MATLAB session displayed in this chapter:

```
>> whos
  Name   Size      Bytes    Class
  ans    1 x 1      226      sym object
  u      1 x 1        8      double array
  v      1 x 1        8      double array
  x      1 x 1      126      sym object
  y      1 x 1      126      sym object
Grand total is 58 elements using 494 bytes
```

We see that there are currently five assigned variables in our MATLAB session. Three are of class "sym object"; that is, they are symbolic objects. The variables **x** and **y** are symbolic because we declared them to be so using **syms**, and **ans** is symbolic because it is the output of the last command we executed, which involved a symbolic expression. The other two variables, **u** and **v**, are of class "double array". That means that they are arrays of double-precision numbers; in this case the arrays are of size 1×1 (that is, scalars). The "Bytes" column shows how much computer memory is allocated to each variable.

Try assigning **u = pi, v = 'pi'**, and **w = sym('pi')**, and then type **whos** to see how the different data types are described.

The command **whos** shows information about all defined variables, but it does not show the values of the variables. To see the value of a variable, simply type the name of the variable and press ENTER or RETURN.

MATLAB commands expect particular classes of data as input, and it is important to know what class of data is expected by a given command; the help text for a command usually indicates the class or classes of input it expects. The wrong class of input usually produces an error message or unexpected output. For example, type **sin('pi')** to see how unexpected output can result from supplying a string to a function that isn't designed to accept strings.

To clear all defined variables, type **clear** or **clear all**. You can also type, for example, **clear x y** to clear only **x** and **y**.

You should generally clear variables before starting a new calculation. Otherwise values from a previous calculation can creep into the new

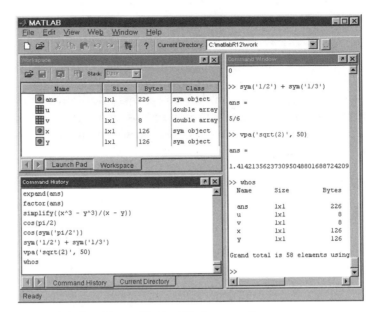

Figure 2-2: Desktop with the Workspace Browser.

calculation by accident. Finally, we observe that the *Workspace browser* presents a graphical alternative to **whos**. You can activate it by clicking on the Workspace tab, by typing **workspace** at the command prompt, or through the **View** item on the menu bar. Figure 2-2 depicts a Desktop in which the Command Window and the Workspace browser contain the same information as displayed above.

Errors in Input

If you make an error in an input line, MATLAB will beep and print an error message. For example, here's what happens when you try to evaluate **3u^2**:

```
>> 3u^2
??? 3u^2
     |
Error: Missing operator, comma, or semicolon.
```

The error is a missing multiplication operator *****. The correct input would be **3*u^2**. Note that MATLAB places a marker (a vertical line segment) at the place where it thinks the error might be; however, the actual error may have occurred earlier or later in the expression.

⇨ **Missing multiplication operators and parentheses are among the most common errors.**

You can edit an input line by using the UP-ARROW key to redisplay the previous command, editing the command using the LEFT- and RIGHT-ARROW keys, and then pressing RETURN or ENTER. The UP- and DOWN-ARROW keys allow you to scroll back and forth through all the commands you've typed in a MATLAB session, and are very useful when you want to correct, modify, or reenter a previous command.

Online Help

There are several ways to get online help in MATLAB. To get help on a particular command, enter **help** followed by the name of the command. For example, **help solve** will display documentation for **solve**. Unless you have a large monitor, the output of **help solve** will not fit in your MATLAB command window, and the beginning of the documentation will scroll quickly past the top of the screen. You can force MATLAB to display information one screenful at a time by typing **more on**. You press the space bar to display the next screenful, or ENTER to display the next line; type **help more** for details. Typing **more on** affects all subsequent commands, until you type **more off**.

The command **lookfor** searches the first line of every MATLAB help file for a specified string (use **lookfor -all** to search all lines). For example, if you wanted to see a list of all MATLAB commands that contain the word "factor" as part of the command name or brief description, then you would type **lookfor factor**. If the command you are looking for appears in the list, then you can use **help** on that command to learn more about it.

The most robust online help in MATLAB 6 is provided through the vastly improved Help Browser. The Help Browser can be invoked in several ways: by typing **helpdesk** at the command prompt, under the **View** item in the menu bar, or through the question mark button on the tool bar. Upon its launch you will see a window with two panes: the first, called the *Help Navigator*, used to find documentation; and the second, called the *display pane*, for viewing documentation. The display pane works much like a normal web browser. It has an address window, buttons for moving forward and backward (among the windows you have visited), live links for moving around in the documentation, the capability of storing favorite sites, and other such tools.

You use the Help Navigator to locate the documentation that you will explore in the display pane. The Help Navigator has four tabs that allow you to arrange your search for documentation in different ways. The first is the *Contents* tab that displays a tree view of all the documentation topics available. The extent of that tree will be determined by how much you (or your system administrator) included in the original MATLAB installation (how many toolboxes, etc.). The second tab is an *Index* that displays all the documentation available in index format. It responds to your key entry of likely items you want to investigate in the usual alphabetic reaction mode. The third tab provides the *Search* mechanism. You type in what you seek, either a function or some other descriptive term, and the search engine locates corresponding documentation that pertains to your entry. Finally, the fourth tab is a roster of your *Favorites*. Clicking on an item that appears in any of these tabs brings up the corresponding documentation in the display pane.

The Help Browser has an excellent tutorial describing its own operation. To view it, open the Browser; if the display pane is not displaying the "Begin Here" page, then click on it in the Contents tab; scroll down to the "Using the Help Browser" link and click on it. The Help Browser is a powerful and easy-to-use aid in finding the information you need on various components of MATLAB. Like any such tool, the more you use it, the more adept you become at its use.

✓ If you type **helpwin** to launch the Help Browser, the display pane will contain the same roster that you see as the result of typing **help** at the command prompt, but the entries will be links.

Variables and Assignments

In MATLAB, you use the *equal sign* to assign values to a variable. For instance,

```
>> x = 7

x =
     7
```

will give the variable **x** the value 7 from now on. Henceforth, whenever MATLAB sees the letter **x**, it will substitute the value 7. For example, if **y** has been defined as a symbolic variable, then

```
>> x^2 - 2*x*y + y

ans =
49-13*y
```

⇨ **To clear the value of the variable x, type `clear x`.**

You can make very general assignments for symbolic variables and then manipulate them. For example,

```
>> clear x; syms x y
>> z = x^2 - 2*x*y + y

z =
x^2-2*x*y+y

>> 5*y*z

ans =
5*y*(x^2-2*x*y+y)
```

A variable name or function name can be any string of letters, digits, and underscores, provided it begins with a letter (punctuation marks are not allowed). MATLAB distinguishes between uppercase and lowercase letters. You should choose distinctive names that are easy for you to remember, generally using lowercase letters. For example, you might use **cubicsol** as the name of the solution of a cubic equation.

⇨ **A common source of puzzling errors is the inadvertent reuse of previously defined variables.**

MATLAB never forgets your definitions unless instructed to do so. You can check on the current value of a variable by simply typing its name.

Solving Equations

You can solve equations involving variables with **solve** or **fzero**. For example, to find the solutions of the quadratic equation $x^2 - 2x - 4 = 0$, type

```
>> solve('x^2 - 2*x - 4 = 0')

ans =
[  5^(1/2)+1]
[  1-5^(1/2)]
```

Note that the equation to be solved is specified as a string; that is, it is surrounded by single quotes. The answer consists of the exact (symbolic) solutions

$1 \pm \sqrt{5}$. To get numerical solutions, type **double(ans)**, or **vpa(ans)** to display more digits.

The command **solve** can solve higher-degree polynomial equations, as well as many other types of equations. It can also solve equations involving more than one variable. If there are fewer equations than variables, you should specify (as strings) which variable(s) to solve for. For example, type **solve('2*x - log(y) = 1', 'y')** to solve $2x - \log y = 1$ for y in terms of x. You can specify more than one equation as well. For example,

```
>> [x, y] = solve('x^2 - y = 2', 'y - 2*x = 5')

x =
[ 1+2*2^(1/2)]
[ 1-2*2^(1/2)]

y =
[ 7+4*2^(1/2)]
[ 7-4*2^(1/2)]
```

This system of equations has two solutions. MATLAB reports the solution by giving the two x values and the two y values for those solutions. Thus the first solution consists of the first value of x together with the first value of y. You can extract these values by typing **x(1)** and **y(1)**:

```
>> x(1)

ans =
1+2*2^(1/2)
>> y(1)

ans =
7+4*2^(1/2)
```

The second solution can be extracted with **x(2)** and **y(2)**.

Note that in the preceding **solve** command, we assigned the output to the *vector* **[x, y]**. If you use **solve** on a system of equations without assigning the output to a vector, then MATLAB does not automatically display the values of the solution:

```
>> sol = solve('x^2 - y = 2', 'y - 2*x = 5')
```

```
sol =
    x: [2x1 sym]
    y: [2x1 sym]
```

To see the vectors of x and y values of the solution, type **sol.x** and **sol.y**. To see the individual values, type **sol.x(1)**, **sol.y(1)**, etc.

Some equations cannot be solved symbolically, and in these cases **solve** tries to find a numerical answer. For example,

```
>> solve('sin(x) = 2 - x')
```

```
ans =
1.1060601577062719106167372970301
```

Sometimes there is more than one solution, and you may not get what you expected. For example,

```
>> solve('exp(-x) = sin(x)')
```

```
ans =
-2.0127756629315111633360706990971
+2.7030745115909622139316148044265*i
```

The answer is a complex number; the **i** at the end of the answer stands for the number $\sqrt{-1}$. Though it is a valid solution of the equation, there are also real number solutions. In fact, the graphs of $\exp(-x)$ and $\sin(x)$ are shown in Figure 2-3; each intersection of the two curves represents a solution of the equation $e^{-x} = \sin(x)$.

You can numerically find the solutions shown on the graph with **fzero**, which looks for a zero of a given function near a specified value of x. A solution of the equation $e^{-x} = \sin(x)$ is a zero of the function $e^{-x} - \sin(x)$, so to find the solution near $x = 0.5$ type

```
>> fzero(inline('exp(-x) - sin(x)'), 0.5)
```

```
ans =
    0.5885
```

Replace **0.5** with **3** to find the next solution, and so forth.

☞ *In the example above, the command* **inline**, *which we will discuss further in the section* User-Defined Functions *below, converts its string argument to a*

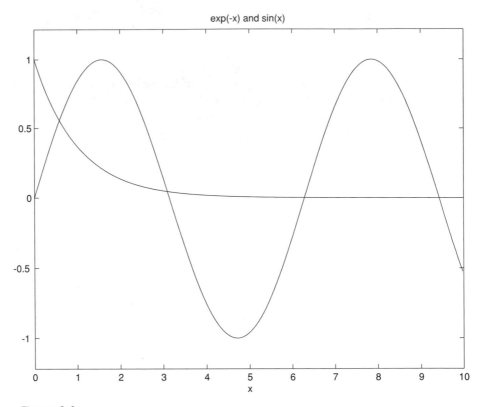

Figure 2-3

function data class. This is the type of input **fzero** *expects as its first argument.*

✓ In current versions of MATLAB, **fzero** also accepts a string expression with independent variable **x**, so that we could have run the command above without using **inline**, but this feature is no longer documented in the help text for **fzero** and may be removed in future versions.

Vectors and Matrices

MATLAB was written originally to allow mathematicians, scientists, and engineers to handle the mechanics of linear algebra — that is, vectors and matrices — as effortlessly as possible. In this section we introduce these concepts.

Vectors

A *vector* is an ordered list of numbers. You can enter a vector of any length in MATLAB by typing a list of numbers, separated by commas or spaces, inside square brackets. For example,

```
>> Z = [2,4,6,8]

Z =
     2     4     6     8

>> Y = [4 -3 5 -2 8 1]

Y =
     4    -3     5    -2     8     1
```

Suppose you want to create a vector of values running from 1 to 9. Here's how to do it without typing each number:

```
>> X = 1:9

X =
     1     2     3     4     5     6     7     8     9
```

The notation **1:9** is used to represent a vector of numbers running from 1 to 9 in increments of 1. The increment can be specified as the second of three arguments:

```
>> X = 0:2:10

X =
     0     2     4     6     8    10
```

You can also use fractional or negative increments, for example, **0:0.1:1** or **100:-1:0**.

The elements of the vector **X** can be extracted as **X(1)**, **X(2)**, etc. For example,

```
>> X(3)

ans =
     4
```

To change the vector **x** from a row vector to a column vector, put a prime ($'$) after **x**:

```
>> x'

ans =
     0
     2
     4
     6
     8
    10
```

You can perform mathematical operations on vectors. For example, to square the elements of the vector **x**, type

```
>> x.^2

ans =
     0     4    16    36    64   100
```

The period in this expression is very important; it says that the numbers in **x** should be squared individually, or *element-by-element*. Typing **x^2** would tell MATLAB to use matrix multiplication to multiply **x** by itself and would produce an error message in this case. (We discuss matrices below and in Chapter 4.) Similarly, you must type **.*** or **./** if you want to multiply or divide vectors element-by-element. For example, to multiply the elements of the vector **x** by the corresponding elements of the vector **y**, type

```
>> x.*y

ans =
     0    -6    20   -12    64    10
```

Most MATLAB operations are, by default, performed element-by-element. For example, you do not type a period for addition and subtraction, and you can type **exp(x)** to get the exponential of each number in **x** (the matrix exponential function is **expm**). One of the strengths of MATLAB is its ability to efficiently perform operations on vectors.

Matrices

A *matrix* is a rectangular array of numbers. Row and column vectors, which we discussed above, are examples of matrices. Consider the 3×4 matrix

$$A = \begin{pmatrix} 1 & 2 & 3 & 4 \\ 5 & 6 & 7 & 8 \\ 9 & 10 & 11 & 12 \end{pmatrix}.$$

It can be entered in MATLAB with the command

```
>> A = [1, 2, 3, 4; 5, 6, 7, 8; 9, 10, 11, 12]
A =

       1       2       3       4
       5       6       7       8
       9      10      11      12
```

Note that the matrix *elements* in any row are separated by commas, and the rows are separated by semicolons. The elements in a row can also be separated by spaces.

If two matrices **A** and **B** are the same size, their (element-by-element) sum is obtained by typing **A + B**. You can also add a scalar (a single number) to a matrix; **A + c** adds **c** to each element in **A**. Likewise, **A - B** represents the difference of **A** and **B**, and **A - c** subtracts the number **c** from each element of **A**. If **A** and **B** are multiplicatively compatible (that is, if **A** is $n \times m$ and **B** is $m \times \ell$), then their product **A*B** is $n \times \ell$. Recall that the element of **A*B** in the ith row and jth column is the sum of the products of the elements from the ith row of **A** times the elements from the jth column of **B**, that is,

$$(\mathbf{A} * \mathbf{B})_{ij} = \sum_{k=1}^{m} \mathbf{A}_{ik}\mathbf{B}_{kj}, \ 1 \le i \le n, \ 1 \le j \le \ell.$$

The product of a number **c** and the matrix **A** is given by **c*A**, and **A'** represents the conjugate transpose of **A**. (For more information, see the online help for **ctranspose** and **transpose**.)

A simple illustration is given by the matrix product of the 3×4 matrix **A** above by the 4×1 column vector **z'**:

```
>> A*z'
ans =
        60
       140
       220
```

The result is a 3×1 matrix, in other words, a column vector.

☞ *MATLAB has many commands for manipulating matrices. You can read about them in the section* More about Matrices *in Chapter 4 and in the online help; some of them are illustrated in the section* Linear Economic Models *in Chapter 9.*

Suppressing Output

Typing a semicolon at the end of an input line suppresses printing of the output of the MATLAB command. The semicolon should generally be used when defining large vectors or matrices (such as **X = -1:0.1:2;**). It can also be used in any other situation where the MATLAB output need not be displayed.

Functions

In MATLAB you will use both built-in functions as well as functions that you create yourself.

Built-in Functions

MATLAB has many built-in functions. These include **sqrt**, **cos**, **sin**, **tan**, **log**, **exp**, and **atan** (for arctan) as well as more specialized mathematical functions such as **gamma**, **erf**, and **besselj**. MATLAB also has several built-in constants, including **pi** (the number π), **i** (the complex number $i = \sqrt{-1}$), and **Inf** (∞). Here are some examples:

```
>> log(exp(3))

ans =
     3
```

The function **log** is the natural logarithm, called "ln" in many texts. Now consider

```
>> sin(2*pi/3)

ans =
    0.8660
```

To get an exact answer, you need to use a symbolic argument:

```
>> sin(sym('2*pi/3'))

ans =
1/2*3^(1/2)
```

User-Defined Functions

In this section we will show how to use **inline** to define your own functions. Here's how to define the polynomial function $f(x) = x^2 + x + 1$:

```
>> f = inline('x^2 + x + 1', 'x')

f =
    Inline function:
    f(x) = x^2 + x + 1
```

The first argument to **inline** is a string containing the expression defining the function. The second argument is a string specifying the independent variable.

☞ *The second argument to **inline** can be omitted, in which case MATLAB will "guess" what it should be, using the rules about "Default Variables" to be discussed later at the end of Chapter 4.*

Once the function is defined, you can evaluate it:

```
>> f(4)

ans =
    21
```

MATLAB functions can operate on vectors as well as scalars. To make an inline function that can act on vectors, we use MATLAB's **vectorize** function. Here is the vectorized version of $f(x) = x^2 + x + 1$:

```
>> f1 = inline(vectorize('x^2 + x + 1'), 'x')

f1 =
    Inline function:
    f1(x) = x.^2 + x + 1
```

Note that ^ has been replaced by .^. Now you can evaluate **f1** on a vector:

```
>> f1(1:5)

ans =
     3     7    13    21    31
```

You can plot **f1**, using MATLAB graphics, in several ways that we will explore in the next section. We conclude this section by remarking that one can also define functions of two or more variables:

```
>> g = inline('u^2 + v^2', 'u', 'v')

g =
     Inline function:
     g(u,v) = u^2+v^2
```

Graphics

In this section, we introduce MATLAB's two basic plotting commands and show how to use them.

Graphing with `ezplot`

The simplest way to graph a function of one variable is with **ezplot**, which expects a string or a symbolic expression representing the function to be plotted. For example, to graph $x^2 + x + 1$ on the interval -2 to 2 (using the string form of **ezplot**), type

```
>> ezplot('x^2 + x + 1', [-2 2])
```

The plot will appear on the screen in a new window labeled "Figure No. 1".
   We mentioned that **ezplot** accepts either a string argument or a symbolic expression. Using a symbolic expression, you can produce the plot in Figure 2-4 with the following input:

```
>> syms x
>> ezplot(x^2 + x + 1, [-2 2])
```

✓   Graphs can be misleading if you do not pay attention to the axes. For example, the input **ezplot(x^2 + x + 3, [-2 2])** produces a graph

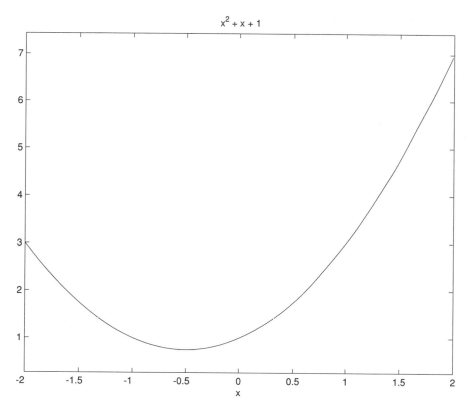

Figure 2-4

that looks identical to the previous one, except that the vertical axis has different tick marks (and MATLAB assigns the graph a different title).

Modifying Graphs

You can modify a graph in a number of ways. You can change the title above the graph in Figure 2-4 by typing (in the Command Window, not the figure window)

```
>> title 'A Parabola'
```

You can add a label on the horizontal axis with **xlabel** or change the label on the vertical axis with **ylabel**. Also, you can change the horizontal and vertical ranges of the graph with **axis**. For example, to confine the vertical range to the interval from 1 to 4, type

```
>> axis([-2 2 1 4])
```

The first two numbers are the range of the horizontal axis; both ranges must be included, even if only one is changed. We'll examine more options for manipulating graphs in Chapter 5.

To close the graphics window select **File**:**Close** from its menu bar, type `close` in the Command Window, or kill the window the way you would close any other window on your computer screen.

Graphing with `plot`

The command **plot** works on vectors of numerical data. The basic syntax is `plot(X, Y)` where **X** and **Y** are vectors of the same length. For example,

```
>> X = [1 2 3];
>> Y = [4 6 5];
>> plot(X, Y)
```

The command **plot(X, Y)** considers the vectors **X** and **Y** to be lists of the x and y coordinates of successive points on a graph and joins the points with line segments. So, in Figure 2-5, MATLAB connects $(1, 4)$ to $(2, 6)$ to $(3, 5)$.

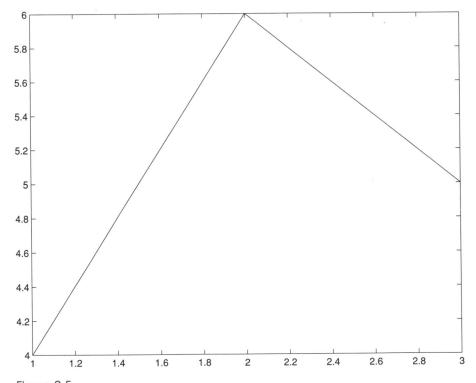

Figure 2-5

To plot $x^2 + x + 1$ on the interval from -2 to 2 we first make a list **X** of x values, and then type **plot(X, X.^2 + X + 1)**. We need to use enough x values to ensure that the resulting graph drawn by "connecting the dots" looks smooth. We'll use an increment of 0.1. Thus a recipe for graphing the parabola is

```
>> X = -2:0.1:2;
>> plot(X, X.^2 + X + 1)
```

The result appears in Figure 2-6. Note that we used a semicolon to suppress printing of the 41-element vector **x**. Note also that the command

```
>> plot(X, f1(X))
```

would produce the same results (**f1** is defined earlier in the section *User-Defined Functions*).

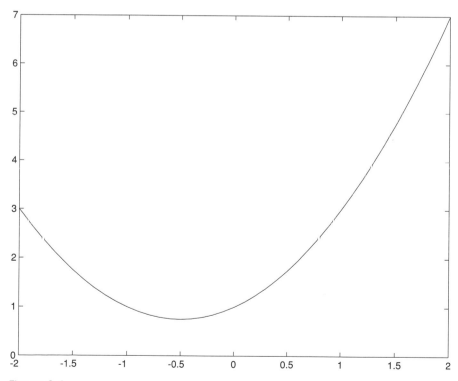

Figure 2-6

The Command Window is where you type the commands and instructions that cause MATLAB to evaluate, compute, draw, and perform all the other wonderful magic that we describe in this book. The Command History window contains a running history of the commands that you type into the Command Window. It is useful in two ways. First, it lets you see at a quick glance a record of the commands that you have entered previously. Second, it can save you some typing time. If you click on an entry in the Command History with the right mouse button, it becomes highlighted and a menu of options appears. You can, for example, select **Copy**, then click with the right mouse button in the Command Window and select **Paste**, whereupon the command you selected will appear at the command prompt and be ready for execution or editing. There are many other options that you can learn by experimenting; for instance, if you double-click on an entry in the Command History then it will be executed immediately in the Command Window.

The Launch Pad window is basically a series of shortcuts that enable you to access various features of the MATLAB software with a double-click. You can use it to start SIMULINK, run demos of various toolboxes, use MATLAB web tools, open the Help Browser, and more. We recommend that you experiment with the entries in the Launch Pad to gain familiarity with its features.

The Workspace browser and Current Directory browser will be described in separate subsections below.

Each of the five windows in the Desktop contains two small buttons in the upper right corner. The × allows you to close the window, while the curved arrow will "undock" the window from the Desktop (you can return it to the Desktop by selecting **Dock** from the **View** menu of the undocked window). You can also customize which windows appear inside the Desktop using its **View** menu.

✓ While the Desktop provides some new features and a common interface for both the Windows and UNIX versions of MATLAB 6, it may also run more slowly than the MATLAB 5 Command Window interface, especially on older computers. You can run MATLAB 6 with the old interface by starting the program with the command **matlab /nodesktop** on a Windows system or **matlab -nodesktop** on a UNIX system. If you are a Windows user, you probably start MATLAB by double-clicking on an icon. If so, you can create an icon to start MATLAB without the Desktop feature as follows. First, click the right mouse button on the MATLAB icon and select **Create Shortcut**. A new, nearly identical icon will appear on your screen (possibly behind a window — you may need to hunt for it). Next, click the right mouse button on the new icon, and select **Properties**. In the panel that pops up, select the

Shortcut tab, and in the "Target" box, add to the end of the executable file name a space followed by **/nodesktop**. (Notice that you can also change the default working directory in the "Start in" box.) Click **OK**, and your new icon is all set; you may want to rename it by clicking on it again with the right mouse button, selecting **Rename**, and typing the new name.

Menu and Tool Bars

The MATLAB Desktop includes a *menu bar* and a *tool bar*; the tool bar contains buttons that give quick access to some of the items you can select through the menu bar. On a Windows system, the MATLAB 5 Command Window has a menu bar and tool bar that are similar, but not identical, to those of MATLAB 6. For example, its menus are arranged differently and its tool bar has buttons that open the *Workspace browser* and *Path Browser*, described below. When referring to menu and tool bar items below, we will describe the MATLAB 6 Desktop interface.

⇨ **Many of the menu selections and tool bar buttons cause a new window to appear on your screen. If you are using a UNIX system, keep in mind the following caveats as you read the rest of this chapter. First, some of the pop-up windows that we describe are available on some UNIX systems but unavailable on others, depending (for instance) on the operating system. Second, we will often describe how to use both the command line and the menu and tool bars to perform certain tasks, though only the command line is available on some UNIX systems.**

The Workspace

In Chapter 2, we introduced the commands **clear** and **whos**, which can be used to keep track of the variables you have defined in your MATLAB session. The complete collection of defined variables is referred to as the Workspace, which you can view using the Workspace browser. You can make the browser appear by typing **workspace** or, in the default layout of the MATLAB Desktop, by clicking on the **Workspace** tab in the Launch Pad window (in a MATLAB 5 Command Window select **File:Show Workspace** instead). The Workspace browser contains a list of the current variables and their sizes (but not their values). If you double-click on a variable, its contents will appear in a new window called the *Array Editor*, which you can use to edit individual entries in a vector or matrix. (The command **openvar** also will open the Array Editor.)

You can remove a variable from the Workspace by selecting it in the Workspace browser and choosing **Edit:Delete**.

If you need to interrupt a session and don't want to be forced to recompute everything later, then you can save the current Workspace with **save**. For example, typing **save myfile** saves the values of all currently defined variables in a file called `myfile.mat`. To save only the values of the variables **X** and **Y**, type

```
>> save myfile X Y
```

When you start a new session and want to recover the values of those variables, use **load**. For example, typing **load myfile** restores the values of all the variables stored in the file `myfile.mat`.

The Working Directory

New files you create from within MATLAB will be stored in your current *working directory*. You may want to change this directory from its default location, or you may want to maintain different working directories for different projects. To create a new working directory you must use the standard procedure for creating a directory in your operating system. Then you can make this directory your current working directory in MATLAB by using **cd**, or by selecting this directory in the "Current Directory" box on the Desktop tool bar.

For example, on a Windows computer, you could create a directory called `C:\ProjectA`. Then in MATLAB you would type

```
>> cd C:\ProjectA
```

to make it your current working directory. You will then be able to read and write files in this directory in your current MATLAB session.

If you only need to be able to read files from a certain directory, an alternative to making it your working directory is to add it to the *path* of directories that MATLAB searches to find files. The current working directory and the directories in your path are the only places MATLAB searches for files, unless you explicitly type the directory name as part of the file name. To add the directory `C:\ProjectA` to your path, type

```
>> addpath C:\ProjectA
```

When you add a directory to the path, the files it contains remain available for the rest of your session regardless of whether you subsequently add another directory to the path or change the working directory. The potential disadvantage of this approach is that you must be careful when naming files. When MATLAB searches for files, it uses the first file with the correct name that it finds in the path list, starting with the current working directory. If you use the same name for different files in different directories in your path, you can run into problems.

You can also control the MATLAB search path from the Path Browser. To open the Path Browser, type **editpath** or **pathtool**, or select **File:Set Path...**. The Path Browser consists of a panel, with a list of directories in the current path, and several buttons. To add a directory to the path list, click on **Add Folder...** or **Add with Subfolders...**, depending on whether or not you want subdirectories to be included as well. To remove a directory, click on **Remove**. The buttons **Move Up** and **Move Down** can be used to reorder the directories in the path. Note that you can use the Current Directory browser to examine the files in the working directory, and even to create subdirectories, move M-files around, etc.

✓ The information displayed in the main areas of the Path Browser can also be obtained from the command line. To see the current working directory, type **pwd**. To list the files in the working directory type either **ls** or **dir**. To see the current path list that MATLAB will search for files, type **path**.

✓ If you have many toolboxes installed, path searches can be slow, especially with **lookfor**. Removing the toolboxes you are not currently using from the MATLAB path is one way to speed up execution.

Using the Command Window

We have already described in Chapters 1 and 2 how to enter commands in the MATLAB Command Window. We continue that description here, presenting an example that will serve as an introduction to our discussion of M files. Suppose you want to calculate the values of

$$\sin(0.1)/0.1, \ \sin(0.01)/0.01, \ \text{and} \ \sin(0.001)/0.001$$

to 15 digits. Such a simple problem can be worked directly in the Command Window. Here is a typical first try at a solution, together with the response that MATLAB displays in the Command Window:

```
>> x = [0.1, 0.01, 0.001];
>> y = sin(x)./x
```

```
y =
0.9983   1.0000    1.0000
```

After completing a calculation, you will often realize that the result is not what you intended. The commands above displayed only 5 digits, not 15. To display 15 digits, you need to type the command **format long** and then repeat the line that defines **y**. In this case you could simply retype the latter line, but in general retyping is time consuming and error prone, especially for complicated problems. How can you modify a sequence of commands without retyping them?

For simple problems, you can take advantage of the command history feature of MATLAB. Use the UP- and DOWN-ARROW keys to scroll through the list of commands that you have used recently. When you locate the correct command line, you can use the LEFT- and RIGHT-ARROW keys to move around in the command line, deleting and inserting changes as necessary, and then press the ENTER key to tell MATLAB to evaluate the modified command. You can also copy and paste previous command lines from the Command Window, or in the MATLAB 6 Desktop from the Command History window as described earlier in this chapter. For more complicated problems, however, it is better to use M-files.

M-Files

For complicated problems, the simple editing tools provided by the Command Window and its history mechanism are insufficient. A much better approach is to create an M-file. There are two different kinds of M-files: script M-files and function M-files. We shall illustrate the use of both types of M-files as we present different solutions to the problem described above.

M-files are ordinary text files containing MATLAB commands. You can create and modify them using any text editor or word processor that is capable of saving files as plain ASCII text. (Such text editors include **notepad** in Windows or **emacs**, **textedit**, and **vi** in UNIX.) More conveniently, you can use the built-in *Editor/Debugger*, which you can start by typing **edit**, either by itself (to edit a new file) or followed by the name of an existing M-file in the current working directory. You can also use the **File** menu or the two leftmost buttons on the tool bar to start the Editor/Debugger, either to create a new file or to open an existing file. Double-clicking on an M-file in the Current Directory browser will also open it in the Editor/Debugger.

Script M-Files

We now show how to construct a script M-file to solve the mathematical problem described earlier. Create a file containing the following lines:

```
format long
x = [0.1, 0.01, 0.001];
y = sin(x)./x
```

We will assume that you have saved this file with the name `task1.m` in your working directory, or in some directory on your path. You can name the file any way you like (subject to the usual naming restrictions on your operating system), but the ".m" suffix is mandatory.

You can tell MATLAB to run (or *execute*) this script by typing **task1** in the Command Window. (You must not type the ".m" extension here; MATLAB automatically adds it when searching for M-files.) The output — but not the commands that produce them — will be displayed in the Command Window. Now the sequence of commands can easily be changed by modifying the M-file `task1.m`. For example, if you also wish to calculate sin(0.0001)/0.0001, you can modify the M-file to read

```
format long
x = [0.1, 0.01, 0.001, 0.0001];
y = sin(x)./x
```

and then run the modified script by typing **task1**. Be sure to save your changes to `task1.m` first; otherwise, MATLAB will not recognize them. Any variables that are set by the running of a script M-file will persist exactly as if you had typed them into the Command Window directly. For example, the program above will cause all future numerical output to be displayed with 15 digits. To revert to 5-digit format, you would have to type **format short**.

Echoing Commands. As mentioned above, the commands in a script M-file will not automatically be displayed in the Command Window. If you want the commands to be displayed along with the results, use **echo**:

```
echo on
format long
x = [0.1, 0.01, 0.001];
y = sin(x)./x
echo off
```

Adding Comments. It is worthwhile to include comments in a lengthly script M-file. These comments might explain what is being done in the calculation, or they might interpret the results of the calculation. Any line in a script M-file that begins with a percent sign is treated as a comment and is not executed by MATLAB. Here is our new version of `task1.m` with a few comments added:

```
echo on
% Turn on 15 digit display
format long
x = [0.1, 0.01, 0.001];
y = sin(x)./x
% These values illustrate the fact that the limit of
% sin(x)/x as x approaches 0 is 1.
echo off
```

When adding comments to a script M-file, remember to put a percent sign at the beginning of each line. This is particularly important if your editor starts a new line automatically while you are typing a comment. If you use **echo on** in a script M-file, then MATLAB will also echo the comments, so they will appear in the Command Window.

Structuring Script M-Files. For the results of a script M-file to be reproducible, the script should be self-contained, unaffected by other variables that you might have defined elsewhere in the MATLAB session, and uncorrupted by leftover graphics. With this in mind, you can type the line **clear all** at the beginning of the script, to ensure that previous definitions of variables do not affect the results. You can also include the **close all** command at the beginning of a script M-file that creates graphics, to close all graphics windows and start with a clean slate.

Here is our example of a complete, careful, commented solution to the problem described above:

```
% Remove old variable definitions
clear all
% Remove old graphics windows
close all
% Display the command lines in the command window
echo on

% Turn on 15 digit display
format long
```

```
% Define the vector of values of the independent variable
x = [0.1, 0.01, 0.001];

% Compute the desired values
y = sin(x)./x
% These values illustrate the fact that the limit of
% sin(x)/x as x approaches 0 is equal to 1.

echo off
```

✓ Sometimes you may need to type, either in the Command Window or in an M-file, a command that is too long to fit on one line. If so, when you get near the end of a line you can type ... (that is, three successive periods) followed by ENTER, and continue the command on the next line. In the Command Window, you will not see a command prompt on the new line.

Function M-Files

You often need to repeat a process several times for different input values of a parameter. For example, you can provide different inputs to a built-in function to find an output that meets a given criterion. As you have already seen, you can use **inline** to define your own functions. In many situations, however, it is more convenient to define a function using an M-file instead of an inline function.

Let us return to the problem described above, where we computed some values of $\sin(x)/x$ with $x = 10^{-b}$ for several values of b. Suppose, in addition, that you want to find the smallest value of b for which $\sin(10^{-b})/(10^{-b})$ and 1 agree to 15 digits. Here is a function M-file called sinelimit.m designed to solve that problem:

```
function y = sinelimit(c)
% SINELIMIT computes sin(x)/x for x = 10^(-b),
% where b = 1, ..., c.
format long
b = 1:c;
x = 10.^(-b);
y = (sin(x)./x)';
```

Like a script M-file, a function M-file is a plain text file that should reside in your MATLAB working directory. The first line of the file contains a **function** statement, which identifies the file as a function M-file. The first line specifies the name of the function and describes both its input arguments (or parameters) and its output values. In this example, the function is called **sinelimit**. The file name and the function name should match.

The function **sinelimit** takes one input argument and returns one output value, called **c** and **y** (respectively) inside the M-file. When the function finishes executing, its output will be assigned to **ans** (by default) or to any other variable you choose, just as with a built-in function. The remaining lines of the M-file define the function. In this example, **b** is a row vector consisting of the integers from **1** to **c**. The vector **y** contains the results of computing $\sin(x)/x$ where $x = 10^{-b}$; the prime makes **y** a column vector. Notice that the output of the lines defining **b**, **x**, and **y** is suppressed with a semicolon. In general, the output of intermediate calculations in a function M-file should be suppressed.

✓ Of course, when we run the M-file above, we do want to see the results of the last line of the file, so a natural impulse would be to avoid putting a semicolon on this last line. But because this is a function M-file, running it will automatically display the contents of the designated output variable **y**. Thus if we did not put a semicolon at the end of the last line, we would see the same numbers twice when we run the function!

☞ *Note that the variables used in a function M-file, such as* **b**, **x**, *and* **y** *in* sinelimit.m, *are* local variables. *This means that, unlike the variables that are defined in a script M-file, these variables are completely unrelated to any variables with the same names that you may have used in the Command Window, and MATLAB does not remember their values after the function M-file is executed. For further information, see the section* Variables in Function M-files *in Chapter 4.*

Here is an example that shows how to use the function **sinelimit**:

```
>> sinelimit(5)

ans =

    0.99833416646828
    0.99998333341667
    0.99999983333334
    0.99999999833333
    0.99999999998333
```

None of the values of b from 1 to 5 yields the desired answer, 1, to 15 digits.

Judging from the output, you can expect to find the answer to the question we posed above by typing **sinelimit(10)**. Try it!

Loops

A *loop* specifies that a command or group of commands should be repeated several times. The easiest way to create a loop is to use a **for** statement. Here is a simple example that computes and displays $10! = 10 \cdot 9 \cdot 8 \cdots 2 \cdot 1$:

```
f = 1;
for n = 2:10
    f = f*n;
end
f
```

The loop begins with the **for** statement and ends with the **end** statement. The command between those statements is executed a total of nine times, once for each value of **n** from 2 to 10. We used a semicolon to suppress intermediate output within the loop. To see the final output, we then needed to type **f** after the end of the loop. Without the semicolon, MATLAB would display each of the intermediate values 2!, 3!, ...

We have presented the loop above as you might type it into an M-file; indentation is not required by MATLAB, but it helps human readers distinguish the commands within the loop. If you type the commands above directly to the MATLAB prompt, you will not see a new prompt after entering the **for** statement. You should continue typing, and after you enter the **end** statement, MATLAB will evaluate the entire loop and display a new prompt.

✓ If you use a loop in a script M-file with **echo on** in effect, the commands will be echoed every time through the loop. You can avoid this by inserting the command **echo off** just before the **end** statement and inserting **echo on** just afterward; then each command in the loop (except **end**) will be echoed once.

Presenting Your Results

Sometimes you may want to show other people the results of a script M-file that you have created. For a polished presentation, you should use an M-book, as described in Chapter 6, or import your results into another program, such as a word processor, or convert your results to HTML format, by the procedures described in Chapter 10. But to share your results more informally, you can give someone else your M-file, assuming that person has a copy of MATLAB on which to run it, or you can provide the output you obtained. Either way, you should remember that the reader is not nearly as familiar with the M-file as you are; it is your responsibility to provide guidance.

✓ You can greatly enhance the readability of your M-file by including frequent comments. Your comments should explain what is being calculated, so that the reader can understand your procedures and strategies. Once you've done the calculations, you can also add comments that interpret the results.

If your audience is going to run your M-files, then you should make liberal use of the command **pause**. Each time MATLAB reaches a **pause** statement, it stops executing the M-file until the user presses a key. Pauses should be placed after important comments, after each graph, and after critical points where your script generates numerical output. These pauses allow the viewer to read and understand your results.

Diary Files

Here is an effective way to save the output of your M-file in a way that others (and you!) can later understand. At the beginning of a script M-file, such as task1.m, you can include the commands

```
delete task1.txt
diary task1.txt
echo on
```

The script M-file should then end with the commands

```
echo off
diary off
```

The first **diary** command causes all subsequent input to and output from the Command Window to be copied into the specified file — in this case, task1.txt. The diary file task1.txt is a plain text file that is suitable for printing or importing into another program.

By using **delete** at the beginning of the M-file, you ensure that the file only contains the output of the current script. If you omit the **delete** command, then the **diary** command will add any new output to the end of an existing file, and the file task1.txt can end up containing the results of several runs of the M-file. (Putting the **delete** command in the script will lead to a harmless warning message about a nonexistent file the first time you run the script.) You can also get extraneous output in a diary file if you type CTRL+C to halt a script containing a **diary** command. If this happens, you should type **diary off** in the Command Window before running the script again.

Presenting Graphics

As indicated in Chapters 1 and 2, graphics appear in a separate window. You can print the current figure by selecting **File : Print...** in the graphics window. Alternatively, the command **print** (without any arguments) causes the figure in the current graphics window to be printed on your default printer. Since you probably don't want to print the graphics every time you run a script, you should not include a bare **print** statement in an M-file. Instead, you should use a form of **print** that sends the output to a file. It is also helpful to give reasonable titles to your figures and to insert **pause** statements into your script so that viewers have a chance to see the figure before the rest of the script executes. For example,

```
xx = 2*pi*(0:0.02:1);
plot(xx, sin(xx))
% Put a title on the figure.
title('Figure A: Sine Curve')
pause
% Store the graph in the file figureA.eps.
print -deps figureA
```

The form of **print** used in this script does not send anything to the printer. Instead, it causes the current figure to be written to a file in the current working directory called figureA.eps in Encapsulated PostScript® format. This file can be printed later on a PostScript printer, or it can be imported into another program that recognizes the EPS format. Type **help print** to see how to save your graph in a variety of other formats that may be suitable for your particular printer or application.

As a final example involving graphics, let's consider the problem of plotting the functions $\sin(x)$, $\sin(2x)$, and $\sin(3x)$ on the same set of axes. This is a typical example; we often want to plot several similar curves whose equations depend on a parameter. Here is a script M-file solution to the problem:

```
echo on
% Define the x values.
x = 2*pi*(0:0.01:1);
```

```
% Remove old graphics, and get ready for several new ones.
close all; axes; hold on

% Run a loop to plot three sine curves.
for c = 1:3
   plot(x, sin(c*x))
   echo off
end
echo on
hold off

% Put a title on the figure.
title('Several Sine Curves')
pause
```

The result is shown in Figure 3-1.

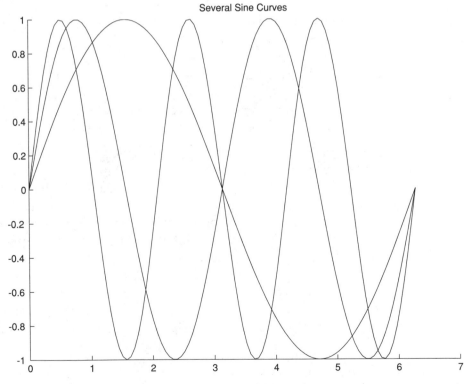

Figure 3-1

Let's analyze this solution. We start by defining the values to use on the x axis. The command **close all** removes all existing graphics windows; **axes** starts a fresh, empty graphics window; and **hold on** lets MATLAB know that we want to draw several curves on the same set of axes. The lines between **for** and **end** constitute a *for loop*, as described above. The important part of the loop is the **plot** command, which plots the desired sine curves. We inserted an **echo off** command so that we only see the loop commands once in the Command Window (or in a diary file). Finally, we turn echoing back on after exiting the loop, use **hold off** to tell MATLAB that the curves we just graphed should not be held over for the next graph that we make, title the figure, and instruct MATLAB to pause so that the viewer can see it.

Pretty Printing

If **s** is a symbolic expression, then typing **pretty(s)** displays **s** in *pretty print* format, which uses multiple lines on your screen to imitate written mathematics. The result is often more easily read than the default one-line output format. An important feature of **pretty** is that it *wraps* long expressions to fit within the margins (80 characters wide) of a standard-sized window. If your symbolic output is long enough to extend past the right edge of your window, it probably will be truncated when you print your output, so you should use **pretty** to make the entire expression visible in your printed output.

A General Procedure

In this section, we summarize the general procedure we recommend for using the Command Window and the Editor/Debugger (or your own text editor) to make a calculation involving many commands. We have in mind here the case when you ultimately want to print your results or otherwise save them in a format you can share with others, but we find that the first steps of this procedure are useful even for exploratory calculations.

1. Create a script M-file in your current working directory to hold your commands. Include **echo on** near the top of the file so that you can see which commands are producing what output when you run the M-file.
2. Alternate between editing and running the M-file until you are satisfied that it contains the MATLAB commands that do what you want. Remember to save the M-file each time between editing and running! Also, see the debugging hints below.

3. Add comments to your M-file to explain the meaning of the intermediate calculations you do and to interpret the results.

4. If desired, insert the **delete** and **diary** statements into the M-file as described above.

5. If you are generating graphs, add **print** statements that will save the graphs to files. Use **pause** statements as appropriate.

6. If needed, run the M-file one more time to produce the final output. Send the diary file and any graphics files to the printer or incorporate them into a document.

7. If you import your diary file into a word processing program, you can insert the graphics right after the commands that generated them. You can also change the fonts of text comments and input to make it easier to distinguish comments, input, and output. This sort of polishing is done automatically by the M-book interface; see Chapter 6.

Fine-Tuning Your M-Files

You can edit your M-file repeatedly until it produces the desired output. Generally, you will run the script each time you edit the file. If the program is long or involves complicated calculations or graphics, it could take a while each time. Then you need a strategy for debugging. Our experience indicates that there is no best paradigm for debugging M-files — what you do depends on the content of your file.

☞ *We will discuss features of the Editor/Debugger and MATLAB debugging commands in the section* Debugging *in Chapter 7 and in the section* Debugging Techniques *in Chapter 11. For the moment, here are some general tips.*

- Include **clear all** and **close all** at the beginning of the M-file.
- Use **echo on** early in your M-file so that you can see "cause" as well as "effect".
- If you are producing graphics, use **hold on** and **hold off** carefully. In general, you should put a **pause** statement after each **hold off**. Otherwise, the next graphics command will obliterate the current one, and you won't see it.
- Do not include bare **print** statements in your M-files. Instead, print to a file.
- Make liberal use of **pause**.

- The command **keyboard** is an interactive version of **pause**. If you have the line **keyboard** in your M-file, then when MATLAB reaches it, execution of your program is interrupted, and a new prompt appears with the letter **K** before it. At this point you can type any normal MATLAB command. This is useful if you want to examine or reset some variables in the middle of a script run. To resume the execution of your script, type **return**; i.e., type the six letters r-e-t-u-r-n and press the ENTER key.

- In some cases, you might prefer **input**. For example, if you include the line **var = input('Input var here: ')** in your script, when MATLAB gets to that point it will print "Input var here:" and pause while you type the value to be assigned to **var**.

- Finally, remember that you can stop a running M-file by typing CTRL+C. This is useful if, at a **pause** or **input** statement, you realize that you want to stop execution completely.

Practice Set A

Algebra and Arithmetic

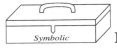 Problems 3–8 require the Symbolic Math Toolbox. The others do not.

1. Compute:
   (a) $1111 - 345$.
   (b) e^{14} and 382801π to 15 digits each. Which is bigger?
   (c) the fractions $2709/1024$, $10583/4000$, and $2024/765$. Which of these is the best approximation to $\sqrt{7}$?

2. Compute to 15 digits:
   (a) $\cosh(0.1)$.
   (b) $\ln(2)$. (*Hint*: The natural logarithm in MATLAB is called **log**, not **ln**.)
   (c) $\arctan(1/2)$. (*Hint*: The inverse tangent function in MATLAB is called **atan**, not **arctan**.)

3. Solve (symbolically) the system of linear equations

   $$\begin{cases} 3x + 4y + 5z = 2 \\ 2x - 3y + 7z = -1 \\ x - 6y + z = 3. \end{cases}$$

   Check your answer using matrix multiplication.

4. Try to solve the system of linear equations

   $$\begin{cases} 3x - 9y + 8z = 2 \\ 2x - 3y + 7z = -1 \\ x - 6y + z = 3. \end{cases}$$

   What happens? Can you see why? Again check your answer using matrix multiplication. Is the answer "correct"?

5. Factor the polynomial $x^4 - y^4$.

6. Use **simplify** or **simple** to simplify the following expressions:
   (a) $1/(1 + 1/(1 + \frac{1}{x}))$
   (b) $\cos^2 x - \sin^2 x$
7. Compute 3^{301}, both as an approximate floating point number and as an exact integer (written in usual decimal notation).
8. Use either **solve** or **fzero**, as appropriate, to solve the following equations:
   (a) $8x + 3 = 0$ (exact solution)
   (b) $8x + 3 = 0$ (numerical solution to 15 places)
   (c) $x^3 + px + q = 0$ (Solve for x in terms of p and q)
   (d) $e^x = 8x - 4$ (*all* real solutions). It helps to draw a picture first.
9. Use **plot** and/or **ezplot**, as appropriate, to graph the following functions:
   (a) $y = x^3 - x$ for $-4 \le x \le 4$.
   (b) $y = \sin(1/x^2)$ for $-2 \le x \le 2$. Try this one with both **plot** and **ezplot**. Are both results "correct"? (If you use **plot**, be sure to plot enough points.)
   (c) $y = \tan(x/2)$ for $-\pi \le x \le \pi$, $-10 \le y \le 10$ (*Hint*: First draw the plot; then use **axis**.)
   (d) $y = e^{-x^2}$ and $y = x^4 - x^2$ for $-2 \le x \le 2$ (on the same set of axes).
10. Plot the functions x^4 and 2^x on the same graph and determine how many times their graphs intersect. (*Hint*: You will probably have to make several plots, using intervals of various sizes, to find all the intersection points.) Now find the approximate values of the points of intersection using **fzero**.

Chapter 4

Beyond the Basics

In this chapter, we describe some of the finer points of MATLAB and review in more detail some of the concepts introduced in Chapter 2. We explore enough of MATLAB's internal structure to improve your ability to work with complicated functions, expressions, and commands. At the end of this chapter, we introduce some of the MATLAB commands for doing calculus.

Suppressing Output

Some MATLAB commands produce output that is superfluous. For example, when you assign a value to a variable, MATLAB echoes the value. You can suppress the output of a command by putting a *semicolon* after the command. Here is an example:

```
>> syms x
>> y = x + 7

y =
x+7

>> z = x + 7;
>> z

z =
x+7
```

The semicolon does not affect the way MATLAB processes the command internally, as you can see from its response to the command **z**.

You can also use semicolons to separate a string of commands when you are interested only in the output of the final command (several examples appear later in the chapter). Commas can also be used to separate commands without suppressing output. If you use a semicolon after a graphics command, it will not suppress the graphic.

⇒ **The most common use of the semicolon is to suppress the printing of a long vector, as indicated in Chapter 2.**

Another object that you may want to suppress is MATLAB's label for the output of a command. The command **disp** is designed to achieve that; typing **disp(x)** will print the value of the variable **x** without printing the label and the equal sign. So,

```
>> x = 7;
>> disp(x)
    7
```

or

```
>> disp(solve('x + tan(y) = 5', 'y'))
-atan(x-5)
```

Data Classes

Every variable you define in MATLAB, as well as every input to, and output from, a command, is an *array* of data belonging to a particular *class*. In this book we use primarily four types of data: floating point numbers, symbolic expressions, character strings, and inline functions. We introduced each of these types in Chapter 2. In Table 4–1, we list for each type of data its class (as given by **whos**) and how you can create it.

Type of data	Class	Created by
Floating point	double	typing a number
Symbolic	sym	using **sym** or **syms**
Character string	char	typing a string inside single quotes
Inline function	inline	using **inline**

Table 4-1

You can think of an array as a two-dimensional grid of data. A single number (or symbolic expression, or inline function) is regarded by MATLAB as a 1×1

array, sometimes called a *scalar*. A $1 \times n$ array is called a *row vector*, and an $m \times 1$ array is called a *column vector*. (A string is actually a row vector of characters.) An $m \times n$ array of numbers is called a *matrix*; see *More on Matrices* below. You can see the class and array size of every variable you have defined by looking in the Workspace browser or typing **whos** (see *Managing Variables* in Chapter 2). The set of variable definitions shown by **whos** is called your *Workspace*.

To use MATLAB commands effectively, you must pay close attention to the class of data each command accepts as input and returns as output. The input to a command consists of one or more arguments separated by commas; some arguments are optional. Some commands, such as **whos**, do not require any input. When you type a pair of words, such as **hold on**, MATLAB interprets the second word as a string argument to the command given by the first word; thus, **hold on** is equivalent to **hold('on')**. The help text (see *Online Help* in Chapter 2) for each command usually tells what classes of inputs the command expects as well as what class of output it returns.

Many commands allow more than one class of input, though sometimes only one data class is mentioned in the online help. This flexibility can be a convenience in some cases and a pitfall in others. For example, the integration command, **int**, accepts strings as well as symbolic input, though its help text mentions only symbolic input. However, suppose that you have already defined **a = 10, b = 5**, and now you attempt to factor the expression $a^2 - b^2$, forgetting your previous definitions and that you have to declare the variables symbolic:

```
>> factor(a^2 - b^2)

ans =
     3     5     5
```

The reason you don't get an error message is that **factor** is the name of a command that factors integers into prime numbers as well as factoring expressions. Since $a^2 - b^2 = 75 = 3 \cdot 5^2$, the numerical version of **factor** is applied. This output is clearly not what you intended, but in the course of a complicated series of commands, you must be careful not to be fooled by such unintended output.

✓ Note that typing **help factor** only shows you the help text for the numerical version of the command, but it does give a cross-reference to the symbolic version at the bottom. If you want to see the help text for the symbolic version instead, type **help sym/factor**. Functions such as **factor** with more than one version are called *overloaded*.

Sometimes you need to convert one data class into another to prepare the output of one command to serve as the input for another. For example, to use **plot** on a symbolic expression obtained from **solve**, it is convenient to use first **vectorize** and then **inline**, because **inline** does not allow symbolic input and **vectorize** converts symbolic expressions to strings. You can make the same conversion without vectorizing the expression using **char**. Other useful conversion commands we have encountered are **double** (symbolic to numerical), **sym** (numerical or string to symbolic), and **inline** itself (string to inline function). Also, the commands **num2str** and **str2num** convert between numbers and strings.

String Manipulation

Often it is useful to concatenate two or more strings together. The simplest way to do this is to use MATLAB's vector notation, keeping in mind that a string is a "row vector" of characters. For example, typing **[string1, string2]** combines **string1** and **string2** into one string.

Here is a useful application of string concatenation. You may need to define a string variable containing an expression that takes more than one line to type. (In most circumstances you can continue your MATLAB input onto the next line by typing **...** followed by ENTER or RETURN, but this is not allowed in the middle of a string.) The solution is to break the expression into smaller parts and concatenate them, as in:

```
>> eqn = ['left hand side of equation = ', ...
'right hand side of equation']

eqn =
left hand side of equation = right hand side of equation
```

Symbolic and Floating Point Numbers

We mentioned above that you can convert between symbolic numbers and floating point numbers with **double** and **sym**. Numbers that you type are, by default, floating point. However, if you mix symbolic and floating point numbers in an arithmetic expression, the floating point numbers are automatically converted to symbolic. This explains why you can type **syms x** and then **x^2** without having to convert **2** to a symbolic number. Here is another example:

```
>> a = 1
```

```
a =
        1
>> b = a/sym(2)
b =
1/2
```

MATLAB was designed so that some floating point numbers are restored to their exact values when converted to symbolic. Integers, rational numbers with small numerators and denominators, square roots of small integers, the number π, and certain combinations of these numbers are so restored. For example,

```
>> c = sqrt(3)

c =
        1.7321
>> sym(c)

ans =
sqrt(3)
```

Since it is difficult to predict when MATLAB will preserve exact values, it is best to suppress the floating point evaluation of a numeric argument to **sym** by enclosing it in single quotes to make it a string, e.g., **sym('1 + sqrt(3)')**. We will see below another way in which single quotes suppress evaluation.

Functions and Expressions

We have used the terms *expression* and *function* without carefully making a distinction between the two. Strictly speaking, if we define $f(x) = x^3 - 1$, then f (written without any particular input) is a function while $f(x)$ and $x^3 - 1$ are expressions involving the variable x. In mathematical discourse we often blur this distinction by calling $f(x)$ or $x^3 - 1$ a function, but in MATLAB the difference between functions and expressions is important.

In MATLAB, an expression can belong to either the string or symbolic class of data. Consider the following example:

```
>> f = 'x^3 - 1';
>> f(7)

ans   =
1
```

This result may be puzzling if you are expecting **f** to act like a function. Since **f** is a string, **f(7)** denotes the seventh character in **f**, which is **1** (the spaces count). Notice that like symbolic output, string output is not indented from the left margin. This is a clue that the answer above is a string (consisting of one character) and not a floating point number. Typing **f(5)** would yield a minus sign and **f(-1)** would produce an error message.

You have learned two ways to define your own functions, using **inline** (see Chapter 2) and using an M-file (see Chapter 3). Inline functions are most useful for defining simple functions that can be expressed in one line and for turning the output of a symbolic command into a function. Function M-files are useful for defining functions that require several intermediate commands to compute the output. Most MATLAB commands are actually M-files, and you can peruse them for ideas to use in your own M-files — to see the M-file for, say, the command **mean** you can enter **type mean**. See also *More about M-files* below.

Some commands, such as **ode45** (a numerical ordinary differential equations solver), require their first argument to be a function — to be precise, either an inline function (as in **ode45(f, [0 2], 1)**) or a *function handle*, that is, the name of a built-in function or a function M-file preceded by the special symbol **@** (as in **ode45(@func, [0 2], 1)**). The **@** syntax is new in MATLAB 6; in earlier versions of MATLAB, the substitute was to enclose the name of the function in single quotes to make it a string. But with or without quotes, typing a symbolic expression instead gives an error message. However, most symbolic commands require their first argument to be either a string or a symbolic expression, and not a function.

An important difference between strings and symbolic expressions is that MATLAB automatically substitutes user-defined functions and variables into symbolic expressions, but not into strings. (This is another sense in which the single quotes you type around a string suppress evaluation.) For example, if you type

```
>> h = inline('t.^3', 't');
>> int('h(t)', 't')

ans =
int(h(t),t)
```

then the integral cannot be evaluated because within a string **h** is regarded as an unknown function. But if you type

```
>> syms t
>> int(h(t), t)

ans =
1/4*t^4
```

then the previous definition of **h** is substituted into the symbolic expression **h(t)** before the integration is performed.

Substitution

In Chapter 2 we described how to create an inline function from an expression. You can then plug numbers into that function, to make a graph or table of values for instance. But you can also substitute numerical values directly into an expression with **subs**. For example,

```
>> syms a x y;
>> a = x^2 + y^2;
>> subs(a, x, 2)

ans =
4+y^2
>> subs(a, [x y], [3 4])

ans =
    25
```

More about M-Files

Files containing MATLAB statements are called M-files. There are two kinds of M-files: *function M-files*, which accept arguments and produce output, and *script M-files*, which execute a series of MATLAB statements. Earlier we created and used both types. In this section we present additional information on M-files.

Variables in Script M-Files

When you execute a script M-file, the variables you use and define belong to your Workspace; that is, they take on any values you assigned earlier in your MATLAB session, and they persist after the script finishes executing. Consider the following script M-file, called scriptex1.m:

```
u = [1 2 3 4];
```

Typing **scriptex1** assigns the given vector to **u** but displays no output. Now consider another script, called scriptex2.m:

```
n = length(u)
```

If you have not previously defined **u**, then typing **scriptex2** will produce an error message. However, if you type **scriptex2** after running **scriptex1**, then the definition of **u** from the first script will be used in the second script and the output n = 4 will be displayed.

If you don't want the output of a script M-file to depend on any earlier computations in your MATLAB session, put the line **clear all** near the beginning of the M-file, as we suggested in *Structuring Script M-files* in Chapter 3.

Variables in Function M-Files

The variables used in a function M-file are *local*, meaning that they are unaffected by, and have no effect on, the variables in your Workspace. Consider the following function M-file, called sq.m:

```
function z = sq(x)
% sq(x) returns the square of x.
z = x.^2;
```

Typing **sq(3)** produces the answer **9**, whether or not **x** or **z** is already defined in your Workspace, and neither defines them, nor changes their definitions, if they have been previously defined.

Structure of Function M-Files

The first line in a function M-file is called the *function definition line*; it defines the function name, as well as the number and order of input and output arguments. Following the function definition line, there can be several comment lines that begin with a percent sign (**%**). These lines are called *help text* and are displayed in response to the command **help**. In the M-file sq.m above, there is only one line of help text; it is displayed when you type **help sq**. The remaining lines constitute the *function body*; they contain the MATLAB statements that calculate the function values. In addition, there can be comment lines (lines beginning with **%**) anywhere in an M-file. All statements in a function M-file that normally produce output should end with a semicolon to suppress the output.

Function M-files can have multiple input and output arguments. Here is an example, called polarcoordinates.m, with two input and two output arguments:

```
function [r, theta] = polarcoordinates(x, y)
% polarcoordinates(x, y) returns the polar coordinates
% of the point with rectangular coordinates (x, y).
```

```
r = sqrt(x^2 + y^2);
theta = atan2(y,x);
```

If you type **polarcoordinates(3,4)**, only the first output argument is returned and stored in **ans**; in this case, the answer is **5**. To see both outputs, you must assign them to variables enclosed in square brackets:

```
>> [r, theta] = polarcoordinates(3,4)
```

```
r =
     5
```

```
theta =
     0.9273
```

By typing **r = polarcoordinates(3,4)** you can assign the first output argument to the variable **r**, but you cannot get only the second output argument; typing **theta = polarcoordinates(3,4)** will still assign the first output, **5**, to **theta**.

Complex Arithmetic

MATLAB does most of its computations using *complex numbers*, that is, numbers of the form $a + bi$, where $i = \sqrt{-1}$ and a and b are real numbers. The complex number i is represented as **i** in MATLAB. Although you may never have occasion to enter a complex number in a MATLAB session, MATLAB often produces an answer involving a complex number. For example, many polynomials with real coefficients have complex roots:

```
>> solve('x^2 + 2*x + 2 = 0')
```

```
ans =
[ -1+i]
[ -1-i]
```

Both roots of this quadratic equation are complex numbers, expressed in terms of the number i. Some common functions also return complex values for certain values of the argument. For example,

```
>> log(-1)
```

```
ans =
     0 + 3.1416i
```

You can use MATLAB to do computations involving complex numbers by entering numbers in the form **a + b*i**:

```
>> (2 + 3*i)*(4 - i)

ans =
     11.0000 + 10.0000i
```

Complex arithmetic is a powerful and valuable feature. Even if you don't intend to use complex numbers, you should be alert to the possibility of complex-valued answers when evaluating MATLAB expressions.

More on Matrices

In addition to the usual algebraic methods of combining matrices (e.g., matrix multiplication), we can also combine them element-wise. Specifically, if **A** and **B** are the same size, then **A.*B** is the *element-by-element* product of **A** and **B**, that is, the matrix whose i, j element is the product of the i, j elements of **A** and **B**. Likewise, **A./B** is the element-by-element quotient of **A** and **B**, and **A.^c** is the matrix formed by raising each of the elements of **A** to the power **c**. More generally, if **f** is one of the built-in functions in MATLAB, or is a user-defined function that accepts vector arguments, then **f(A)** is the matrix obtained by applying **f** element-by-element to **A**. See what happens when you type **sqrt(A)**, where **A** is the matrix defined at the beginning of the *Matrices* section of Chapter 2.

Recall that **x(3)** is the third element of a vector **x**. Likewise, **A(2,3)** represents the 2, 3 element of **A**, that is, the element in the second row and third column. You can specify submatrices in a similar way. Typing **A(2,[2 4])** yields the second and fourth elements of the second row of **A**. To select the second, third, and fourth elements of this row, type **A(2,2:4)**. The submatrix consisting of the elements in rows 2 and 3 and in columns 2, 3, and 4 is generated by **A(2:3,2:4)**. A colon by itself denotes an entire row or column. For example, **A(:,2)** denotes the second column of **A**, and **A(3,:)** yields the third row of **A**.

MATLAB has several commands that generate special matrices. The commands **zeros(n,m)** and **ones(n,m)** produce $n \times m$ matrices of zeros and ones, respectively. Also, **eye(n)** represents the $n \times n$ identity matrix.

Solving Linear Systems

Suppose **A** is a nonsingular $n \times n$ matrix and **b** is a column vector of length n. Then typing **x = A\b** numerically computes the unique solution to **A*x = b**. Type **help mldivide** for more information.

If either **A** or **b** is symbolic rather than numeric, then **x = A\b** computes the solution to **A*x = b** symbolically. To calculate a symbolic solution when both inputs are numeric, type **x = sym(A)\b**.

Calculating Eigenvalues and Eigenvectors

The eigenvalues of a square matrix **A** are calculated with **eig(A)**. The command **[U, R] = eig(A)** calculates both the eigenvalues and eigenvectors. The eigenvalues are the diagonal elements of the diagonal matrix **R**, and the columns of **U** are the eigenvectors. Here is an example illustrating the use of **eig**:

```
>> A = [3 -2 0; 2 -2 0; 0 1 1];
>> eig (A)
ans =
     1
    -1
     2
>> [U, R] = eig(A)
U =
          0     -0.4082     -0.8165
          0     -0.8165     -0.4082
     1.0000      0.4082     -0.4082
R =
     1      0      0
     0     -1      0
     0      0      2
```

The eigenvector in the first column of **U** corresponds to the eigenvalue in the first column of **R**, and so on. These are numerical values for the eigenpairs. To get symbolically calculated eigenpairs, type **[U, R] = eig(sym(A))**.

Doing Calculus with MATLAB

MATLAB has commands for most of the computations of basic calculus in its Symbolic Math Toolbox. This toolbox includes part of a separate program called Maple®, which processes the symbolic calculations.

Differentiation

You can use **diff** to differentiate symbolic expressions, and also to approximate the derivative of a function given numerically (say by an M-file):

```
>> syms x; diff(x^3)

ans =
3*x^2
```

Here MATLAB has figured out that the variable is **x**. (See *Default Variables* at the end of the chapter.) Alternatively,

```
>> f = inline('x^3', 'x'); diff(f(x))

ans =
3*x^2
```

The syntax for second derivatives is **diff(f(x), 2)**, and for *n*th derivatives, **diff(f(x), n)**. The command **diff** can also compute partial derivatives of expressions involving several variables, as in **diff(x^2*y, y)**, but to do multiple partials with respect to mixed variables you must use **diff** repeatedly, as in **diff(diff(sin(x*y/z), x), y)**. (Remember to declare **y** and **z** symbolic.)

There is one instance where differentiation must be represented by the letter **D**, namely when you need to specify a differential equation as input to a command. For example, to use the symbolic ODE solver on the differential equation $xy' + 1 = y$, you enter

```
dsolve('x*Dy + 1 = y', 'x')
```

Integration

MATLAB can compute definite and indefinite integrals. Here is an indefinite integral:

```
>> int ('x^2', 'x')

ans =
1/3*x^3
```

As with **diff**, you can declare **x** to be symbolic and dispense with the character string quotes. Note that MATLAB does not include a constant of integration; the output is a single antiderivative of the integrand. Now here is a definite integral:

```
>> syms x; int(asin(x), 0, 1)

ans =
1/2*pi-1
```

You are undoubtedly aware that not every function that appears in calculus can be symbolically integrated, and so numerical integration is sometimes necessary. MATLAB has three commands for numerical integration of a function $f(x)$: **quad**, **quad8**, and **quadl** (the latter is new in MATLAB 6). We recommend **quadl**, with **quad8** as a second choice. Here's an example:

```
>> syms x; int(exp(-x^4), 0, 1)
Warning: Explicit integral could not be found.
> In /data/matlabr12/toolbox/symbolic/@sym/int.m at line 58

ans =
int(exp(-x^4),x = 0 .. 1)
>> quadl(vectorize(exp(-x^4)), 0, 1)

ans =
     0.8448
```

➩ **The commands quad, quad8, and quadl will not accept Inf or -Inf as a limit of integration (though int will). The best way to handle a numerical improper integral over an infinite interval is to evaluate it over a** *very large* **interval.**

✓ You have another option. If you type **double(int( ))**, then Maple's numerical integration routine will evaluate the integral — even over an infinite range.

MATLAB can also do multiple integrals. The following command computes the double integral

$$\int_0^\pi \int_0^{\sin x} (x^2 + y^2)\, dy\, dx\; :$$

```
>> syms x y; int(int(x^2 + y^1, y, 0, sin(x)), 0, pi)
```

```
ans =
pi^2-32/9
```

Note that MATLAB presumes that the variable of integration in **int** is **x** unless you prescribe otherwise. Note also that the order of integration is as in calculus, from the "inside out". Finally, we observe that there is a numerical double integral command **dblquad**, whose properties and use we will allow you to discover from the online help.

Limits

You can use **limit** to compute right- and left-handed limits and limits at infinity. For example, here is $\lim_{x \to 0} \sin(x)/x$:

```
>> syms x; limit(sin(x)/x, x, 0)
```

```
ans =
1
```

To compute one-sided limits, use the **'right'** and **'left'** options. For example,

```
>> limit(abs(x)/x, x, 0, 'left')
```

```
ans =
-1
```

Limits at infinity can be computed using the symbol **Inf**:

```
>> limit((x^4 + x^2 - 3)/(3*x^4 - log(x)), x, Inf)
```

```
ans =
1/3
```

Sums and Products

Finite numerical sums and products can be computed easily using the vector capabilities of MATLAB and the commands **sum** and **prod**. For example,

```
>> X = 1:7;
>> sum(X)

ans =
      28
>> prod(X)

ans =
    5040
```

You can do finite and infinite symbolic sums using the command **symsum**. To illustrate, here is the telescoping sum

$$\sum_{k=1}^{n} \left(\frac{1}{k} - \frac{1}{1+k} \right) :$$

```
>> syms k n; symsum(1/k - 1/(k + 1), 1, n)

ans =
-1/(n+1)+1
```

And here is the well-known infinite sum

$$\sum_{n=1}^{\infty} \frac{1}{n^2} :$$

```
>> symsum(1/n^2, 1, Inf)

ans =
1/6*pi^2
```

Another familiar example is the sum of the infinite geometric series:

```
>> syms a k; symsum(a^k, 0, Inf)

ans =
-1/(a-1)
```

Note, however, that the answer is only valid for $|a| < 1$.

Taylor Series

You can use **taylor** to generate Taylor polynomial expansions of a specified order at a specified point. For example, to generate the Taylor polynomial up to order 10 at 0 of the function $\sin x$, we enter

```
>> syms x; taylor(sin(x), x, 10)

ans =
x-1/6*x^3+1/120*x^5-1/5040*x^7+1/362880*x^9
```

You can compute a Taylor polynomial at a point other than the origin. For example,

```
>> taylor(exp(x), 4, 2)

ans =
exp(2)+exp(2)*(x-2)+1/2*exp(2)*(x-2)^2+1/6*exp(2)*(x-2)^3
```

computes a Taylor polynomial of e^x centered at the point $x = 2$.

The command **taylor** can also compute Taylor expansions at infinity:

```
>> taylor(exp(1/x^2), 6, Inf)

ans =
1+1/x^2+1/2/x^4
```

Default Variables

You can use any letters to denote variables in functions — either MATLAB's or the ones you define. For example, there is nothing special about the use of **t** in the following, any letter will do as well:

```
>> syms t; diff(sin(t^2))

ans =
2*cos(t^2)*t
```

However, if there are multiple variables in an expression and you employ a MATLAB command that does not make explicit reference to one of them, then either you must make the reference explicit or MATLAB will use a built-in hierarchy to decide which variable is the "one in play". For example, `solve('x + y = 3')` solves for **x**, not **y**. If you want to solve for **y** in this example, you need to enter `solve('x + y = 3', 'y')`. MATLAB's default variable for `solve` is **x**. If there is no **x** in the equation(s), MATLAB looks for the letter nearest to **x** in alphabetical order (where **y** takes precedence over **w**, but **w** takes precedence over **z**, etc). Similarly for `diff`, `int`, and many other symbolic commands. Thus `syms w z; diff w*z` yields **z** as an answer. On occasion MATLAB assigns a different primary default variable — for example, the default independent variable for MATLAB's symbolic ODE solver `dsolve` is **t**. This is mentioned clearly in the online help for `dsolve`. If you have doubt about the default variables for any MATLAB command, you should check the online help.

Chapter 5

MATLAB Graphics

In this chapter we describe more of MATLAB's graphics commands and the most common ways of manipulating and customizing them. You can get a list of MATLAB graphics commands by typing **help graphics** (for general graphics commands), **help graph2d** (for two-dimensional graphing), **help graph3d** (for three-dimensional graphing), or **help specgraph** (for specialized graphing commands).

We have already discussed the commands **plot** and **ezplot** in Chapter 2. We will begin this chapter by discussing more uses of these commands, as well as the other most commonly used plotting commands in two and three dimensions. Then we will discuss some techniques for customizing and manipulating graphics.

Two-Dimensional Plots

Often one wants to draw a curve in the x-y plane, but with y not given explicitly as a function of x. There are two main techniques for plotting such curves: parametric plotting and contour or implicit plotting. We discuss these in turn in the next two subsections.

Parametric Plots

Sometimes x and y are both given as functions of some parameter. For example, the circle of radius 1 centered at (0,0) can be expressed in *parametric* form as $x = \cos(2\pi t)$, $y = \sin(2\pi t)$ where t runs from 0 to 1. Though y is not expressed as a function of x, you can easily graph this curve with **plot**, as follows:

```
>> T = 0:0.01:1;
```

```
>> plot(cos(2*pi*T), sin(2*pi*T))
>> axis square
```

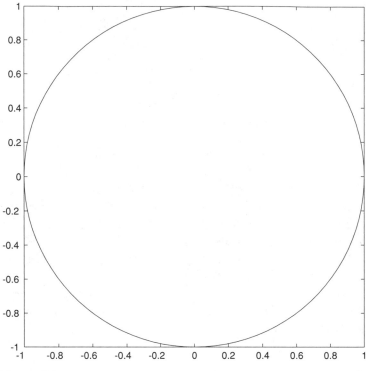

Figure 5-1

The output is shown in Figure 5.1. If you had used an increment of only 0.1 in the **T** vector, the result would have been a polygon with clearly visible corners, an indication that you should repeat the process with a smaller increment until you get a graph that looks smooth.

Symbolic   If you have version 2.1 or higher of the Symbolic Math Toolbox (corresponding to MATLAB version 5.3 or higher), then parametric plotting is also possible with **ezplot**. Thus one can obtain almost the same picture as Figure 5-1 with the command

```
>> ezplot('cos(t)', 'sin(t)', [0 2*pi]); axis square
```

Contour Plots and Implicit Plots

A *contour plot* of a function of two variables is a plot of the *level curves* of the function, that is, sets of points in the *x-y* plane where the function assumes a constant value. For example, the level curves of $x^2 + y^2$ are circles centered at the origin, and the *levels* are the squares of the radii of the circles. Contour plots are produced in MATLAB with **meshgrid** and **contour**. The command **meshgrid** produces a grid of points in a specified rectangular region, with a specified spacing. This grid is used by **contour** to produce a contour plot in the specified region.

We can make a contour plot of $x^2 + y^2$ as follows:

```
>> [X Y] = meshgrid(-3:0.1:3, -3:0.1:3);
>> contour(X, Y, X.^2 + Y.^2)
>> axis square
```

The plot is shown in Figure 5-2. We have used MATLAB's vector notation to

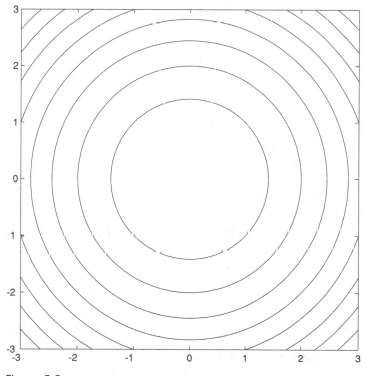

Figure 5-2

produce a grid with spacing 0.1 in both directions. We have also used **axis square** to force the same scale on both axes.

You can specify particular level sets by including an additional vector argument to **contour**. For example, to plot the circles of radii 1, $\sqrt{2}$, and $\sqrt{3}$, type

```
>> contour(X, Y, X.^2 + Y.^2, [1 2 3])
```

The vector argument must contain at least two elements, so if you want to plot a single level set, you must specify the same level twice. This is quite useful for implicit plotting of a curve given by an equation in x and y. For example, to plot the circle of radius 1 about the origin, type

```
>> contour(X, Y, X.^2 + Y.^2, [1 1])
```

Or to plot the lemniscate $x^2 - y^2 = (x^2 + y^2)^2$, rewrite the equation as

$$(x^2 + y^2)^2 - x^2 + y^2 = 0$$

and type

```
>> [X Y] = meshgrid(-1.1:0.01:1.1, -1.1:0.01:1.1);
>> contour(X, Y, (X.^2 + Y.^2).^2 - X.^2 + Y.^2, [0 0])
>> axis square
>> title('The lemniscate x^2-y^2=(x^2+y^2)^2')
```

The command **title** labels the plot with the indicated string. (In the default string interpreter, ^ is used for inserting an exponent and _ is used for subscripts.) The result is shown in Figure 5-3.

If you have the Symbolic Math Toolbox, contour plotting can also be done with the command **ezcontour**, and implicit plotting of a curve $f(x, y) = 0$ can also be done with **ezplot**. One can obtain almost the same picture as Figure 5-2 with the command

```
>> ezcontour('x^2 + y^2', [-3, 3], [-3, 3]); axis square
```

and almost the same picture as Figure 5-3 with the command

```
>> ezplot('(x^2 + y^2)^2 - x^2 + y^2', ...
[-1.1, 1.1], [-1.1, 1.1]); axis square
```

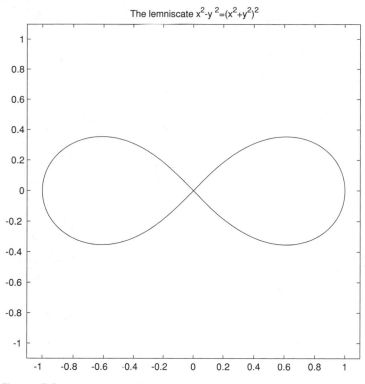

Figure 5-3

Field Plots

The MATLAB routine **quiver** is used to plot vector fields or arrays of arrows. The arrows can be located at equally spaced points in the plane (if x and y coordinates are not given explicitly), or they can be placed at specified locations. Sometimes some fiddling is required to scale the arrows so that they don't come out looking too big or too small. For this purpose, **quiver** takes an optional scale factor argument. The following code, for example, plots a vector field with a "saddle point," corresponding to a combination of an attractive force pointing toward the x axis and a repulsive force pointing away from the y axis:

```
>> [x, y] = meshgrid(-1.1:.2:1.1, -1.1:.2:1.1);
>> quiver(x, -y); axis equal; axis off
```

The output is shown in Figure 5-4.

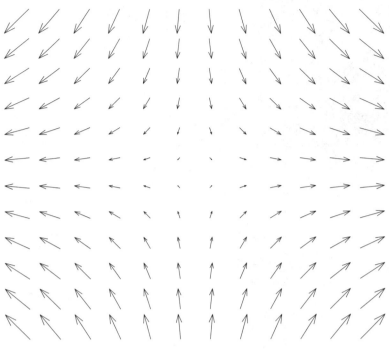

Figure 5-4

Three-Dimensional Plots

MATLAB has several routines for producing three-dimensional plots.

Curves in Three-Dimensional Space

For plotting curves in 3-space, the basic command is **plot3**, and it works like **plot**, except that it takes three vectors instead of two, one for the x coordinates, one for the y coordinates, and one for the z coordinates. For example, we can plot a helix (see Figure 5-5) with

```
>> T = -2:0.01:2;
>> plot3(cos(2*pi*T), sin(2*pi*T), T)
```

Again, if you have the Symbolic Math Toolbox, there is a shortcut using **ezplot3**; you can instead plot the helix with

```
>> ezplot3('cos(2*pi*t)', 'sin(2*pi*t)', 't', [-2, 2])
```

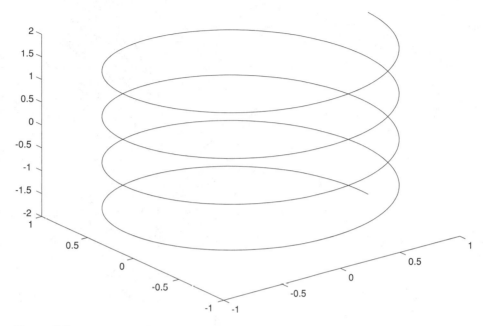

Figure 5-5

Surfaces in Three-Dimensional Space

There are two basic commands for plotting surfaces in 3-space: **mesh** and **surf**. The former produces a transparent "mesh" surface; the latter produces an opaque shaded one. There are two different ways of using each command, one for plotting surfaces in which the z coordinate is given as a function of x and y, and one for *parametric surfaces* in which x, y, and z are all given as functions of two other parameters. Let us illustrate the former with **mesh** and the latter with **surf**.

To plot $z = f(x, y)$, one begins with a **meshgrid** command as in the case of **contour**. For example, the "saddle surface" $z = x^2 - y^2$ can be plotted with

```
>> [X,Y] = meshgrid(-2:.1:2, -2:.1:2);
>> Z = X.^2 - Y.^2;
>> mesh(X, Y, Z)
```

The result is shown in Figure 5-6, although it looks much better on the screen since MATLAB shades the surface with a color scheme depending on the z coordinate. We could have gotten an opaque surface instead by replacing **mesh** with **surf**.

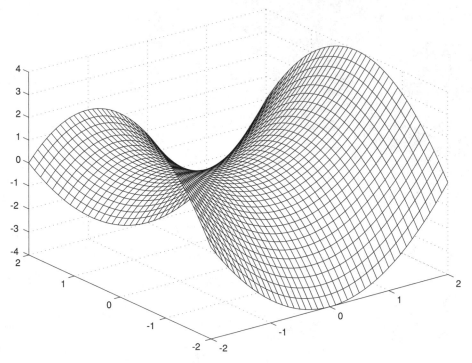

Figure 5-6

With the Symbolic Math Toolbox, there is a shortcut command **ezmesh**, and you can obtain a result very similar to Figure 5-6 with

```
>> ezmesh('x^2 - y^2', [-2, 2], [-2, 2])
```

If one wants to plot a surface that cannot be represented by an equation of the form $z = f(x, y)$, for example the sphere $x^2 + y^2 + z^2 = 1$, then it is better to parameterize the surface using a suitable coordinate system, in this case cylindrical or spherical coordinates. For example, we can take as parameters the vertical coordinate z and the polar coordinate θ in the x-y plane. If r denotes the distance to the z axis, then the equation of the sphere becomes $r^2 + z^2 = 1$, or $r = \sqrt{1 - z^2}$, and so $x = \sqrt{1 - z^2} \cos\theta$, $y = \sqrt{1 - z^2} \sin\theta$. Thus we can produce our plot with

```
>> [theta, Z] = meshgrid((0:0.1:2)*pi, (-1:0.1:1));
>> X = sqrt(1 - Z.^2).*cos(theta);
```

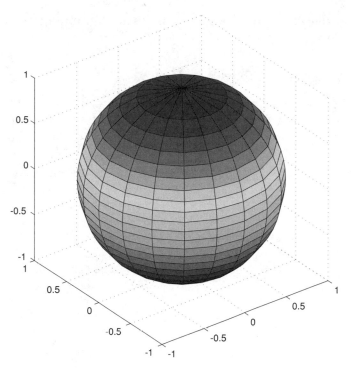

Figure 5-7

```
>> Y = sqrt(1 - Z.^2).*sin(theta);
>> surf(X, Y, Z); axis square
```

The result is shown in Figure 5-7.

With the Symbolic Math Toolbox, parametric plotting of surfaces has been greatly simplified with the commands **ezsurf** and **ezmesh**, and you can obtain a result very similar to Figure 5-7 with

```
>> ezsurf('sqrt(1-s^2)*cos(t)', 'sqrt(1-s^2)*sin(t)', ...
's', [-1, 1, 0, 2*pi]); axis equal
```

Special Effects

So far we have only discussed graphics commands that produce or modify a single static figure window. But MATLAB is also capable of combining several

figures in one window, or of producing animated graphics that change with
time.

Combining Figures in One Window

The command **subplot** divides the figure window into an array of smaller
figures. The first two arguments give the dimensions of the array of sub-
plots, and the last argument gives the number of the subplot (counting left
to right across the first row, then left to right across the next row, and so on)
in which to put the next figure. The following example, whose output appears
as Figure 5-8, produces a 2×2 array of plots of the first four Bessel functions
J_n, $0 \le n \le 3$:

```
>> x = 0:0.05:40;
>> for j = 1:4, subplot(2,2,j)
       plot(x, besselj(j*ones(size(x)), x))
end
```

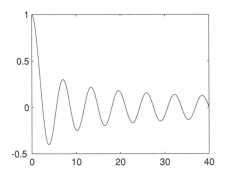
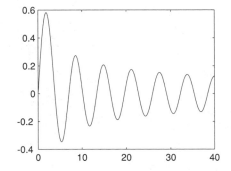
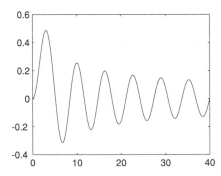
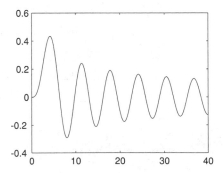

Figure 5-8

Animations

The simplest way to produce an animated picture is with **comet**, which produces a parametric plot of a curve (the way **plot** does), except that you can see the curve being traced out in time. For example,

```
>> t = 0:0.01*pi:2*pi;
>> figure; axis equal; axis([-1 1 -1 1]); hold on
>> comet(cos(t), sin(t))
```

displays uniform circular motion.

For more complicated animations, you can use **getframe** and **movie**. The command **getframe** captures the active figure window for one frame of the movie, and **movie** then plays back the result. For example, the following (in MATLAB 5.3 or later — earlier versions of the software used a slightly different syntax) produces a movie of a vibrating string:

```
>> x = 0:0.01:1;
>> for j = 0:50
     plot(x, sin(j*pi/5)*sin(pi*x)), axis([0, 1, -2, 2])
     M(j+1) = getframe;
end
>> movie(M)
```

It is worth noting that the **axis** command here is important, to ensure that each frame of the movie is drawn with the same coordinate axes. (Otherwise the scale of the axes will be different in each frame and the resulting movie will be totally misleading.) The semicolon after the **getframe** command is also important; it prevents the spewing forth of a lot of numerical data with each frame of the movie. Finally, make sure that while MATLAB executes the loop that generates the frames, you do not cover the active figure window with another window (such as the Command Window). If you do, the contents of the other window will be stored in the frames of the movie.

✓ MATLAB 6 has a new command **movieview** that you can use in place of **movie** to view the animation in a separate window, with a button to replay the movie when it is done.

Customizing and Manipulating Graphics

☞ *This is a more advanced topic; if you wish you can skip it on a first reading.*

So far in this chapter, we have discussed the most commonly used MATLAB routines for generating plots. But often, to get the results one wants, one needs to customize or manipulate the graphics these commands produce. Knowing how to do this requires understanding a few basic principles concerning the way MATLAB stores and displays graphics. For most purposes, the discussion here will be sufficient. But if you need more information, you might eventually want to consult one of the books devoted exclusively to MATLAB graphics, such as *Using MATLAB Graphics*, which comes free (in PDF format) with the software and can be accessed in the "MATLAB Manuals" subsection of the "Printable Documentation" section in the Help Browser (or under "Full Documentation Set" from the **helpdesk** in MATLAB 5.3 and earlier versions), or *Graphics and GUIs with MATLAB*, 2nd ed., by P. Marchand, CRC Press, Boca Raton, FL, 1999.

In a typical MATLAB session, one may have many figure windows open at once. However, only one of these can be "active" at any one time. One can find out which figure is active with the command **gcf**, short for "get current figure," and one can change the active figure to, say, figure number 5 with the command **figure(5)**, or else by clicking on figure window 5 with the mouse. The command **figure** (with no arguments) creates a blank figure window. (This is sometimes useful if you want to avoid overwriting an existing plot.)

Once a figure has been created and made active, there are two basic ways to manipulate it. The active figure can be modified by MATLAB commands in the command window, such as the commands **title** and **axis square** that we have already encountered. Or one can modify the figure by using the menus and/or tools in the figure window itself. Let's consider a few examples. To insert labels or text into a plot, one may use the commands **text**, **xlabel**, **ylabel**, **zlabel**, and **legend**, in addition to **title**. As the names suggest, **xlabel**, **ylabel**, and **zlabel** add text next to the coordinate axes, **legend** puts a "legend" on the plot, and **text** adds text at a specific point. These commands take various optional arguments that can be used to change the font family and font size of the text. As an example, let's illustrate how to modify our plot of the lemniscate (Figure 5-3) by adding and modifying text:

```
>> figure(3)
>> title('The lemniscate x^2-y^2=(x^2+y^2)^2',...
```

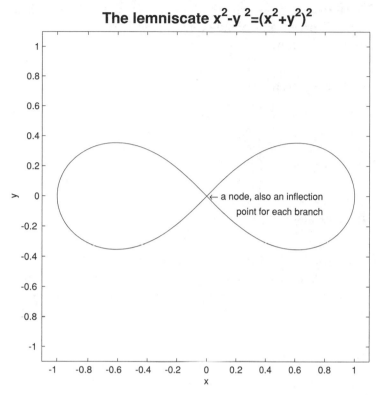

Figure 5-9

```
'FontSize', 16, 'FontName', 'Helvetica',...
'FontWeight', 'bold')
>> text(0, 0, '\leftarrow a node, also an inflection')
>> text(0.2, -0.1, 'point for each branch')
>> xlabel('x'); ylabel('y')
```

The result is shown in Figure 5-9. Note that many symbols (an arrow pointing to the left in this case) can be inserted into a text string by calling them with names starting with \. (If you've used the scientific typesetting program TₑX, you'll recognize the convention here.) In most cases the names are self-explanatory. For example, you get a Greek π by typing **\pi**, a summation sign $\sum$ by typing either **\Sigma** (for a capital sigma) or **\sum**, and arrows pointing in various directions with **\leftarrow**, **\uparrow**, and so on. For more details and a complete list of available symbols, see the listing for "Text Properties" in the Help Browser.

An alternative is to make use of the tool bar at the top of the figure window. The button indicated by the letter "A" adds text to a figure, and the menu item

Text Properties... in the Tools menu (in MATLAB 5.3), or else the menu item Figure Properties... in the Edit menu (in MATLAB 6), can be used to change the font style and font size.

Change of Viewpoint

Another common and important way to vary a graphic is to change the viewpoint in 3-space. This can be done with the command **view**, and also (at least in MATLAB 5.3 and higher) by using the **Rotate 3D** option in the **Tools** menu at the top of the figure window. The command **view(2)** projects a figure into the x-y plane (by looking down on it from the positive z axis), and the command **view(3)** views it from the default direction in 3-space, which is in the direction looking toward the origin from a point far out on the ray $z = 0.5t$, $x = -0.5272t$, $y = -0.3044t$, $t > 0$.

⇨ **In MATLAB, any two-dimensional plot can be "viewed in 3D," and any three-dimensional plot can be projected into the plane. Thus Figure 5-5 above (the helix), if followed by the command view(2), produces a circle.**

Change of Plot Style

Another important way to change the style of graphics is to modify the color or line style in a plot or to change the scale on the axes. Within a **plot** command, one can change the color of a graph, or plot with a dashed or dotted line, or mark the plotted points with special symbols, simply by adding a string as a third argument for every x-y pair. Symbols for colors are **'y'** for yellow, **'m'** for magenta, **'c'** for cyan, **'r'** for red, **'g'** for green, **'b'** for blue, **'w'** for white, and **'k'** for black. Symbols for point markers include **'o'** for a circle, **'x'** for an X-mark, **'+'** for a plus sign, and **'*'** for a star. Symbols for line styles include **'-'** for a solid line, **':'** for a dotted line, and **'--'** for a dashed line. If a point style is given but no line style, then the points are plotted but no curve is drawn connecting them. The same methods work with **plot3** in place of **plot**. For example, one can produce a solid red sine curve along with a dotted blue cosine curve, marking all the local maximum points on each curve with a distinctive symbol of the same color as the plot, as follows:

```
>> X = (-2:0.02:2)*pi; Y1 = sin(X); Y2 = cos(X);
>> plot(X, Y1, 'r-', X, Y2, 'b:'); hold on
>> X1 = [-3*pi/2 pi/2]; Y3 = [1 1]; plot(X1, Y3, 'r+')
>> X2 = [-2*pi 0 2*pi]; Y4 = [1 1 1]; plot(X2, Y4, 'b*')
```

Here we would probably want the tick marks on the x axis located at multiples of π. This can be done with the **set** command applied to the properties of the axes (and/or by selecting **Edit** : **Axes Properties...** in MATLAB 6, or **Tools** : **Axes Properties...** in MATLAB 5.3). The command **set** is used to change various properties of graphics. To apply it to "Axes", it has to be combined with the command **gca**, which stands for "get current axes". The code

```
>> set(gca, 'XTick', (-2:2)*pi, 'XTickLabel',...
'-2pi|-pi|0|pi|2pi')
```

in combination with the code above gets the current axes, sets the ticks on the x axis to go from -2π to 2π in multiples of π, and then labels these ticks the way one would want (rather than in decimal notation, which is ugly here). The result is shown in Figure 5-10. Incidentally, you might wonder how to label the ticks as -2π, $-\pi$, etc., instead of **-2pi**, **-pi**, and so on. This is trickier but you can do it by typing

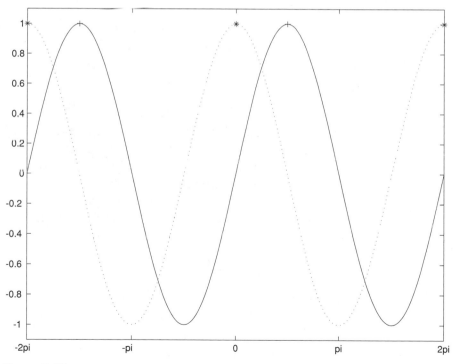

Figure 5-10

```
>> set(gca, 'FontName', 'Symbol')
>> set(gca, 'XTickLabel', '-2p|-p|0|p|2p')
```

since in the Symbol font, π occupies the slot held by **p** in text fonts.

Full-Fledged Customization

What about changes to other aspects of a plot? The useful commands **get** and **set** can be used to obtain a complete list of the properties of a graphics window, and then to modify them. These properties are arranged in a hierarchical structure, identified by markers (which are simply numbers) called *handles*. If you type **get(gcf)**, you will "get" a (rather long) list of properties of the current figure (whose number is returned by the function **gcf**). Some of these might read

```
Color = [0.8  0.8  0.8]
CurrentAxes = [72.0009]
PaperSize = [8.5 11]
Children = [72.0009]
```

Here **PaperSize** is self-explanatory; **Color** gives the background color of the plot in RGB (red-green-blue) coordinates, where [0 0 0] is black and [1 1 1] is white. ([0.8 0.8 0.8] is light gray.) Note that **CurrentAxes** and **Children** in this example have the same value, the one-element vector containing the funny-looking number 72.0009. This number would also be returned by the command **gca** ("get current axes"); it is the handle to the axis properties of the plot. The fact that this also shows up under **Children** indicates that the axis properties are "children" of the figure, this is, they lie one level down in the hierarchical structure. Typing **get(gca)** or **get(72.0009)** would then give you a list of axis properties, including further **Children** such as **Line** objects, within which you would find the **XData** and **YData** encoding the actual plot.

Once you have located the properties you're interested in, they can be changed with **set**. For example,

```
>> set(gcf, 'Color', [1  0  0])
```

changes the background color of the border of the figure window to red, and

```
>> set(gca, 'Color', [1  1  0])
```

changes the background color of the plot itself (a child of the figure window) to yellow (which in the RGB scheme is half red, half green).

This "one at a time" method for locating and modifying figure properties can be speeded up using the command **findobj** to locate the handles of all the descendents (the main figure window, its children, children of children, etc.) of the current figure. One can also limit the search to handles containing elements of a specific type. For example, **findobj('Type', 'Line')** hunts for all handles of objects containing a Line element. Once one has located these, **set** can be used to change the **LineStyle** from solid to dashed, etc. In addition, the low-level graphics commands **line, rectangle, fill, surface,** and **image** can be used to create new graphics elements within a figure window.

As an example of these techniques, the following code creates a chessboard on a white background, as shown in Figure 5-11:

```
>> white = [1 1 1]; gray = 0.7*white;
>> a = [0 1 1 0]; b = [0 0 1 1]; c = [1 1 1 1];
```

Figure 5-11

```
>> figure; hold on
>> for k = 0:1, for j = 0:2:6
      fill(a'*c + c'*(0:2:6) + k, b'*c + j + k, gray)
end, end
>> plot(8*a', 8*b', 'k')
>> set(gca, 'XTickLabel', [], 'YTickLabel', [])
>> set(gcf, 'Color', white); axis square
```

Here **white** and **gray** are the RGB codings for white and gray. The double **for** loop draws the 32 dark squares on the chessboard, using **fill**, with **j** indexing the dark squares in a single vertical column, with **k = 0** giving the odd-numbered rows, and with **k = 1** giving the even-numbered rows. Note that **fill** here takes three arguments: a matrix, each of whose columns gives the x coordinates of the vertices of a polygon to be filled (in this case a square), a second matrix whose corresponding columns give the y coordinates of the vertices, and a color. We've constructed the matrices with four columns, one for each of the solid squares in a single horizontal row. The **plot** command draws the solid black line around the outside of the board. Finally, the first **set** command removes the printed labels on the axes, and the second **set** command resets the background color to white.

Quick Plot Editing in the Figure Window

Almost all of the command-line changes one can make in a figure have counterparts that can be executed using the menus in the figure window. So why bother learning both techniques? The reason is that editing in the figure window is often more convenient, especially when one wishes to "experiment" with various changes, while editing a figure with MATLAB code is often required when writing M-files. So the true MATLAB expert uses both techniques. The figure window menus are a bit different in MATLAB 6 than in MATLAB 5.3. In MATLAB 6, you can zoom in and out and rotate the figure using the **Tools** menu, you can insert labels and text with the **Insert** menu, and you can view and edit the figure properties (just as you would with **set**) with the **Edit** menu. For example you can change the ticks and labels on the axes by selecting **Edit : Edit Axes...**. In MATLAB 5.3, editing of the figure properties is done with the **Property Editor**, located under the **File** menu of the figure window. By default this opens to the figure properties, and double-clicking on "Children" then enables you to access the axes properties, etc.

Sound

You can use **sound** to generate sound on your computer (provided that your computer is suitably equipped). Although, strictly speaking, **sound** is not a graphics command, we have placed it in this chapter since we think of "sight" and "sound" as being allied features. The command **sound** takes a vector, views it as the waveform of a sound, and "plays" it. The length of the vector, divided by 8192, is the length of the sound in seconds. A "sinusoidal" vector corresponds to a pure tone, and the frequency of the sinusoidal signal determines the pitch. Thus the following example plays the motto from Beethoven's 5th Symphony:

```
>> x=0:0.1*pi:250*pi; y=zeros(1,200); z=0:0.1*pi:1000*pi;
>> sound([sin(x),y,sin(x),y,sin(x),y,sin(z*4/5),y,...
sin(8/9*x),y,sin(8/9*x),y,sin(8/9*x),y,sin(z*3/4)]);
```

Note that the zero vector **y** in this example creates a very short pause between successive notes.

Practice Set B

Calculus, Graphics, and Linear Algebra

Symbolic Problems 2, 3, 5–7, and parts of 10–12 require the Symbolic Math Tool-box. The others do not.

1. Use **contour** to do the following:
   (a) Plot the level curves of the function $f(x, y) = 3y + y^3 - x^3$ in the region where x and y are between -1 and 1 (to get an idea of what the curves look like near the origin), and in some larger regions (to get the big picture).
   (b) Plot the curve $3y + y^3 - x^3 = 5$.
   (c) Plot the level curve of the function $f(x, y) = y \ln x + x \ln y$ that contains the point $(1, 1)$.

2. Find the derivatives of the following functions. If possible, simplify each answer.
   (a) $f(x) = 6x^3 - 5x^2 + 2x - 3$.
   (b) $f(x) = \frac{2x-1}{x^2+1}$.
   (c) $f(x) = \sin(3x^2 + 2)$.
   (d) $f(x) = \arcsin(2x + 3)$.
   (e) $f(x) = \sqrt{1 + x^4}$.
   (f) $f(x) = x^r$.
   (g) $f(x) = \arctan(x^2 + 1)$.

3. See if MATLAB can do the following integrals symbolically. For the indefinite integrals, check the results by differentiating.
   (a) $\int_0^{\pi/2} \cos x \, dx$.
   (b) $\int x \sin(x^2) \, dx$.
   (c) $\int \sin(3x)\sqrt{1 - \cos(3x)} \, dx$.

(d) $\int x^2 \sqrt{x+4}\,dx$.

(e) $\int_{-\infty}^{\infty} e^{-x^2}\,dx$.

4. Compute the following integrals numerically, using **quad8** or **quadl**:

(a) $\int_0^{\pi} e^{\sin x}\,dx$.

(b) $\int_0^1 \sqrt{x^3+1}\,dx$.

(c) $\int_{-\infty}^{\infty} e^{-x^2}\,dx$. In this case, also approximate the error in the numerical answer, by comparing with the exact answer found in Problem 3.

5. Evaluate the following limits:

(a) $\lim_{x\to 0} \frac{\sin x}{x}$.

(b) $\lim_{x\to -\pi} \frac{1+\cos x}{x+\pi}$.

(c) $\lim_{x\to\infty} x^2 e^{-x}$.

(d) $\lim_{x\to 1^-} \frac{1}{x-1}$.

(e) $\lim_{x\to 0^+} \sin\left(\frac{1}{x}\right)$.

6. Compute the following sums:

(a) $\sum_{k=1}^{n} k^2$.

(b) $\sum_{k=0}^{n} r^k$.

(c) $\sum_{k=0}^{\infty} \frac{x^k}{k!}$. You may need the gamma function $\Gamma(x) = \int_0^{\infty} e^{-t} t^{x-1}\,dt$, called **gamma** in MATLAB, which satisfies $\Gamma(k+1) = k!$.

(d) $\sum_{k=-\infty}^{\infty} \frac{1}{(z-k)^2}$.

7. Find the Taylor polynomial of the indicated order n at the indicated point c for the following functions:

(a) $f(x) = e^x$, $n = 7$, $c = 0$.

(b) $f(x) = \sin x$, $n = 5$ and 6, $c = 0$.

(c) $f(x) = \sin x$, $n = 6$, $c = 2$.

(d) $f(x) = \tan x$, $n = 7$, $c = 0$.

(e) $f(x) = \ln x$, $n = 5$, $c = 1$

(f) $f(x) = \text{erf}(x)$, $n = 9$, $c = 0$.

8. Plot the following surfaces:

(a) $z = \sin x \sin y$ for $-3\pi < x \le 3\pi$ and $-3\pi \le y \le 3\pi$.

(b) $z = (x^2 + y^2)\cos(x^2 + y^2)$ for $-1 \le x \le 1$ and $1 \le y \le 1$.

9. Create a 17-frame movie, whose frames show filled red circles of radius $1/2$ centered at the points $\left(4\cos(j\pi/8), 4\sin(j\pi/8)\right)$, $j = 0, 1, \ldots, 16$. Make sure all the circles are drawn on the same set of axes, and that they look like circles, not ellipses.

10. In this problem we use the *backslash* operator, or "left-matrix-divide" operator introduced in the *Solving Linear Systems* section of Chapter 4.

(a) Use the backslash operator to solve the system of linear equations in Problem 3 of Practice Set A.

(b) Now try the same method on Problem 4 of Practice Set A. MATLAB finds one, but not all, answer(s). Can you explain why? If not, see Problem 11 below, as well as part (d) of this problem.

(c) Next try the method on this problem:

$$w + 3x - 2y + 4z = 1$$
$$-2w + 3x + 4y - z = 1$$
$$-4w - 3x + y + 2z = 1$$
$$2w + 3x - 4y + z = 1.$$

Check your answer by matrix multiplication.

(d) Finally, try the matrix division method on:

$$ax + by = u$$
$$cx + dy = v.$$

Don't forget to declare the variables to be symbolic. Your answer should involve a fraction, and so will be valid only when its denominator is nonzero. Evaluate **det** on the coefficient matrix of the system. Compare with the denominator.

11. We deal in this problem with 3×3 matrices, although the concepts are valid in any dimension.

(a) Consider the rows of a square matrix A. They are vectors in 3-space and so span a subspace of dimension 3, 2, 1, or possibly 0 (if all the entries of A are zero). That number is called the *rank* of A. The MATLAB command **rank** computes the rank of a matrix. Try it on the four coefficient matrices in each of the parts of Problem 10. Comment on MATLAB's answer for the fourth one.

(b) An $n \times n$ matrix is *nonsingular* if its rank is n. Which of the four matrices you computed in part (a) are nonsingular?

(c) Another measure of nonsingularity is given by the *determinant* — a fundamental result in linear algebra is that a matrix is nonsingular precisely when its determinant is nonzero. In that case a unique matrix B exists that satisfies $AB = BA =$ the identity matrix. We denote this inverse matrix by A^{-1}. MATLAB can compute inverses with **inv**. Compute **det(A)** for the four coefficient matrices, and for the nonsingular ones, find their inverses. Note: The matrix equation $Ax = b$ has a unique solution, namely $x = A^{-1}b = $ **A\b**, when A is nonsingular.

12. As explained in Chapter 4, when you compute **[U, R] = eig(A)**, each column of U is an eigenvector of A associated to the eigenvalue that

appears in the corresponding column of the diagonal matrix R. This says exactly that $AU = UR$.

(a) Verify the equality $AU = UR$ for each of the coefficient matrices in Problem 10.

(b) In fact, $\text{rank}(A) = \text{rank}(U)$, so when A is nonsingular, then

$$U^{-1}AU = R.$$

Thus if two diagonalizable matrices A and B have the same set of eigenvectors, then the fact that diagonal matrices commute implies the same for A and B. Verify these facts for the two matrices

$$A = \begin{pmatrix} 1 & 0 & 2 \\ -1 & 0 & 4 \\ -1 & -1 & 5 \end{pmatrix}, \quad B = \begin{pmatrix} 5 & 2 & -8 \\ 3 & 6 & -10 \\ 3 & 3 & -7 \end{pmatrix};$$

that is, show that the matrices of eigenvectors are the "same" — that is, the columns are the same up to scalar multiples — and verify that $AB = BA$.

13. This problem, having to do with genetic inheritance, is based on Chapter 12 in *Applications of Linear Algebra*, 3rd ed., by C. Rorres and H. Anton, John Wiley & Sons, 1984. In a typical inheritance model, a trait in the off-spring is determined by the passing of a genotype from the parents, where there are two independent possibilities from each parent, say A and a, and each is equally likely. (A is the dominant gene, and a is recessive.) Then we have the following table of probabilities of the possible geno-types for the offspring for all possible combinations of the genotypes of the parents:

		AA-AA	AA-Aa	AA-aa	Aa-Aa	Aa-aa	aa-aa
Genotype	AA	1	1/2	0	1/4	0	0
of	Aa	0	1/2	1	1/2	1/2	0
Offspring	aa	0	0	0	1/4	1/2	1

Genotype of Parents

Now suppose one has a population in which mating only occurs with one's identical genotype. (That's not far-fetched if we are considering con-trolled plant or vegetable populations.) Next suppose that x_0, y_0, and z_0 denote the percentage of the population with genotype AA, Aa, and aa respectively at the outset of observation. We then denote by x_n, y_n, and z_n the percentages in the nth generation. We are interested in knowing these numbers for large n and how they depend on the initial population. Clearly

$$x_n + y_n + z_n = 1, \quad n \geq 0.$$

Now we can use the table to express a relationship between the nth and $(n+1)$st generations. Because of our presumption on mating, only the first, fourth, and sixth columns are relevant. Indeed a moment's reflection reveals that we have

$$x_{n+1} = x_n + \frac{1}{4}y_n$$

$$y_{n+1} = \frac{1}{2}y_n \qquad\qquad (*)$$

$$z_{n+1} = z_n + \frac{1}{4}y_n.$$

(a) Write the equations (*) as a single matrix equation $X_{n+1} = MX_n$, $n \geq 0$. Explain carefully what the entries of the column matrix X_n are and what the coefficients of the square matrix M are.

(b) Apply the matrix equation recursively to express X_n in terms of X_0 and powers of M.

(c) Next use MATLAB to compute the eigenvalues and eigenvectors of M.

(d) From Problem 12 you know that $MU = UR$, where R is the diagonal matrix of eigenvalues of M. Solve that equation for M. Now it should be evident to you what $R_\infty = \lim_{n\to\infty} R^n$ is. Use that and your expression of M in terms of R to compute $M_\infty = \lim_{n\to\infty} M^n$.

(e) Describe the eventual population distribution by computing $M_\infty X_0$.

(f) Check your answer by directly computing M^n for large specific values of M. (*Hint*: MATLAB can compute the powers of a matrix **M** by entering **M^10**, for example.)

(g) You can alter the fundamental presumption in this problem by assuming, alternatively, that all members of the nth generation must mate only with a parent whose genotype is purely dominant. Compute the eventual population distribution of that model. Chapters 12–14 in Rorres and Anton have other interesting models.

Chapter 6

M-Books

MATLAB is exceptionally strong in linear algebra, numerical methods, and graphical interpretation of data. It is easily programmed and relatively easy to learn to use. As such it has proven invaluable to engineers and scientists who are working on problems that rely on scientific techniques and methods at which MATLAB excels. Very often the individuals and groups that so employ MATLAB are primarily interested in the numbers and graphs that emerge from MATLAB commands, processes, and programs. Therefore, it is enough for them to work in a MATLAB Command Window, from which they can easily print or export their desired output. At most, the production technique described in Chapter 3 involving diary files is sufficient for their presentation needs.

However, other practitioners of mathematical software find themselves with two additional requirements. They need a mathematical software package embedded in an interactive environment — one in which the output is not necessarily "linear", that is, one that they can manipulate and massage without regard to chronology or geographical location. Second, they need a higher-level presentation mode, which affords graphics integrated with text, with different formats for input and output, and one that can communicate effortlessly with other software applications. Some of MATLAB's competitors have focused on such needs in designing the interfaces (or front ends) behind which their mathematical software runs. MATLAB has decided to concentrate on the software rather than the interface — and for the reasons and purposes outlined above, that is clearly a wise decision. But for academic users (both faculty and especially students), for authors, and even for applied scientists who want to use MATLAB to generate slick presentations, the interface demands can become very important. For them, MATLAB has provided the *M-book* interface, which we describe in this chapter.

The M-book interface allows the user to operate MATLAB from a special Microsoft Word document instead of from a MATLAB Command Window. In this mode, the user should think of Word as running in the foreground and MATLAB as running in the background. Lines that you enter into your Word document are passed to the MATLAB engine in the background and executed there, whereupon the output is returned to Word (through the intermediary of Visual Basic®), and then both input and output are automatically formatted. One obtains a living document in the sense that one can edit the document as one normally edits a word processing document. So one can revisit input lines that need adjustment, change them, and reexecute on the spot — after which the old outdated output is automatically overwritten with new output. The graphical output that results from MATLAB graphics commands appear in the Word document, immediately after the commands that generated them. Erroneous input and output are easily expunged, enhanced formatting can be done in a way that is no more complicated than what one does in a word processor, and in the end the result of your MATLAB session can be an attractive, easily readable, and highly informative document. Of course, one can "cheat" by editing one's output — we shall discuss that and other pitfalls and strengths in what follows.

Enabling M-Books

To run the M-book interface you must have Microsoft Word on your computer. It is possible to run the interface with earlier versions of Word, but we find that it works best if you have Word 97. (In fact, we find that it runs better in Word 97 than it does in Word 2000, though the difference is not usually significant.) The interface is enabled when you install MATLAB. This is done in one of three ways depending on which version of MATLAB you have. In some instances, during installation, you will be prompted to enter the location of the Word executable file and the Word template directory. These are usually easily located; for example, on many PCs the former is in `MSOffice\Office\Winword.exe`, and the latter is in `MSOffice\ Templates`. You may also be asked to specify a template file — in that case, select `normal.dot` in the `Templates` directory. The installation program will create a new template called `m-book.dot`, which is the Word template file associated with M-book documents.

✓ If you don't know where the Word files are located on your PC, go to **Find** from the **Start** menu on the Task Bar, and search your hard drive for the files `Winword.exe` and `normal.dot`.

In other instances, you may not notice any prompt for Word information during installation. This can mean that your computer found the Word executable and template information and set up the associations automatically; or it can mean that it ignored the M-book configuration completely. In either eventuality, it is best, after installation, to type `notebook -setup` from the Command Window. Follow the ensuing instructions, which will be essentially the same as in the first possibility described in the last paragraph.

Starting M-Books

The most common way to start up the M-book interface is to type `notebook` at the Command Window prompt. This is the only way to start the M-book interface if it is your first foray into the venue. After you type `notebook`, you will see Microsoft Word launch and a blank Word document will fill your screen. We will refer to this document as an M-book. The difference between a blank M-book and a normal Word document is only apparent if you peruse the menu bar. There you will see an entry that is not present in a normal Word document — namely, the **Notebook** menu. Click on it and examine the menu items that appear. We will describe each of them and their functions in our discussion below. If this is not your first experience with M-books, and you have already saved an M-book, say under the name `Problem1.doc`, then you can open it by typing `notebook Problem1.doc` at the Command Window prompt. Even though you may not see it, the MATLAB Command Window is alive, but it is hidden behind the M-book.

⇨ **On some systems, you may see a DOS command window appear after typing `notebook`, but before the M-book appears. We recommend that you close that window before working in the M-book.**

✓ For M-books to work properly, you need to have "Macros Enabled" in your Word installation. If an M-book opens as a regular Word document, without M-book functionality, it probably means that macros have been disabled. To enable them, first close the document (without saving changes), then go to **Tools : Macro : Security...** from the Word menu bar, and reset your security level to Medium or Low. Then reopen the M-book.

✓ An alternate, and on some systems (especially networked systems) a preferable, launch method is first to open a previously saved M-book — either directly through **File : Open...** in Word or by double-clicking on the file name in Windows Explorer. Word recognizes that the document is an M-book, so automatically launches MATLAB if it is not already running. A word of caution: If you have more than one version of MATLAB installed, Word will launch the version you installed last. To override this, you can open the MATLAB version you want *before* you open the M-book.

You can now type into the M-book in the usual way. In fact you could prepare a document in this screen in precisely the same manner that you would in a normal Word screen. The background features of MATLAB are only activated if you do one of two things: either access the items in the **Notebook** menu or press the key combination CTRL+ENTER. Type into your M-book the line 23/45 and press CTRL+ENTER. After a short delay you will see what you entered change font to bold New Courier, encased in brackets, and then the output

```
ans =
     0.5111
```

will appear below, also in New Courier font (but not bold). It is also likely that the input and output will be colored (the input in green, the output in blue). Your cursor should be on the line following the output, but if it is at the end of the output line, move it down a line and type **solve('x^2 - 5*x + 5 = 0')** followed by CTRL+ENTER. After some thought MATLAB feeds the answer to the M-book:

```
ans=
[5/2+1/2*5^(1/2)]
[5/2-1/2*5^(1/2)]
```

Finally, try typing **ezplot('x^3 - x')**, then CTRL+ENTER, and watch the graph appear. At this point your M-book should look like Figure 6-1.

You may note that your commands take a little longer to evaluate than they would inside a normal MATLAB Command Window. This is not surprising considering the amount of information that is passing back and forth between MATLAB and Word. Continue entering MATLAB commands that are familiar to you (always followed by CTRL+ENTER), and observe that you obtain the output you expect, except that it is formatted and integrated into your M-book.

✓ If you want to start a fresh M-book, click on **File**:**New M-book** in the Menu Bar, or **File**:**New**, and then click on m-book.dot.

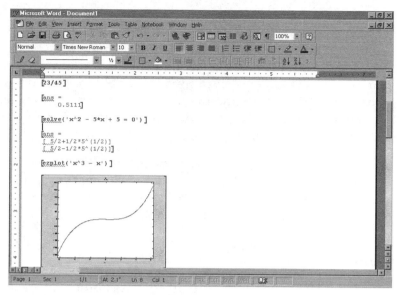

Figure 6-1: A Simple M-Book.

Working with M-Books

You interact with data in your M-book in two ways — via the keyboard or through the menu bar.

Editing Input

Place your cursor in the line containing the second command of the previous section — where we solved the quadratic equation

$$x^2 - 5x + 5 = 0.$$

Click to the left of the equal sign, hit BACKSPACE, type **6** (that is, replace the second **5** by a **6**), and press CTRL+ENTER. You will see your output replaced by

```
ans =
 [ 2]
 [ 3]
```

By changing the quadratic equation we have altered its roots. You can edit any of the input lines in your M-book in this way, including the one that generated the graph. See what happens if you click in the **ezplot** command line, change the cubic expression, and press CTRL+ENTER.

It is important to understand that your M-book can be handled in exactly the same way that you would any Word document. In particular, you can save the file, print the document, change fonts or margins, move or export a graphic, etc. This has the advantage of allowing you to present the results of your MATLAB session in an attractively formatted style. It also has the disadvantage of affording the user the opportunity to muck with MATLAB's input or output and so to create input and output that may not truly correspond to each other. One must be very careful!

✓ Note that the **help** item on the menu bar is Word help, not MATLAB help. If you want to invoke MATLAB help, then either type **help** (with CTRL+ENTER of course) or bring the MATLAB Command Window to the foreground (see below) and use MATLAB help in the usual fashion.

The Notebook Menu

Next let's examine the items in the **Notebook** menu. First comes **Define Input Cell**. If you put your cursor on any line and select **Define Input Cell**, then that line will become an input line. But to evaluate it, you still need to press CTRL+ENTER. The advantage to this item is apparent when you want to create an input cell containing more than one line. For example, type

```
syms x y
factor(x^2 - y^2)
```

and then select both lines (by clicking and dragging over them) and choose **Define Input Cell**. CTRL+ENTER will then cause *both* lines to be evaluated. You can recognize that both lines are incorporated into one input cell by looking at the brackets, or *Cell Markers*. The menu item **Hide Cell Markers** will cause the Cell Markers to disappear; in fact that menu item is a toggle switch that turns the Markers on and off. If you have several input cells, you can convert them into one input cell by selecting them and choosing **Group Cells**. You can break them apart by choosing **Ungroup Cells**. If you click in an input cell and choose **Undefine Cells**, that cell ceases to be an input cell; its formatting reverts to the default Word format, as does the corresponding output cell. If you "undefine" an output cell, it loses its format, but the corresponding input cell remains unchanged.

If you select some portion of your M-book (for example, the entire M-book by using **Edit : Select All**) and then choose **Purge Output Cells**, all output cells in the selection will be deleted. This is particularly useful if you wish to change some data on which the output in your selection depends, and then reevaluate the entire selection by choosing **Evaluate Cell**. You can reevaluate the entire M-book at any time by choosing **Evaluate M-book**. If your M-book contains a loop, you can evaluate it by selecting it and choosing **Evaluate Loop**, or for that matter **Evaluate Cell**, provided the entire loop is inside a single input cell.

It is often handy to purge all output from an M-book before saving, to economize on storage space or on time upon reopening, especially if there are complicated graphs in the document. If there are any input cells that you want to automatically evaluate upon opening of the M-book, select them and click on **Define Auto Init Cell**. The color of the text in those cells will change. If you want to separate out a series of commands, say for repeated evaluation, then select the cells and click on **Define Calc Zone**. The commands selected will be encased in a Word section (with section breaks before and after it). If you click in the section and select **Evaluate Calc Zone** from the **Notebook** menu, the commands in only that zone will be (re)evaluated.

The last two buttons are also useful. The button **Bring MATLAB to Front** does exactly that; it reveals the MATLAB Command Window that has been hiding behind the M-book. You may want to enter a command directly into the Command Window (for example, a help entry) and not have it in your M-book. Finally, the last button, **Notebook Options** brings up a panel in which you can do some customization of your M-book: set the numerical format, establish the size of graphics figures, etc. We find it most useful to decrease the default graphics size — the "factory setting" is generally too large. Decreasing the figure size with **Notebook Options** may not work with Word 2000, though it is still possible to change the size of figures one at a time, by right clicking on the figure and then choosing the "Size" tab from **Format Object....**

M-Book Graphics

All MATLAB commands that generate graphics work in M-books. The figure produced by a graphics command appears immediately below that command. However, one must be a little careful in planning and executing graphics statements. For example, if in an attempt to reproduce Figure 5-3, you type `ezcontour('x^2 + y^2', [-3 3], [-3 3])` and CTRL+ENTER, this will yield the level curves of $x^2 + y^2$, but they will appear elliptical because you forgot the command `axis square`. If you enter that command on the next line, you will get a second picture that will be correct. But a much better strategy — and one that we strongly recommend — is to return to the original input cell and edit it by adding a semicolon (or a carriage return) and the `axis`

square statement. In general, as you refine your graphics in an M-book, you will find it is more desirable to modify the input cells that generated them, rather than to produce more pictures by repeating the command with new options. So when adding things such as **xlabel**, **ylabel**, **legend**, **title**, etc., it is usually best to just add them to the graphics input cell and reevaluate. As a result, input cells generating graphics in M-books often end up being several lines long.

In instances where you really do want to generate a new picture, then you need to think about whether you want to have **hold** set to **on** or **off**. This feature works exactly as in a Command Window — if **hold** is set to **on**, whatever graphic results from your next command will be combined with whatever last graphic you produced; and if **hold** is **off**, then previous graphics will not influence any graphic you generate.

Since there are no separate graphics windows, the command **figure** is of limited use in M-books; you probably should not use it. If you do, it will produce a blank graph. Similarly, there are other graphics commands that are not so suitable for use in M-books, for example **close**.

✓   There is one exception to this rule: Sometimes you might want to use a figure window along with an M-book, for example to rotate a plot with the mouse. If you type **figure** from the Command Window to open a figure window, then subsequent graphics from the M-book will appear *simultaneously* in the figure window and in the M-book itself.

Finally, we note the button **Toggle Graph Output for Cell**, the only button on the **Notebook** menu not previously described. If you select a cell containing a graphics command and click on this button, no graphical output will result from the evaluation of this command. This can be useful when used in conjunction with **hold on** if you want to produce a single graphic using multiple command lines.

More Hints for Effective Use of M-Books

If an interactive mode and/or attractive output beyond what you can achieve with M-files and diary files is your goal, then you should get used to working in the M-book interface rather than in a Command Window. Even experienced MATLAB users will find that in time they will get use to the environment. Here are a few more hints to smooth your transition.

In Chapter 3 we outlined some strategies for effective use of M-files, especially in the realm of debugging. Many of the techniques we described are unnecessary in the M-book mode. For example, the commands **pause** and **keyboard** serve no purpose. In addition the UP- and DOWN-ARROW keys on the keyboard cannot be used as they are in a Command Window. Those keys cause your cursor to travel in the Word screen rather than to scroll through previous input commands. For navigating in the M-book, you will likely find the scroll bar and the mouse to be more useful than the arrow keys.

You may want to run script or function M-files in an M-book. You still must take care of path business as you do in a Command Window. But assuming you have done so, M-files are executed in an M-book exactly as in a Command Window. You invoke them simply by typing their name and pressing CTRL+ENTER. The outputs they generate, both intermediate and final, are determined as before. In particular, semicolons at ends of lines are important; the command **echo** works as before; and so do loops. One thing that does not work so well is the command **more**. We have found that, even if **more on** is executed, help commands that run on for more than a page do not come out staggered in an M-book. Thus you may want to bring MATLAB to the foreground and enter your help requests in the Command Window.

Another standard MATLAB feature that does not work so well in M-books is the **. . .** construct for continuing a long command entry on a second line. Word automatically converts three dots into a single special ellipsis character and so confuses MATLAB. There are two ways around this difficulty. Either do not use ellipses (rather simply continue typing and allow Word to wrap as usual — the command will be interpreted properly when passed to MATLAB) or turn off the "Auto Correct" feature of Word that converts the three dots into an ellipsis. This is most easily done by typing CTRL+Z after the three dots. Alternatively, open **Tools : Auto Correct...** and change the settings that appear there.

One final comment is in order. Another reason to bring MATLAB to the foreground is if you want to use the Current Directory browser, Workspace browser, or Editor/Debugger. The relevant icons on the tool bar or buttons on the menu bar can only be found in the MATLAB Desktop, not in the Word screen. However, you can also type **pathtool**, **workspace**, or **edit** directly into the M-book, followed by CTRL+ENTER of course.

A Warning

The ellipsis difficulty described in the last section is not an isolated difficulty. The various kinds of automatic formatting that Word carries out can truly confuse MATLAB. Several such instances that we find particularly annoying are: fractions (1/2 is converted to a single character $^1/_2$ representing one-half);

the character combination ":)", a construct often used when specifying the rows of a matrix, which Word converts to a "smiley face" ☺; and various dashes that wreak havoc with MATLAB's attempts to interpret an ordinary hyphen as a minus sign. Examine these in **Tools : Auto Correct...** and, if you use M-books regularly, consider turning them off.

A more insidious problem is the following. If you cut and paste character strings into an input cell, the characters in the original font may be converted into something you don't anticipate in the Courier input cell. Mysterious and unfathomable error messages upon execution are a tip-off to this problem. In general, you should not copy cells for evaluation unless it is from a cell that has already been evaluated successfully — it is safer to type in the line anew.

Finally, we have seen instances in which a cell, for no discernible reason, fails to evaluate. If this happens, try typing CTRL+ENTER again. If that fails, you may have to delete and retype the cell. We have also occasionally experienced the following problem: Reevaluation of a cell causes its output to appear in an unpredictable place elsewhere in the M-book — sometimes even obliterating unrelated output in that locale. If that happens, click on the **Undo** button on the Word tool bar, retype the input cell before evaluating, and delete the old input cell.

Chapter 7

MATLAB Programming

Every time you create an M-file, you are writing a computer program using the MATLAB programming language. You can do quite a lot in MATLAB using no more than the most basic programming techniques that we have already introduced. In particular, we discussed simple loops (using **for**) and a rudimentary approach to debugging in Chapter 3. In this chapter, we will cover some further programming commands and techniques that are useful for attacking more complicated problems with MATLAB. If you are already familiar with another programming language, much of this material will be quite easy for you to pick up!

✓ Many MATLAB commands are themselves M-files, which you can examine using **type** or **edit** (for example, enter **type isprime** to see the M-file for the command **isprime**). You can learn a lot about MATLAB programming techniques by inspecting the built-in M-files.

Branching

For many user-defined functions, you can use a function M-file that executes the same sequence of commands for each input. However, one often wants a function to perform a different sequence of commands in different cases, depending on the input. You can accomplish this with a branching command, and as in many other programming languages, branching in MATLAB is usually done with the command **if**, which we will discuss now. Later we will describe the other main branching command, **switch**.

Branching with if

For a simple illustration of branching with **if**, consider the following function M-file `absval.m`, which computes the absolute value of a real number:

```
function y = absval(x)
if x >= 0
    y = x;
else
    y = -x;
end
```

The first line of this M-file states that the function has a single input **x** and a single output **y**. If the input **x** is nonnegative, the **if** statement is determined by MATLAB to be true. Then the command between the **if** and the **else** statements is executed to set **y** equal to **x**, while MATLAB skips the command between the **else** and **end** statements. However, if **x** is negative, then MATLAB skips to the **else** statement and executes the succeeding command, setting **y** equal to **-x**. As with a **for** loop, the indentation of commands above is optional; it is helpful to the human reader and is done automatically by MATLAB's built-in Editor/Debugger.

✓ Most of the examples in this chapter will give peculiar results if their input is of a different type than intended. The M-file `absval.m` is designed only for scalar real inputs **x**, not for complex numbers or vectors. If **x** is complex for instance, then **x >= 0** checks only if the real part of **x** is nonnegative, and the output **y** will be complex in either case. MATLAB has a built-in function **abs** that works correctly for vectors of complex numbers.

In general, **if** must be followed on the same line by an expression that MATLAB will test to be true or false; see the section below on *Logical Expressions* for a discussion of allowable expressions and how they are evaluated. After some intervening commands, there must be (as with **for**) a corresponding **end** statement. In between, there may be one or more **elseif** statements (see below) and/or an **else** statement (as above). If the test is true, MATLAB executes all commands between the **if** statement and the first **elseif**, **else**, or **end** statement and then skips all other commands until after the **end** statement. If the test is false, MATLAB skips to the first **elseif**, **else**, or **end** statement and proceeds from there, making a new test in the case of an **elseif** statement. In the example below, we reformulate `absval.m` so that no commands are necessary if the test is false, eliminating the need for an **else** statement.

```
function y = absval(x)
y = x;
if y < 0
    y = -y;
end
```

The **elseif** statement is useful if there are more than two alternatives and they can be distinguished by a sequence of true/false tests. It is essentially equivalent to an **else** statement followed immediately by a nested **if** statement. In the example below, we use **elseif** in an M-file signum.m, which evaluates the mathematical function

$$\text{sgn}(x) = \begin{cases} 1 & x > 0, \\ 0 & x = 0, \\ -1 & x < 0. \end{cases}$$

(Again, MATLAB has a built-in function **sign** that performs this function for more general inputs than we consider here.)

```
function y = signum(x)
if x > 0
    y = 1;
elseif x == 0
    y = 0;
else
    y = -1;
end
```

Here if the input **x** is positive, then the output **y** is set to **1** and all commands from the **elseif** statement to the **end** statement are skipped. (In particular, the test in the **elseif** statement is not performed.) If **x** is not positive, then MATLAB skips to the **elseif** statement and tests to see if **x** equals **0**. If so, **y** is set to **0**; otherwise **y** is set to **-1**. Notice that MATLAB requires a double equal sign **==** to test for equality; a single equal sign is reserved for the assignment of values to variables.

✓ Like **for** and the other programming commands you will encounter, **if** and its associated commands can be used in the Command Window. Doing so can be useful for practice with these commands, but they are intended mainly for use in M-files. In our discussion of branching, we consider primarily the case of function M-files; branching is less often used in script M-files.

Logical Expressions

In the examples above, we used *relational operators* such as `>=`, `>`, and `==` to form a logical expression, and we instructed MATLAB to choose between different commands according to whether the expression is true or false. Type **help relop** to see all of the available relational operators. Some of these operators, such as `&` (AND) and `|` (OR), can be used to form logical expressions that are more complicated than those that simply compare two numbers. For example, the expression `(x > 0) | (y > 0)` will be true if `x` or `y` (or both) is positive, and false if neither is positive. In this particular example, the parentheses are not necessary, but generally compound logical expressions like this are both easier to read and less prone to errors if parentheses are used to avoid ambiguities.

Thus far in our discussion of branching, we have only considered expressions that can be evaluated as true or false. While such expressions are sufficient for many purposes, you can also follow **if** or **elseif** with any expression that MATLAB can evaluate numerically. In fact, MATLAB makes almost no distinction between logical expressions and ordinary numerical expressions. Consider what happens if you type a logical expression by itself in the Command Window:

```
>> 2 > 3

ans =
     0
```

When evaluating a logical expression, MATLAB assigns it a value of **0** (for FALSE) or **1** (for TRUE). Thus if you type `2 < 3`, the answer is **1**. The relational operators are treated by MATLAB like arithmetic operators, inasmuch as their output is numeric.

✓ MATLAB makes a subtle distinction between the output of relational operators and ordinary numbers. For example, if you type **whos** after the command above, you will see that **ans** is a *logical array*. We will give an example of how this feature can be used shortly. Type **help logical** for more information.

Here is another example:

```
>> 2 | 3

ans =
     1
```

The OR operator | gives the answer **0** if both operands are zero and **1** otherwise. Thus while the output of relational operators is always **0** or **1**, any nonzero input to operators such as **&** (AND), **|** (OR), and **~** (NOT) is regarded by MATLAB to be true, while only **0** is regarded to be false.

If the inputs to a relational operator are vectors or matrices rather than scalars, then as for arithmetic operations such as **+** and **.***, the operation is done term-by-term and the output is an array of zeros and ones. Here are some examples:

```
>> [2 3] < [3 2]

ans =
      1      0
>> x = -2:2; x >= 0

ans =
      0      0      1      1      1
```

In the second case, **x** is compared term-by-term to the scalar **0**. Type **help relop** or more information.

You can use the fact that the output of a relational operator is a logical array to select the elements of an array that meet a certain condition. For example, the expression **x(x >= 0)** yields a vector consisting of only the nonnegative elements of **x** (or more precisely, those with nonzero real part). So, if **x = -2:2** as above,

```
>> x(x >= 0)

ans =
      0      1      2
```

If a logical array is used to choose elements from another array, the two arrays must have the same size. The elements corresponding to the ones in the logical array are selected while the elements corresponding to the zeros are not. In the example above, the result is the same as if we had typed **x(3:5)**, but in this case **3:5** is an ordinary numerical array specifying the numerical indices of the elements to choose.

Next, we discuss how **if** and **elseif** decide whether an expression is true or false. For an expression that evaluates to a scalar real number, the criterion is the same as described above — namely, a nonzero number is treated as true while **0** is treated as false. However, for complex numbers only the real part is considered. Thus, in an **if** or **elseif** statement, any number with nonzero real part is treated as true, while numbers with zero real part are treated as false. Furthermore, if the expression evaluates to a vector or matrix, an **if** or **elseif** statement must still result in a single true-or-false decision. The convention MATLAB uses is that all elements must be true (i.e., all elements must have nonzero real part) for an expression to be treated as true. If any element has zero real part, then the expression is treated as false.

You can manipulate the way branching is done with vector input by inverting tests with ~ and using the commands **any** and **all**. For example, the statements **if x == 0; ...; end** will execute a block of commands (represented here by · · ·) when all the elements of **x** are zero; if you would like to execute a block of commands when *any* of the elements of **x** is zero you could use the form **if x ~= 0; else; ...; end**. Here ~= is the relational operator for "does not equal", so the test fails when any element of **x** is zero, and execution skips past the **else** statement. You can achieve the same effect in a more straightforward manner using **any**, which outputs true when any element of an array is nonzero: **if any(x == 0); ...; end** (remember that if any element of **x** is zero, the corresponding element of **x == 0** is nonzero). Likewise **all** outputs true when all elements of an array are nonzero.

Here is a series of examples to illustrate some of the features of logical expressions and branching that we have just described. Suppose you want to create a function M-file that computes the following function:

$$f(x) = \begin{cases} \sin(x)/x & x \neq 0, \\ 1 & x = 0. \end{cases}$$

You could construct the M-file as follows:

```
function y = f(x)
if x == 0
    y = 1;
else
    y = sin(x)/x;
end
```

This will work fine if the input **x** is a scalar, but not if **x** is a vector or matrix. Of course you could change **/** to **./** in the second definition of **y**, and change the first definition to make **y** the same size as **x**. But if **x** has both zero and nonzero elements, then MATLAB will declare the **if** statement to be false and use the second definition. Then some of the entries in the output array **y** will be **NaN**, "not a number," because **0/0** is an indeterminate form.

One way to make this M-file work for vectors and matrices is to use a loop to evaluate the function element-by-element, with an **if** statement inside the loop:

```
function y = f(x)
y = ones(size(x));
for n = 1:prod(size(x))
    if x(n) ~= 0
        y(n) = sin(x(n))/x(n);
    end
end
```

In the M-file above, we first create the eventual output **y** as an array of ones with the same size as the input **x**. Here we use **size(x)** to determine the number of rows and columns of **x**; recall that MATLAB treats a scalar or a vector as an array with one row and/or one column. Then **prod(size(x))** yields the number of elements in **x**. So in the **for** statement **n** varies from **1** to this number. For each element **x(n)**, we check to see if it is nonzero, and if so we redefine the corresponding element **y(n)** accordingly. (If **x(n)** equals **0**, there is no need to redefine **y(n)** since we defined it initially to be **1**.)

✓ We just used an important but subtle feature of MATLAB, namely that each element of a matrix can be referred to with a single index; for example, if **x** is a 3 × 2 array then its elements can be enumerated as **x(1)**, **x(2)**, ..., **x(6)**. In this way, we avoided using a loop within a loop. Similarly, we could use **length(x(:))** in place of **prod(size(x))** to count the total number of entries in **x**. However, one has to be careful. If we had not predefined **y** to have the same size as **x**, but rather used an **else** statement inside the loop to let **y(n)** be **1** when **x(n)** is **0**, then **y** would have ended up a 1 × 6 array rather than a 3 × 2 array. We then could have used the command **y = reshape(y, size(x))** at the end of the M-file to make **y** have the same shape as **x**. However, even if the shape of the output array is not important, it is generally best to predefine an array of the appropriate size before computing it element-by-element in a loop, because the loop will then run faster.

Next, consider the following modification of the M-file above:

```
function y = f(x)
if x ~= 0
    y = sin(x)./x;
    return
end
```

```
y = ones(size(x));
for n = 1:prod(size(x))
    if x(n) ~= 0
        y(n) = sin(x(n))/x(n);
    end
end
```

Above the loop we added a block of four lines whose purpose is to make the M-file run faster if all the elements of the input **x** are nonzero. The difference in running time can be significant (more than a factor of 10) if **x** has a large number of elements. Here is how the new block of four lines works. The first **if** statement will be true provided all the elements of **x** are nonzero. In this case, we define the output **y** using MATLAB's vector operations, which are generally much more efficient than running a loop. Then we use the command **return** to stop execution of the M-file without running any further commands. (The use of **return** here is a matter of style; we could instead have indented all of the remaining commands and put them between **else** and **end** statements.) If, however, **x** has some zero elements, then the **if** statement is false and the M-file skips ahead to the commands after the next **end** statement.

Often you can avoid the use of loops and branching commands entirely by using logical arrays. Here is another function M-file that performs the same task as in the previous examples; it has the advantage of being more concise and more efficient to run than the previous M-files, since it avoids a loop in all cases:

```
function y = f(x)
y = ones(size(x));
n = (x ~= 0);
y(n) = sin(x(n))./x(n);
```

Here **n** is a logical array of the same size as **x** with a **1** in each place where **x** has a nonzero element and zeros elsewhere. Thus the line that defines **y(n)** only redefines the elements of **y** corresponding to nonzero values of **x** and leaves the other elements equal to **1**. If you try each of these M-files with an array of about 100,000 elements, you will see the advantage of avoiding a loop!

Branching with `switch`

The other main branching command is **switch**. It allows you to branch among several cases just as easily as between two cases, though the cases must be described through equalities rather than inequalities. Here is a simple example, which distinguishes between three cases for the input:

```
function y = count(x)
switch x
case 1
    y = 'one';
case 2
    y = 'two';
otherwise
    y = 'many';
end
```

Here the **switch** statement evaluates the input **x** and then execution of the M-file skips to whichever **case** statement has the same value. Thus if the input **x** equals **1**, then the output **y** is set to be the string **'one'**, while if **x** is **2**, then **y** is set to **'two'**. In each case, once MATLAB encounters another **case** statement or since an **otherwise** statement, it skips to the **end** statement, so that at most one case is executed. If no match is found among the **case** statements, then MATLAB skips to the (optional) **otherwise** statement, or else to the **end** statement. In the example above, because of the **otherwise** statement, the output is **'many'** if the input is not **1** or **2**.

Unlike **if**, the command **switch** does not allow vector expressions, but it does allow strings. Type **help switch** to see an example using strings. This feature can be useful if you want to design a function M-file that uses a string input argument to select among several different variants of a program you write.

✓ Though strings cannot be compared with relational operators such as **==** (unless they happen to have the same length), you can compare strings in an **if** or **elseif** statement by using the command **strcmp**. Type **help strcmp** to see how this command works; for an example of its use in conjunction with **if** and **elseif**, enter **type hold**.

More about Loops

In Chapter 3 we introduced the command **for**, which begins a loop — a sequence of commands to be executed multiple times. When you use **for**, you effectively specify the number of times to run the loop in advance (though this number may depend for instance on the input to a function M-file). Sometimes you may want to keep running the commands in a loop until a certain condition is met, without deciding in advance on the number of iterations. In MATLAB, the command that allows you to do so is **while**.

⇨ Using `while`, one can easily end up accidentally creating an "infinite loop", one that will keep running indefinitely because the condition you set is never met. Remember that you can generally interrupt the execution of such a loop by typing CTRL+C; otherwise, you may have to shut down MATLAB.

Open-Ended Loops

Here is a simple example of a script M-file that uses `while` to numerically sum the infinite series $1/1^4 + 1/2^4 + 1/3^4 + \cdots$, stopping only when the terms become so small (compared to the machine precision) that the numerical sum stops changing:

```
n = 1;
oldsum = -1;
newsum = 0;
while newsum > oldsum
    oldsum = newsum;
    newsum = newsum + n^(-4);
    n = n + 1;
end
newsum
```

Here we initialize **newsum** to **0** and **n** to **1**, and in the loop we successively add **n^(-4)** to **newsum**, add **1** to **n**, and repeat. The purpose of the variable **oldsum** is to keep track of how much **newsum** changes from one iteration to the next. Each time MATLAB reaches the end of the loop, it starts over again at the **while** statement. If **newsum** exceeds **oldsum**, the expression in the **while** statement is true, and the loop is executed again. But the first time the expression is false, which will happen when **newsum** and **oldsum** are equal, MATLAB skips to the **end** statement and executes the next line, which displays the final value of **newsum** (the result is 1.0823 to five significant digits). The initial value of **-1** that we gave to **oldsum** is somewhat arbitrary, but it must be negative so that the first time the **while** statement is executed, the expression therein is true; if we set **oldsum** to **0** initially, then MATLAB would skip to the **end** statement without ever running the commands in the loop.

✓ Even though you can construct an M-file like the one above without deciding exactly how many times to run the loop, it may be useful to consider roughly how many times it will need to run. Since the floating point computations on most computers are accurate to about 16 decimal digits, the loop above should run until $n^{(-4)}$ is about $10^{(-16)}$, that is, until n is about 10^4. Thus the computation will take very little time on most computers. However, if the exponent were 2 and not 4, the computation would take about 10^8 operations, which would take a long time on most (current) computers — long enough to make it wiser for you to find a more efficient way to sum the series, for example using **symsum** if you have the Symbolic Math Toolbox!

☞ *Though we have classified it here as a looping command,* **while** *also has features of a branching command. Indeed, the types of expressions allowed and the method of evaluation for a* **while** *statement are exactly the same as for an* **if** *statement. See the section* Logical Expressions *above for a discussion of the possible expressions you can put in a* **while** *statement.*

Breaking from a Loop

Sometimes you may want MATLAB to jump out of a **for** loop prematurely, for example if a certain condition is met. Or, in a **while** loop, there may be an auxiliary condition that you want to check in addition to the main condition in the **while** statement. Inside either type of loop, you can use the command **break** to tell MATLAB to stop running the loop and skip to the next line after the end of the loop. The command **break** is generally used in conjunction with an **if** statement. The following script M-file computes the same sum as in the previous example, except that it places an explicit upper limit on the number of iterations:

```
newsum = 0;
for n = 1:100000
    oldsum = newsum;
    newsum = newsum + n^(-4);
    if newsum == oldsum
        break
    end
end newsum
```

In this example, the loop stops after **n** reaches **100000** or when the variable **newsum** stops changing, whichever comes first. Notice that **break** ignores the **end** statement associated with **if** and skips ahead past the nearest **end** statement associated with a loop command, in this case **for**.

Other Programming Commands

In this section we describe several more advanced programming commands and techniques.

Subfunctions

In addition to appearing on the first line of a function M-file, the command **function** can be used later in the M-file to define an auxiliary function, or *subfunction*, which can be used anywhere within the M-file but will not be accessible directly from the command line. For example, the following M-file sums the cube roots of a vector **x** of real numbers:

```
function y = sumcuberoots(x)
y = sum(cuberoot(x));
% ---- Subfunction starts here.
function z = cuberoot(x)
z = sign(x).*abs(x).^(1/3);
```

Here the subfunction **cuberoot** takes the cube root of **x** element-by-element, but it cannot be used from the command line unless placed in a separate M-file. You can only use subfunctions in a function M-file, not in a script M-file. For examples of the use of subfunctions, you can examine many of MATLAB's built-in function M-files. For example, **type ezplot** will display three different subfunctions.

Commands for Parsing Input and Output

You may have noticed that many MATLAB functions allow you to vary the type and/or the number of arguments you give as input to the function. You can use the commands **nargin**, **nargout**, **varargin**, and **varargout** in your own M-files to handle variable numbers of input and/or output arguments, whereas to treat different types of input arguments differently you can use commands such as **isnumeric** and **ischar**.

When a function M-file is executed, the functions **nargin** and **nargout** report respectively the number of input and output arguments that were specified on the command line. To illustrate the use of **nargin**, consider the following M-file add.m that adds either 2 or 3 inputs:

```
function s = add(x, y, z)
if nargin < 2
```

```
        error('At least two input arguments are required.')
end
if nargin == 2
    s = x + y;
else
    s = x + y + z;
end
```

First the M-file checks to see if fewer than 2 input arguments were given, and if so it prints an error message and quits. (See the next section for more about **error** and related commands.) Since MATLAB automatically checks to see if there are more arguments than specified on the first line of the M-file, there is no need to do so within the M-file. If the M-file reaches the second **if** statement in the M-file above, we know there are either 2 or 3 input arguments; the **if** statement selects the proper course of action in either case. If you type, for instance, **add(4,5)** at the command line, then within the M-file, **x** is set to **4**, **y** is set to **5**, and **z** is left undefined; thus it is important to use **nargin** to avoid referring to **z** in cases where it is undefined.

To allow a greater number of possible inputs to add.m, we could add additional arguments on the first line of the M-file and add more cases for **nargin**. A better way to do this is to use the specially named input argument **varargin**:

```
function s = add(varargin)
s = sum([varargin{:}]);
```

In this example, all of the input arguments are assigned to the *cell array* **varargin**. The expression **varargin{:}** returns a comma-separated list of the input arguments. In the example above, we convert this list to a vector by enclosing it in square brackets, forming suitable input for **sum**.

The sample M-files above assume their input arguments are numeric and will attempt to add them even if they are not. This may be desirable in some cases; for instance, both M-files above will correctly add a mixture of numeric and symbolic inputs. However, if some of the input arguments are strings, the result will be either an essentially meaningless numerical answer or an error message that may be difficult to decipher. MATLAB has a number of test functions that you can use to make an M-file treat different types of input arguments differently — either to perform different calculations or to produce a helpful error message if an input is of an unexpected type. For a list of some of these test functions, look up the commands beginning with **is** in the *Programming Commands* section of the *Glossary*.

As an example, here we use **isnumeric** in the M-file add.m to print an error message if any of the inputs are not numeric:

```
function s = add(varargin)
if ~isnumeric([varargin{:}])
    error('Inputs must be floating point numbers.')
end
s = sum([varargin{:}]);
```

When a function M-file allows multiple output arguments, then if fewer output arguments are specified when the function is called, the remaining outputs are simply not assigned. Recall that if no output arguments are explicitly specified on the command line, then a single output is returned and assigned to the variable **ans**. For example, consider the following M-file rectangular.m that changes coordinates from polar to rectangular:

```
function [x, y] = rectangular(r, theta)
x = r.*cos(theta);
y = r.*sin(theta);
```

If you type **rectangular(2, 1)** at the command line, then the answer will be just the x coordinate of the point with polar coordinates $(2, 1)$. The following modification to rectangular.m adjusts the output in this case to be a complex number $x + iy$ containing both coordinates:

```
function [x, y] = rectangular(r, theta)
x = r.*cos(theta);
y = r.*sin(theta);
if nargout < 2
    x = x + i*y;
end
```

See the online help for **varargout** and the functions described above for additional information and examples.

User Input and Screen Output

In the previous section we used **error** to print a message to the screen and then terminate execution of an M-file. You can also print messages to the screen without stopping execution of the M-file with **disp** or **warning**. Not surprisingly, **warning** is intended to be used for warning messages, when the M-file detects a problem that might affect the validity of its result but is not necessarily serious. You can suppress warning messages, either from the command prompt or within an M-file, with the command **warning off**. There are several other options for how MATLAB should handle warning messages; type **help warning** for details.

In Chapter 4 we used **disp** to display the output of a command without printing the "ans =" line. You can also use **disp** to display informational messages on the screen while an M-file is running, or to combine numerical output with a message on the same line. For example, the commands

```
x = 2 + 2; disp(['The answer is ' num2str(x) '.'])
```

will set **x** equal to **4** and then print The answer is 4.

MATLAB also has several commands to solicit input from the user running an M-file. At the end of Chapter 3 we discussed three of them: **pause**, **keyboard**, and **input**. Briefly, **pause** simply pauses execution of an M-file until the user hits a key, while **keyboard** both pauses and gives the user a prompt to use like the regular command line. Typing **return** continues executing the M-file. Lastly, **input** displays a message and allows the user to enter input for the program on a single line. For example, in a program that makes successive approximations to an answer until some accuracy goal is met, you could add the following lines to be executed after a large number of steps have been taken:

```
answer = input(['Algorithm is converging slowly; ', ...
    'continue (yes/no)? '], 's');
if ~isequal(answer, 'yes')
    return
end
```

Here the second argument **'s'** to **input** directs MATLAB not to evaluate the answer typed by the user, just to assign it as a character string to the variable **answer**. We use **isequal** to compare the answer to the string **'yes'** because **==** can only be used to compare arrays (in this case strings) of the same length. In this case we decided that if the user types anything but the full word **yes**, the M-file should terminate. Other approaches would be to only compare the first letter **answer(1)** to **'y'**, to stop only if the answer is **'no'**, etc.

If a figure window is open, you can use **ginput** to get the coordinates of a point that the user selects with the mouse. As an example, the following M-file prints an "X" where the user clicks:

```
function xmarksthespot
if isempty(get(0, 'CurrentFigure'))
```

```
        error('No current figure.')
    end
    flag = ~ishold;
    if flag
        hold on
    end
    disp('Click on the point where you want to plot an X.')
    [x, y] = ginput(1);
    plot(x, y, 'xk')
    if flag
        hold off
    end
```

First the M-file checks to see if there is a current figure window. If so, it proceeds to set the variable **flag** to 1 if **hold off** is in effect and 0 if **hold on** is in effect. The reason for this is that we need **hold on** in effect to plot an "X" without erasing the figure, but afterward we want to restore the figure window to whichever state it was in before the M-file was executed. The M-file then displays a message telling the user what to do, gets the coordinates of the point selected with **ginput(1)**, and plots a black **"X"** at those coordinates. The argument **1** to **ginput** means to get the coordinates of a single point; using **ginput** with no input argument would collect coordinates of several points, stopping only when the user presses the ENTER key.

In the next chapter we describe how to create a GUI (Graphical User Interface) within MATLAB to allow more sophisticated user interaction.

Evaluation

The commands **eval** and **feval** allow you to run a command that is stored in a string as if you had typed the string on the command line. If the entire command you want to run is contained in a string **str**, then you can execute it with **eval(str)**. For example, typing **eval('cos(1)')** will produce the same result as typing **cos(1)**. Generally **eval** is used in an M-file that uses variables to form a string containing a command; see the online help for examples.

You can use **feval** on a function handle or on a string containing the name of a function you want to execute. For example, typing **feval('atan2', 1, 0)** or **feval(@atan2, 1, 0)** is equivalent to typing **atan2(1, 0)**. Often **feval** is used to allow the user of an M-file to input the name of a function to use in a computation. The following M-file iterate.m takes the name of a function and an initial value and iterates the function a specified number of times:

```
function final = iterate(func, init, num)
final = init;
for k = 1:num
    final = feval(func, final);
end
```

Typing **iterate('cos', 1, 2)** yields the numerical value of $\cos(\cos(1))$, while **iterate('cos', 1, 100)** yields an approximation to the real number x for which $\cos(x) = x$. (Think about it!) Most MATLAB commands that take a function name argument use **feval**, and as with all these commands, if you give the name of an inline function to **feval**, you should not enclose it in quotes.

Debugging

In Chapter 3 we discussed some rudimentary debugging procedures. One suggestion was to insert the command **keyboard** into an M-file, for instance right before the line where an error occurs, so that you can examine the Workspace of the M-file at that point in its execution. A more effective and flexible way to do this kind of debugging is to use **dbstop** and related commands. With **dbstop** you can set a *breakpoint* in an M-file in a number of ways, for example, at a specific line number, or whenever an error occurs. Type **help dbstop** for a list of available options.

When a breakpoint is reached, a prompt beginning with the letter **K** will appear in the Command Window, just as if **keyboard** were inserted in the M-file at the breakpoint. In addition, the location of the breakpoint is highlighted with an arrow in the Editor/Debugger (which is opened automatically if you were not already editing the M-file). At this point you can examine in the Command Window the variables used in the M-file, set another breakpoint with **dbstop**, clear breakpoints with **dbclear**, etc. If you are ready to continue running the M-file, type **dbcont** to continue or **dbstep** to step through the file line-by-line. You can also stop execution of the M-file and return immediately to the usual command prompt with **dbquit**.

☞ *You can also perform all the command-line functions that we described in this section with the mouse and/or keyboard shortcuts in the Editor/Debugger. See the section* Debugging Techniques *in Chapter 11 for more about debugging commands and features of the Editor/Debugger.*

Interacting with the Operating System

☞ *This section is somewhat advanced, as is the following chapter. On a first reading, you might want to skip ahead to Chapter 9.*

Calling External Programs

MATLAB allows you to run other programs on your computer from its command line. If you want to enter UNIX or DOS file manipulation commands, you can use this feature as a convenience to avoid opening a separate window. Or you may want to use MATLAB to graph the output of a program written in a language such as FORTRAN or C. For large-scale computations, you may wish to combine routines written in another programming language with routines you write in MATLAB.

The simplest way to run an external program is to type an exclamation point at the beginning of a line, followed by the operating system command you want to run. For example, typing **!dir** on a Windows system or **!ls -l** on a UNIX system will generate a more detailed listing of the files in the current working directory than the MATLAB command **dir**. In Chapter 3 we described **dir** and other MATLAB commands, such as **cd**, **delete**, **pwd**, and **type**, that mimic similar commands from the operating system. However, for certain operations (such as renaming a file) you may need to run an appropriate command from the operating system.

✓ If you use the operating system interface in an M-file that you want to run on either a Windows or UNIX system, you should use the test functions **ispc** and/or **isunix** to set off the appropriate commands for each type of system, for example, **if isunix; ...; else; ...; end**. If you need to distinguish between different versions of UNIX (Linux, Solaris, etc.), you can use **computer** instead of **isunix**.

The output from an operating system command preceded by **!** can only be displayed to the screen. To assign the output of an operating system command to a variable, you must use **dos** or **unix**. Though each is only documented to work for its respective operating system, in current versions of MATLAB they work interchangeably. For example, if you type **[stat, data]= dos('myprog 0.5 1000')**, the program **myprog** will be run with command line arguments **0.5** and **1000** and its "standard output" (which would normally appear on the screen) will be saved as a string in the variable **data**. (The variable **stat** will contain the exit status of the program you run, normally **0** if the program runs without error.) If the output of your program consists only of numbers, then **str2num(data)** will yield a row vector containing those numbers. You can also use **sscanf** to extract numbers from the string **data**; type **help sscanf** for details.

⇨ **A program you run with !, dos, or unix must be in the current directory or elsewhere in the path your system searches for executable files; the MATLAB path will not be searched.**

If you are creating a program that will require extensive communication between MATLAB and an external FORTRAN or C program, then compiling the external program as a *MEX file* will be more efficient than using **dos** or **unix**. To do so, you must write some special instructions into the external program and compile the program from within MATLAB using the command **mex**. This will result in a file with the extension .mex that you can run from within MATLAB just as you would run an M-file. The advantage is that a compiled program will generally run much faster than an M-file, especially when loops are involved.

The instructions you need to write into your program to compile it with **mex** are described in **MATLAB : Using MATLAB : External Interfaces/API** in the Help Browser and in the "MEX, API, & Compilers" section of the web site

```
http://www.mathworks.com/support/tech-notes
```

Look for the page entitled "Is there a tutorial for creating MEX-files with emphasis on C MEX-files?" The instructions depend to some extent on whether your program is written in FORTRAN or C, but they are not hard to learn if you already know one of these languages. MATLAB version 6 also provides the *MATLAB Java Interface*, which enables you to create and access Java objects from within MATLAB.

File Input and Output

In Chapter 3 we discussed how to use **save** and **load** to transfer variables between the Workspace and a disk file. By default the variables are written and read in MATLAB's own binary format, which is signified by the file extension .mat. You can also read and write text files, which can be useful for sharing data with other programs. With **save** you type **-ascii** at the end of the line to save numbers as text rounded to 8 digits, or **-ascii -double** for 16-digit accuracy. With **load** the data are assumed to be in text format if the file name does not end in .mat. This provides an alternative to importing data with **dos** or **unix** in case you have previously run an external program and saved the results in a file.

✓ MATLAB 6 also offers an interactive tool called the *Import Wizard* to read data from files (or the system clipboard) in different formats; to start it type **uiimport** (optionally followed by a file name) or select **File**: **Import Data...**.

For more control over file input and output — for example to annotate numeric output with text — you can use **fopen**, **fprintf**, and related commands. MATLAB also has commands to read and write graphics and sound files. Type **help iofun** for an overview of input and output functions.

Chapter 8

SIMULINK and GUIs

In this chapter we describe SIMULINK, a MATLAB accessory for simulating dynamical processes, and GUIDE, a built-in tool for creating your own graphical user interfaces. These brief introductions are not comprehensive, but together with the online documentation they should be enough to get you started.

SIMULINK

If you want to learn about SIMULINK in depth, you can read the massive PDF document SIMULINK: *Dynamic System Simulation for* MATLAB that comes with the software. Here we give a brief introduction for the casual user who wants to get going with SIMULINK quickly. You start SIMULINK by double-clicking on SIMULINK in the Launch Pad, by clicking on the SIMULINK button on the MATLAB Desktop tool bar, or simply by typing `simulink` in the Command Window. This opens the SIMULINK library window, which is shown for UNIX systems in Figure 8-1. On Windows systems, you see instead the SIMULINK Library Browser, shown in Figure 8-2.

To begin to use SIMULINK, click **New** . **Model** from the **File** menu. This opens a blank model window. You create a SIMULINK model by copying units, called *blocks*, from the various SIMULINK libraries into the model window. We will explain how to use this procedure to model the homogeneous linear ordinary differential equation $u'' + 2u' + 5u = 0$, which represents a damped harmonic oscillator.

First we have to figure out how to represent the equation in a way that SIMULINK can understand. One way to do this is as follows. Since the time variable is *continuous*, we start by opening the "Continuous" library, in UNIX

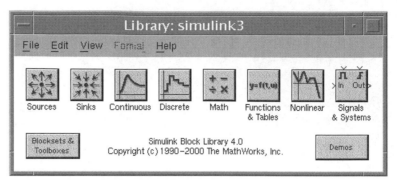

Figure 8-1: The SIMULINK Library in UNIX.

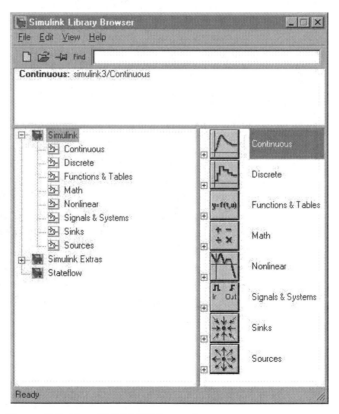

Figure 8-2: The SIMULINK Library Browser.

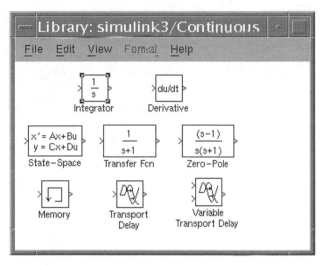

Figure 8-3: The Continuous Library.

by double-clicking on the third icon from the left in Figure 8-1, or in Windows either by clicking on the ⊞ to the left of the "Continuous" icon at the top right of Figure 8-2, or else by clicking on the small icon to the left of the word "Continuous" in the left panel of the SIMULINK Library Browser. When opened, the "Continuous" library looks like Figure 8-3.

Notice that u and u' are obtained from u' and u'' (respectively) by integrating. Therefore, drag two copies of the Integrator block into the model window, and line them up with the mouse. Relabel them (by positioning the mouse at the end of the text under the block, hitting the BACKSPACE key a few times to erase what you don't want, and typing something new in its place) to read u' and u. Note that each Integrator block has an input port and an output port. Align the output port of the u' Integrator with the input port of the u Integrator and join them with an arrow, using the left button on the mouse. Your model window should now look like this:

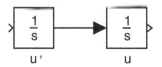

This models the fact that u is obtained by integration from u'. Now the differential equation can be rewritten $u'' = -(5u + 2u')$, and u' is obtained by integration from u''. So we want to add other blocks to implement these relationships. For this purpose we add three Gain blocks, which implement multiplication by a constant, and one Sum block, used for addition. These are all chosen from the "Math" library (fourth from the right in Figure 8-1, or fourth from the top in Figure 8-2). Hooking them up the same way we did with the Integrator blocks gives a model window that looks something like this:

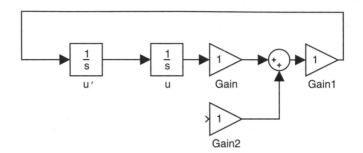

We need to go back and edit the properties of the Gain blocks, to change the constants by which they multiply from the default of 1 to 5 (in "Gain"), −1 (in "Gain1"), and 2 (in "Gain2"). To do this, double-click on each Gain block in turn. A *Block Parameters* box will open in which you can change the Gain parameter to whatever you need. Next, we need to send u', the output of the first Integrator block, to the input port of block "Gain2". This presents a problem, since an Integrator block only has one output port and it's already connected to the next Integrator block. So we need to introduce a *branch line*. Position the mouse in the middle of the arrow connecting the two Integrators, hold down the CTRL key with one hand, simultaneously push down the left mouse button with the other hand, and drag the mouse around to the input port of the block entitled "Gain2". At this point we're almost done; we just need a block for viewing the output. Open up the "Sinks" library and drag a copy of the Scope block into the model window. Hook this up with a branch line (again using the CTRL key) to the line connecting the second Integrator and the Gain block. At this point you might want to relabel some more of the blocks (by editing the text under each block), and also label some of the arrows (by double-clicking on the arrow shaft to open a little box in which you can type a label). We end up with the model shown in Figure 8-4.

Now we're ready to run our simulation. First, it might be a good idea to save the model, using **Save as...** from the **File** menu. One might choose to give it the name `linearODE`. (MATLAB automatically adds the file extension `.mdl`.) To see what is happening during the simulation, double-click on the Scope block to open an "oscilloscope" that will plot u as a function of t. Of course one needs to set initial conditions also; this can be done by double-clicking on

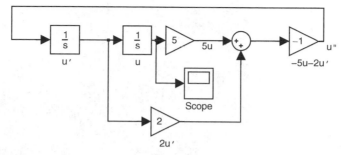

Figure 8-4: A Finished SIMULINK Model.

the Integrator blocks and changing the line of the Block Parameters box that reads "Initial condition". For example, suppose we set the initial condition for u' (in the first Integrator block) to 5 and the condition for u (in the second Integrator block) to 1. In other words, we are solving the system

$$\begin{cases} u'' + 2u' + 5u = 0, \\ \qquad u(0) = 1, \\ \qquad u'(0) = 5, \end{cases}$$

which happens to have the exact solution

$$u(t) = 3e^{-t}\sin(2t) + e^{-t}\cos(2t).$$

✓ Your first instinct might be to rely on the Derivative block, rather than the Integrator block, in simulating differential equations. But this has two drawbacks: It is harder to put in the initial conditions, and also numerical differentiation is much less stable than numerical integration.

Now go to the **Simulation** menu and hit **Start**. You should see in the Scope window something like Figure 8-5 This of course is simply the graph of the function $3e^{-t}\sin(2t) + e^{-t}\cos(2t)$. (By the way, you might need to change the scale on the vertical axis of the Scope window. Clicking on the "binoculars" icon does an "automatic" rescale, and right-clicking on the vertical axis opens an **Axes Properties...** menu that enables you to manually select the minimum and maximum values of the dependent variable.) It is easy to go back and change some of the parameters and rerun the simulation again.

Finally, suppose one now wants to study the *inhomogeneous* equation for "forced oscillations," $u'' + 2u' + 5u = g(t)$, where g is a specified "forcing" term.

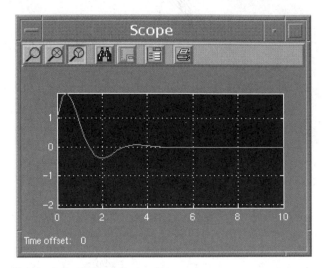

Figure 8-5: Scope Output.

For this, all we have to do is add another block to the model from the "Sources" library. Click on the shaft of the arrow at the top of the model going into the first Integrator and use **Cut** from the **Edit** menu to remove it. Then drag in another "Sum" block before the first Integrator and input a suitable source to one input port of the "Sum" block. For example, if $g(t)$ is to represent "noise," drag the Band-Limited White Noise block from the "Sources" library into the model and hook everything up as shown in Figure 8-6.

The output from this revised model (with the default values of 0.1 for the noise power and 0.1 for the noise sample time) looks like Figure 8-7. The effect of noise on the system is clearly visible from the simulation.

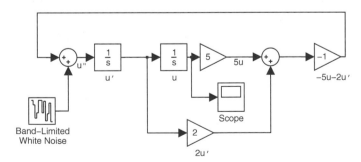

Figure 8-6: Model for the Inhomogeneous Equation.

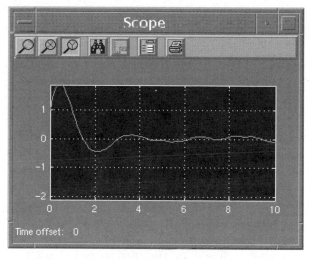

Figure 8-7: Scope Output for the Inhomogeneous Equation.

Graphical User Interfaces (GUIs)

With MATLAB you can create your own *Graphical User Interface*, or GUI, which consists of a Figure window containing menus, buttons, text, graphics, etc., that a user can manipulate interactively with the mouse and keyboard. There are two main steps in creating a GUI: One is designing its layout, and the other is writing *callback functions* that perform the desired operations when the user selects different features.

GUI Layout and GUIDE

Specifying the location and properties of different objects in a GUI can be done with commands such as **uicontrol**, **uimenu**, and **uicontextmenu** in an M-file. MATLAB also provides an interactive tool (a GUI itself!) called GUIDE that greatly simplifies the task of building a GUI. We will describe here how to get started writing GUIs with the MATLAB 6 version of GUIDE, which has been significantly enhanced over previous versions.

✓ One possible drawback of GUIDE is that it equips your GUI with commands that are new in MATLAB 6 and it saves the layout of the GUI in a binary .fig file. If your goal is to create a robust GUI that many different users can use with different versions of MATLAB, you may still be better off writing the GUI from scratch as an M-file.

To open GUIDE, select **File:New:GUI** from the Desktop menu bar or type **guide** in the Command Window. If this is the first time you have run GUIDE, you will next see a window that encourages you to click on "View GUIDE Application Options dialog". We recommend that you do so to see what your options are, but leave the settings as is for now. After you click "OK", the Layout Editor will appear, containing a large white area with a grid. As with most MATLAB windows, the Layout Editor has a tool bar with shortcuts to many of the menu functions we describe below.

You can start building a GUI by clicking on one of the buttons to the left of the grid, then moving to a desired location in the grid, and clicking again to place an object on the grid. To see what type of object each button corresponds to, move the mouse over the button but don't click; soon a yellow box with the name of the button will appear. Once you have placed an object on the grid, you can click and drag (hold down the left mouse button and move the mouse) on the middle of the object to move it or click and drag on a corner to resize the object. After you have placed several objects, you can select multiple objects by clicking and dragging on the background grid to enclose them with a rectangle. Then you can move the objects as a block with the mouse, or align them by selecting **Align Objects** from the **Layout** menu.

To change properties of an object such as its color, the text within it, etc., you must open the *Property Inspector* window. To do so, you can double-click on an object, or choose **Property Inspector** from the **Tools** menu and then select the object you want to alter with the left mouse button. You can leave the Property Inspector open throughout your GUIDE session and go back and forth between it and the Layout Editor. Let's consider an example that illustrates several of the more important properties.

Figure 8-8 shows an example of what the Layout Editor window looks like after several objects have been placed and their properties adjusted. The purpose of this sample GUI is to allow the user to type a MATLAB plotting command, see the result appear in the same window, and modify the graph in a few ways. Let us describe how we created the objects that make up the GUI.

The boxes on the top row, as well as the one labeled "Set axis scaling:", are *Static Text* boxes, which the user of the GUI will not be allowed to manipulate. To create each of them, we first clicked on the "Static Text" button — the one to the right of the grid labeled "TXT" — and then clicked in the grid where we wanted to add the text. Next, to set the text for the box we opened the

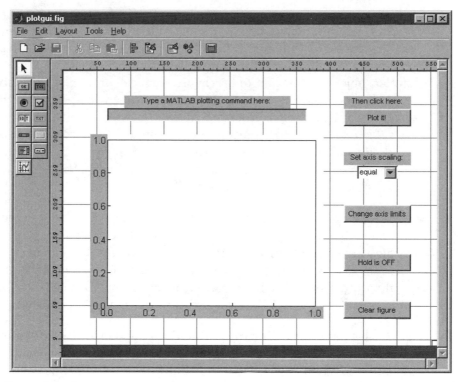

Figure 8-8: The Layout Editor Window.

Property Inspector and clicked on the square button next to "String", which opens a new window in which to change the default text. Finally, we resized each box according to the length of its text.

The buttons labeled "Plot it!", "Change axis limits", and "Clear Figure" are all *Push Button* objects, created using the button to the left of the grid labeled "OK". To make these buttons all the same size, we first created one of them and then after sizing it, we duplicated it (twice) by clicking the right mouse button on the existing object and selecting **Duplicate**. We then moved each new Push Button to a different position and changed its text in the same way as we did for the Static Text boxes.

The blank box near the top of the grid is an *Edit Text* box, which allows the user to enter text. We created it with the button to the left of the grid labeled "EDIT" and then cleared its default text in the same way that we changed text before. Below the Edit Text box is a large *Axes* box, created with the button containing a small graph, and in the lower right the button labeled "Hold is OFF" is a *Toggle Button*, created with the button labeled "TGL". For toggling (on–off) commands you could also use a *Radio Button* or a *Checkbox*, denoted respectively by the buttons with a dot and a check mark in them. Finally, the box on the right that says "equal" is a *Popup Menu* — we'll let you find its button in the Layout Editor since it is hard to describe! Popup Menus and *Listbox* objects allow you to let the user choose among several options.

We moved, resized, and in most cases changed the properties of each object similarly to the way we described above. In the case of the Popup Menu, after we selected the "String" button in the Property Inspector, we entered into the window that appeared three words on three separate lines: `equal`, `normal`, and `square`. Using multiple lines is necessary to give the user multiple choices in a Popup Menu or Listbox object.

✓ In addition to populating your GUI with the objects we described above, you can create a menu bar for it using the Menu Editor, which you can open by selecting **Edit Menubar** from the **Layout** menu. You can also use the Menu Editor to create a *context menu* for an object; this is a menu that appears when you click the right mouse button on the object. See the online documentation for GUIDE to learn how to use the Menu Editor.

We also gave our GUI a title, which will appear in the titlebar of its window, as follows. We clicked on the grid in the Layout Editor to select the entire GUI (as opposed to an object within it) and went to the Property Inspector. There we changed the text to the right of "Name" from "Untitled" to "Simple Plot GUI".

Saving and Running a GUI

To save a GUI, select **Save As...** from the **File** menu. Type a file name for your GUI without any extension; for the GUI described above we chose `plotgui`. Saving creates two files, an M-file and a binary file with extension `.fig`, so in our case the resulting files were named `plotgui.m` and `plotgui.fig`. When you save a GUI for the first time, the M-file for the GUI will appear in a separate Editor/Debugger window. We will describe how and why to modify this M-file in the next section.

⇨ **The instructions in this and the following section assume the default settings of the Application Options, which you may have inspected upon starting GUIDE, as described above. Otherwise, you can access them from the Tools menu. We assume in particular that "Generate .fig file and .m file", "Generate callback function prototypes", and "Application allows only one instance to run" are selected.**

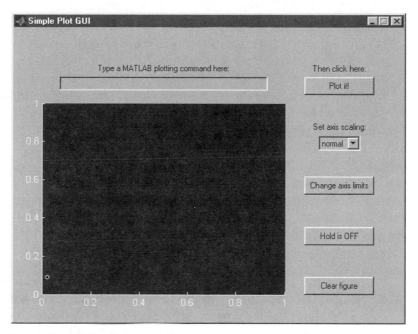

Figure 8-9: A Simple GUI.

Once saved, you can run the GUI from the Command Window by typing its name, in our case **plotgui**, whether or not GUIDE is running. Both the .fig file and the .m file must be in your current directory or MATLAB path. You can also run it from the Layout Editor by typing CTRL+T or selecting **Activate Figure** from the **Tools** menu. A copy of the GUI will appear in a separate window, without all the surrounding menus and buttons of the Layout Editor. (If you have added new objects since the last time you saved or activated the GUI, the M-file associated to the GUI will also be brought to the front.) Figure 8-9 shows how the GUI we created above looks when activated.

Notice that the appearance of the GUI is slightly different than in the GUIDE window; in particular, the font size may differ. For this reason you may have to go back to the GUIDE window after activating a GUI and resize some objects accordingly. The changes you make will not immediately appear in the active GUI; to see their effect you must activate the GUI again.

The objects you create in the Layout Editor are inert within that window — you can't type text in the Edit Text box, you can't see the additional options by clicking on the Popup Menu, etc. But in an activated GUI window, objects such as Toggle Buttons and Popup Menus will respond to mouse clicks. However, they will not actually perform any functions until you write a callback function for each of them.

GUI Callback Functions

When you are ready to create a callback function for a given object, click the right mouse button on the object and select **Edit Callback**. The M-file associated with the GUI will be brought to the front in an Editor/Debugger window, with the cursor in a block of lines like the ones below. (If you haven't yet saved the GUI, you will be prompted to do so first, so that GUIDE knows what name to give the M-file.)

```
function varargout = pushbutton1_Callback(h, eventdata, handles, varargin)
% Stub for Callback of the uicontrol handles.pushbutton1.
disp('pushbutton1 Callback not implemented yet.')
% ------------------ end pushbutton1_Callback ----------------------
```

In this case we have assumed that the object you selected was the first Push Button that you created in the Layout Editor; the string "pushbutton1" above is its default *tag*. (Another way to find the tag for a given object is to select it and look next to "Tag" in the Property Inspector.) All you need to do now to bring this Push Button to life is to replace the **disp** command line in the template shown above with the commands that you want performed when the user clicks on the button. Of course you also need to save the M-file, which you can do in the usual way from the Editor/Debugger, or by activating the GUI from the Layout Editor. Each time you save or activate a GUI, a block of four lines like the ones above is automatically added to the GUI's M-file for any new objects or menu items that you have added to the GUI and that should have callback functions.

In the example **plotgui** from the previous section, there is one case where we used an existing MATLAB command as a callback function. For the Push Button labeled "Change axis limits", we simply entered **axlimdlg** into its callback function in plotgui.m. This command opens a *dialog box* that allows a user to type new values for the ranges of the x and y axes. MATLAB has a number of dialog boxes that you can use either as callback functions or in an ordinary M-file. For example, you can use **inputdlg** in place of **input**. Type **help uitools** for information on the available dialog boxes.

For the Popup Menu on the right side of the GUI, we put the following lines into its callback function template:

```
switch get(h, 'Value')
case 1
   axis equal
case 2
   axis normal
```

```
case 3
   axis square
end
```

Each time the user of the GUI selects an item from a Popup Menu, MATLAB sets the "Value" property of the object to the line number selected and runs the associated callback function. As we described in Chapter 5, you can use **get** to retrieve the current setting of a property of a graphics object. When you use the callback templates provided by GUIDE as we have described, the variable **h** will contain the handle (the required first argument of **get** and **set**) for the associated object. (If you are using another method to write callback functions, you can use the MATLAB command **gcbo** in place of **h**.) For our sample GUI, line 1 of the Popup Menu says "equal", and if the user selects line 1, the callback function above runs **axis equal**; line 2 says "normal"; etc.

✓ You may have noticed that in Figure 8-9 the Popup Menu says "normal" rather than "equal" as in Figure 8-8; that's because we set its "Value" property to 2 when we created the GUI, using the Property Inspector. In this way you can make the default selection something other than the first item in a Popup Menu or Listbox.

For the Push Button labeled "Plot it!", we wrote the following callback function:

```
set(handles.figure1, 'HandleVisibility', 'callback')
eval(get(handles.edit1, 'String'))
```

Here **handles.figure1** and **handles.edit1** are the handles for the entire GUI window and for the Edit Text box, respectively. Again these variables are provided by the callback templates in GUIDE, and if you do not use this feature you can generate the appropriate handles with **gcbf** and **findobj(gcbf, 'Tag', 'edit1')**, respectively. The second line of the callback function above uses **get** to find the text in the Edit Text box and then runs the corresponding command with **eval**. The first line uses **set** to make the GUI window accessible to graphics commands used within callback functions; if we did not do this, a plotting command run by the second line would open a separate figure window.

✓ Another way to enable plotting within a GUI window is to select **Application Options** from the **Tools** menu in the Layout Editor, and within the window that appears change "Command-line accessibility" to "On". This has the possible drawback of allowing plotting commands the user types in the Command Window to affect the GUI window. A safer approach is to set "Command-line accessibility" to "User-specified", click on the grid in the Layout Editor to select the entire GUI, go to the Property Inspector, and change "HandleVisibility" to "callback". This would eliminate the need to select this property with **set** in each of the callback functions above and below that run graphics commands.

Here is our callback function for the Push Button labeled "Clear figure":

```
set(handles.edit1, 'String', '')
set(handles.figure1, 'HandleVisibility', 'callback')
cla reset
```

The first line clears the text in the Edit Text box and the last line clears the Axes box in the GUI window. (If your GUI contains more than one Axes box, you can use **axes** to select the one you want to manipulate in each of your callback functions.)

We used the following callback function for the Toggle Button labeled "Hold is OFF":

```
set(handles.figure1, 'HandleVisibility', 'callback')
if get(h, 'Value')
    hold on
    set(h, 'String', 'Hold is ON');
else
    hold off
    set(h, 'String', 'Hold is OFF');
end
```

We get the "Value" property of the Toggle Button in the same way as in the the Popup Menu callback function above, but for a Toggle Button this value is either 0 if the button is "out" (the default) or 1 if the button is pressed "in". (Radio Buttons and Checkboxes also have a "Value" property of either 0 or 1.) When the user first presses the Toggle Button, the callback function above runs **hold on** and resets the string displayed on the Toggle Button to reflect the change. The next time the user presses the button, these operations are reversed.

✓ We can also associate a callback function with the Edit Text box; this function will be run each time the user presses the ENTER key after typing text in the box. The callback function **eval(get(h, 'String'))** will run the command just typed, providing an alternative to (or making superfluous) the "Plot it!" button.

Finally, if you create a GUI with an Axes box like we did, you may notice that GUIDE puts in the GUI's M-file a template like a callback template but labeled "ButtondownFcn" instead. When the user clicks in an Axes object, this type of function is called rather than a callback function, but within the template you can write the function just as you would write a callback function. You can also associate such a function with an object that already has a callback function by clicking the right mouse button on the object in the Layout Editor and selecting **Edit ButtondownFcn**. This function will be run when the user clicks the right mouse button (as opposed to the left mouse button for the callback function). You can associate functions with several other types of user events as well; to learn more, see the online documentation, or experiment by clicking the right mouse button on various objects and on the grid behind them in the Layout Editor.

Chapter 9

Applications

In this chapter, we present examples showing you how to apply MATLAB to problems in several different disciplines. Each example is presented as a MATLAB M-book. These M-books are illustrations of the kinds of polished, integrated, interactive documents that you can create with MATLAB, as augmented by the Word interface. The M-books are:

- Illuminating a Room
- Mortgage Payments
- Monte Carlo Simulation
- Population Dynamics
- Linear Economic Models
- Linear Programming
- The 360° Pendulum
- Numerical Solution of the Heat Equation
- A Model of Traffic Flow

We have not explained all the MATLAB commands that we use; you can learn about the new commands from the online help. SIMULINK is used in *A Model of Traffic Flow* and as an optional accessory in *Population Dynamics* and *Numerical Solution of the Heat Equation*. Running the M-book on *Linear Programming* also requires an M-file found (in slightly different forms) in the SIMULINK and Optimization toolboxes.

The M-books require different levels of mathematical background and expertise in other subjects. *Illuminating a Room, Mortgage Payments*, and *Population* Dynamics use only high school mathematics. *Monte Carlo Simulation* uses some probability and statistics; *Linear Economic Models* and *Linear Programming*, some linear algebra; *The 360° Pendulum*, some ordinary differential equations; *Numerical Solution of the Heat Equation*, some partial differential equations; and *A Model of Traffic Flow*, differential equations, linear algebra, and familiarity with the function e^z for z a complex number. Even if you don't have the background for a particular example, you should be able to learn something about MATLAB from the M-book.

Illuminating a Room

Suppose we need to decide where to put light fixtures on the ceiling of a room, measuring 10 meters by 4 meters by 3 meters high, in order to best illuminate it. For aesthetic reasons, we are asked to use a small number of incandescent bulbs. We want the bulbs to total a maximum of 300 watts. For a given number of bulbs, how should they be placed to maximize the intensity of the light in the darkest part of the room? We also would like to see how much improvement there is in going from one 300-watt bulb to two 150-watt bulbs to three 100-watt bulbs, and so on. To keep things simple, we assume that there is no furniture in the room and that the light reflected from the walls is insignificant compared with the direct light from the bulbs.

One 300-Watt Bulb

If there is only one bulb, then we want to put the bulb in the center of the ceiling. Let's picture how well the floor is illuminated. We introduce coordinates x running from 0 to 10 in the long direction of the room and y running from 0 to 4 in the short direction. The intensity at a given point, measured in watts per square meter, is the power of the bulb, 300, divided by 4π times the square of the distance from the bulb. Since the bulb is 3 meters above the point $(5, 2)$ on the floor, we can express the intensity at a point (x, y) on the floor as follows:

```
syms x y; illum = 300/(4*pi*((x - 5)^2 + (y - 2)^2 + 3^2))

illum =
75/pi/((x-5)^2+(y-2)^2+9)
```

We can use **ezcontourf** to plot this expression over the entire floor. We use **colormap** to arrange for a color gradation that helps us to see the illumination. (See the online help for **graph3d** for more **colormap** options.)

```
ezcontourf(illum,[0 10 0 4]); colormap(gray);
axis equal tight
```

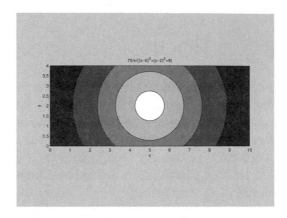

The darkest parts of the floor are the corners. Let us find the intensity of the light at the corners, and at the center of the room.

```
subs(illum, {x, y}, {0, 0})
subs(illum, {x, y}, {5, 2})

ans =
    0.6282
ans =
    2.6526
```

The center of the room, at floor level, is about 4 times as bright as the corners when there is only one bulb on the ceiling. Our objective is to light the room more uniformly using more bulbs with the same total amount of power. Before proceeding to deal with multiple bulbs, we observe that the use of **ezcontourf** is somewhat confining, as it does not allow us to control the number of contours in our pictures. Such control will be helpful in seeing the light intensity; therefore we shall plot numerically rather than symbolically; that is, we shall use **contourf** instead of **ezcontourf**.

Two 150-Watt Bulbs

In this case we need to decide where to put the two bulbs. Common sense tells us to arrange the bulbs symmetrically along a line down the center of the room in the long direction, that is, along the line $y = 2$. Define a function that gives the intensity of light at a point (x, y) on the floor due to a 150-watt bulb at a position $(d, 2)$ on the ceiling.

```
light2 = inline(vectorize('150/(4*pi*((x - d)^2 + (y - 2)^2 +
3^2))'), 'x', 'y', 'd')

light2 =
     Inline function:
     light2(x,y,d) = 150./(4.*pi.*((x - d).^2 + (y - 2).^2 +
3.^2))
```

Let's get an idea of the illumination pattern if we put one light at $d = 3$ and the other at $d = 7$. We specify the drawing of 20 contours in this and the following plots.

```
[X,Y] = meshgrid(0:0.1:10, 0:0.1:4); contourf(light2(X, Y, 3)
+ light2(X, Y, 7), 20); axis equal tight
```

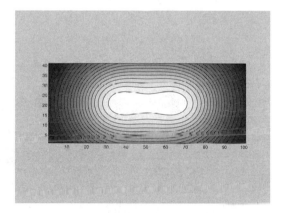

The floor is more evenly lit than with one bulb, but it looks as if the bulbs are closer together than they should be. If we move the bulbs further apart, the center of the room will get dimmer but the corners will get brigher. Let's try changing the location of the lights to $d = 2$ and $d = 8$.

```
contourf(light2(X, Y, 2) + light2(X, Y, 8), 20);
axis equal tight
```

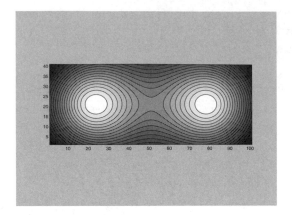

This is an improvement. The corners are still the darkest spots of the room, though the light intensity along the walls toward the middle of the room (near $x = 5$) is diminishing as we move the bulbs further apart. To better illuminate the darkest spots we should keep moving the bulbs apart. Let's try lights at $d = 1$ and $d = 9$.

```
contourf(light2(X, Y, 1) + light2(X, Y, 9), 20);
axis equal tight
```

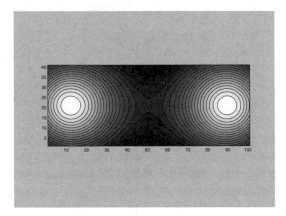

Looking along the long walls, the room is now darker toward the middle than at the corners. This indicates that we have spread the lights too far apart.

We could proceed with further contour plots, but instead let's be systematic about finding the best position for the lights. In general, we can put one light at $x = d$ and the other symmetrically at $x = 10 - d$ for d between 0 and 5. Judging from the examples above, the darkest spots will be either at the corners or at the midpoints of the two long walls. By symmetry, the intensity will be the same at all four corners, so let's graph the intensity at one of the corners (0, 0) as a function of d.

```
d = 0:0.1:5; plot(d, light2(0, 0, d) + light2(0, 0, 10 - d))
```

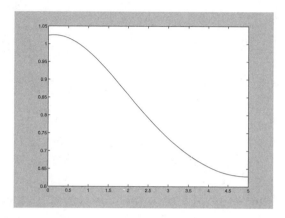

As expected, the smaller d is, the brighter the corners are. In contrast, the graph for the intensity at the midpoint (5, 0) of a long wall (again by symmetry it does not matter which of the two long walls we choose) should grow as d increases toward 5.

```
plot(d, light2(5, 0, d) + light2(5, 0, 10 - d))
```

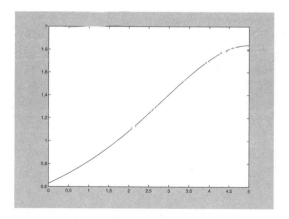

We are after the value of d for which the lower of the two numbers on the above graphs (corresponding to the darkest spot in the room) is as high as possible. We can find this value by showing both curves on one graph.

```
hold on; plot(d, light2(0, 0, d) + light2(0, 0, 10 - d));
hold off
```

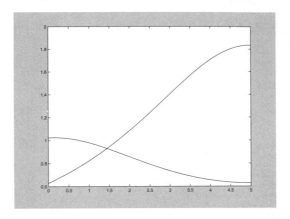

The optimal value of d is at the point of intersection, near 1.4, with minimum intensity a little under 1. To get the optimum value of d, we find exactly where the two curves intersect.

```
syms d; eqn = inline(char(light2(0, 0, d) + light2(0, 0, 10 -
d) - light2(5, 0, d) - light2(5, 0, 10 - d)))
```

```
eqn =
     Inline function:
     eqn(d) = 75/2/pi/(d^2+13)+75/2/pi/((-10+d)^2+13)-
75/2/pi/((5-d)^2+13)-75/2/pi/((-5+d)^2+13)
```

```
fzero(eqn, [0 5])
```

```
ans =
     1.4410
```

So the lights should be placed about 1.44 meters from the short walls. For this configuration, the approximate intensity at the darkest spots on the floor is as follows:

```
light2(0, 0, 1.441) + light2(0, 0, 10 - 1.441)
```

```
ans =
     0.9301
```

The darkest spots in the room have intensity around 0.93, as opposed to 0.63 for a single bulb. This represents an improvement of about 50%.

Three 100-Watt Bulbs

We redefine the intensity function for 100-watt bulbs:

```
light3 = inline(vectorize('100/(4*pi*((x - d)^2 + (y - 2)^2 +
3^2))'), 'x', 'y', 'd')
```

```
light3 =
    Inline function:
    light3(x,y,d) = 100./(4.*pi.*((x - d).^2 + (y - 2).^2 +
3.^2))
```

Assume we put one bulb at the center of the room and place the other two symmetrically as before. Here we show the illumination of the floor when the off-center bulbs are one meter from the short walls.

```
[X,Y] = meshgrid(0:0.1:10, 0:0.1:4); contourf(light3(X, Y, 1)
+ light3(X, Y, 5) + light3(X, Y, 9), 20);
axis equal tight
```

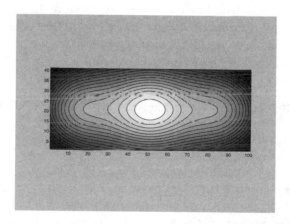

It appears that we should put the bulbs even closer to the walls. (This may not please everyone's aesthetics!) Let d be the distance of the bulbs from the short walls. We define a function giving the intensity at position x along a long wall and then graph the intensity as a function of d for several values of x.

```
d = 0:0.1:5;
for x = 0:0.5:5
    plot(d, light3(x, 0, d) + light3(x, 0, 5) + ...
    light3(x, 0, 10 - d))
    hold on
end
hold off
```

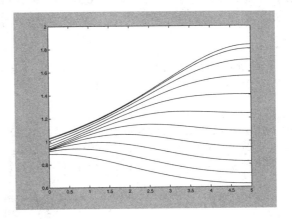

We know that for d near 5, the intensity will be increasing as x increases from 0 to 5, so the bottom curve corresponds to $x = 0$ and the top curve to $x = 5$. Notice that the $x = 0$ curve is the lowest one for all d, and it rises as d decreases. Thus $d = 0$ maximizes the intensity of the darkest spots in the room, which are the corners (corresponding to $x = 0$). There the intensity is as follows:

```
light3(0, 0, 0) + light3(0, 0, 5) + light3(0, 0, 10)
```

```
ans =
    0.8920
```

This is surprising; we do worse than with two bulbs. In going from two bulbs to three, with a decrease in wattage per bulb, we are forced to move wattage away from the ends of the room and bring it back to the center. We could probably improve on the two-bulb scenario if we used brighter bulbs at the ends of the room and a dimmer bulb in the center, or if we used four 75-watt bulbs. But our results so far indicate that the amount to be gained in going to more than two bulbs is likely to be small compared with the amount we gained by going from one bulb to two.

Mortgage Payments

We want to understand the relationships among the mortgage payment rate of a fixed rate mortgage, the principal (the amount borrowed), the annual interest rate, and the period of the loan. We are going to assume (as is usually the case in the United States) that payments are made monthly, even though the interest rate is given as an annual rate. Let's define

```
peryear = 1/12; percent = 1/100;
```

So the number of payments on a 30-year loan is

```
30*12
```

```
ans =
    360
```

and an annual percentage rate of 8% comes out to a monthly rate of

```
8*percent*peryear
```

```
ans =
    0.0067
```

Now consider what happens with each monthly payment. Some of the payment is applied to interest on the outstanding principal amount, P, and some of the payment is applied to reduce the principal owed. The total amount, R, of the monthly payment remains constant over the life of the loan. So if J denotes the monthly interest rate, we have $R - J * P$ (amount applied to principal), and the new principal after the payment is applied is

$$P + J * P - R = P * (1 + J) - R = P * m - R,$$

where $m = 1 + J$. So a table of the amount of the principal still outstanding after n payments is tabulated as follows for a loan of initial amount A, for n from 0 to 6:

```
syms m J P R A
P = A;
for n = 0:6,
    disp([n, P]),
    P = simplify(-R + P*m);
end
```

```
[ 0, A]
[       1,  -R+A*m]
[             2,  -R-m*R+A*m^2]
[                   3,  -R-m*R-m^2*R+A*m^3]
[                         4,  -R-m*R-m^2*R-m^3*R+A*m^4]
[                               5,  -R-m*R-m^2*R-m^3*R-
m^4*R+A*m^5]
[                                     6,  -R-m*R-m^2*R-m^3*R-
m^4*R-m^5*R+A*m^6]
```

We can write this in a simpler way by noticing that $P = A * m^n +$ (terms divisible by R). For example, with $n = 7$ we have

```
factor(p - A*m^7)
```

```
ans =
-R*(1+m+m^2+m^3+m^4+m^5+m^6)
```

But the quantity inside the parentheses is the sum of a geometric series

$$\sum_{k=1}^{n-1} m^k = \frac{m^n - 1}{m - 1}.$$

So we see that the principal after n payments can be written as

$$P = A * m^n - R * (m^n - 1)/(m - 1).$$

Now we can solve for the monthly payment amount R under the assumption that the loan is paid off in N installments, that is, P is reduced to 0 after N payments:

```
syms N; solve(A*m^N - R*(m^N - 1)/(m - 1), R)
```

```
ans =
A*m^N*(m-1)/(m^N-1)
```

```
R = subs(ans, m, J + 1)
```

```
R=
A*(J+1)^N*J/((J+1)^N-1)
```

For example, with an initial loan amount A = \$150,000 and a loan lifetime of 30 years (360 payments), we get the following table of payment amounts as a function of annual interest rate:

```
format bank; disp(' Interest Rate        Payment')
for rate = 1:10,
  disp([rate, double(subs(R, [A, N, J], [150000, 360,...
  rate*percent*peryear]))])
end
```

```
Interest Rate    Payment
         1.00     482.46
         2.00     554.43
         3.00     632.41
         4.00     716.12
         5.00     805.23
         6.00     899.33
         7.00     997.95
         8.00    1100.65
         9.00    1206.93
        10.00    1316.36
```

Note the use of **format bank** to write the floating point numbers with two digits after the decimal point.

There's another way to understand these calculations that's a little slicker and that uses MATLAB's linear algebra capability. Namely, we can write the fundamental equation

$$P_{new} = P_{old} * m - R$$

in matrix from as

$$v_{new} = Bv_{old},$$

where v is the column vector $\binom{P}{1}$ and B is the square matrix

$$\begin{pmatrix} m & -R \\ 0 & 1 \end{pmatrix}.$$

We can check this using matrix multiplication:

```
syms R P; B = [m -R; 0 1]; v = [P; 1]; B*v
```

```
ans =
[ m*P-R]
[     1]
```

which agrees with the formula we had above. (Note the use of **syms** to reset **R** and **P** to *undefined* symbolic quantities.) Thus the column vector $[P; 1]$ resulting after n payments can be computed by left-multiplying the starting vector $[A; 1]$ by the matrix B^n. Assuming $m > 1$, that is, a positive rate of interest, the calculation

```
[eigenvectors, diagonalform] = eig(B)

eigenvectors =
[        1,        1]
[        0, (m-1)/R]
diagonalform =
[ m, 0]
[ 0, 1]
```

shows us that the matrix B has eigenvalues m and 1, and corresponding eigenvectors $[1; 0]$ and $[1; (m - 1)/R] = [1; J/R]$. Now we can write the vector $[A; 1]$ as a linear combination of the eigenvectors: $[A; 1] = x[1; 0] + y[1; J/R]$. We can solve for the coefficients:

```
[x, y] = solve('A = x*1 + y*1', '1 = x*0 + y*J/R')

x =
(A*J-R)/J
y =
R/J
```

and so

$$[A; 1] = (A - (R/J)) * [1; 0] + (R/J) * [1; J/R]$$

and

$$B^n \cdot [A; 1] = (A - (R/J)) * m^n * [1; 0] + (R/J) * [1; J/R].$$

Therefore the principal remaining after n payments is

$$P = ((A * J - R) * m^n + R)/J = A * m^n - R * (m^n - 1)/J.$$

This is the same result we obtained earlier.

To conclude, let's determine the amount of money A one can afford to borrow as a function of what one can afford to pay as the monthly payment R. We simply solve for A in the equation that $P = 0$ after N payments.

```
solve(A*m^N - R*(m^N - 1)/(m - 1), A)

ans =
R*(m^N-1)/(m^N)/(m-1)
```

For example, if one is shopping for a house and can afford to pay $1500 per month for a 30-year fixed-rate mortgage, the maximum loan amount as a function of the interest rate is given by

```
disp(' Interest Rate      Loan Amt.')
for rate = 1:10,
  disp([rate, double(subs(ans, [R, N, m], [1500, 360,...
  1 + rate*percent*peryear]))])
end
```

```
Interest Rate      Loan Amt.
         1.00      466360.60
         2.00      405822.77
         3.00      355784.07
         4.00      314191.86
         5.00      279422.43
         6.00      250187.42
         7.00      225461.35
         8.00      204425.24
         9.00      186422.80
        10.00      170926.23
```

Monte Carlo Simulation

In order to make statistical predictions about the long-term results of a random process, it is often useful to do a simulation based on one's understanding of the underlying probabilities. This procedure is referred to as the *Monte Carlo* method.

As an example, consider a casino game in which a player bets against the house and the house wins 51% of the time. The question is: How many games have to be played before the house is reasonably sure of coming out ahead? This scenario is common enough that mathematicians long ago figured out very precisely what the statistics are, but here we want to illustrate how to get a good idea of what can happen in practice without having to absorb a lot of mathematics.

First we construct an expression that computes the net revenue to the house for a single game, based on a random number chosen between 0 and 1 by the MATLAB function **rand**. If the random number is less than or equal to 0.51, the house wins one betting unit, whereas if the number exceeds 0.51, the house loses one unit. (In a high-stakes game, each bet may be worth $1000 or more. Thus it is important for the casino to know how bad a losing streak it may have to weather to turn a profit — so that it doesn't go bankrupt first!) Here is an expression that returns 1 if the output of **rand** is less than 0.51 and −1 if the output of rand is greater than 0.51 (it will also return 0 if the output of **rand** is exactly 0.51, but this is extremely unlikely):

```
revenue = sign(0.51 - rand)
```

```
revenue =
    -1
```

In the game simulated above, the house lost. To simulate several games at once, say 10 games, we can generate a vector of 10 random numbers with the command **rand(1, 10)** and then apply the same operation.

```
revenues = sign(0.51 - rand(1, 10))
```

```
revenues =
    1   -1    1   -1   -1    1    1   -1    1   -1
```

In this case the house won 5 times and lost 5 times, for a net profit of 0 units. For a larger number of games, say 100, we can let MATLAB sum the revenue from the individual bets as follows:

```
profit = sum(sign(0.51 - rand (1, 100)))
```

```
profit =
    -4
```

For this trial, the house had a net loss of 4 units after 100 games. On average, every 100 games the house should win 51 times and the player(s) should win 49 times, so the house should make a profit of 2 units (on average). Let's see what happens in a few trial runs.

```
profits = sum(sign(0.51 - rand(100, 10)))
```

```
profits =
    14   -12    6    2   -4    0   -10   12    0   12
```

We see that the net profit can fluctuate significantly from one set of 100 games to the next, and there is a sizable probability that the house has lost money after 100 games. To get an idea of how the net profit is likely to be distributed in general, we can repeat the experiment a large number of times and make a histogram of the results. The following function computes the net profits for k different trials of n games each:

```
profits = inline('sum(sign(0.51 - rand(n, k)))', 'n', 'k')

profits =
    Inline function:
    profits(n,k) = sum(sign(0.51 - rand(n, k)))
```

What this function does is to generate an $n \times k$ matrix of random numbers and then perform the same operations as above on each entry of the matrix to obtain a matrix with entries 1 for bets the house won and -1 for bets it lost. Finally it sums the columns of the matrix to obtain a row vector of k elements, each of which represents the total profit from a column of n bets.

Now we make a histogram of the output of **profits** using $n = 100$ and $k = 100$. Theoretically the house could win or lose up to 100 units, but in practice we find that the outcomes are almost always within 30 or so of 0. Thus we let the bins of the histogram range from -40 to 40 in increments of 2 (since the net profit is always even after 100 bets).

```
hist(profits(100, 100), -40:2:40); axis tight
```

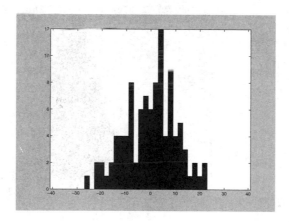

The histogram confirms our impression that there is a wide variation in the outcomes after 100 games. The house is about as likely to have lost money as to have profited. However, the distribution shown above is irregular enough to indicate that we really should run more trials to see a better approximation to the actual distribution. Let's try 1000 trials.

```
hist(profits(100, 1000), -40:2:40); axis tight
```

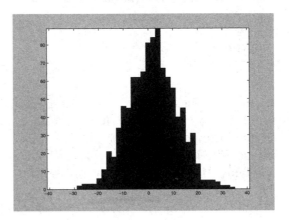

According to the *Central Limit Theorem*, when both n and k are large, the histogram should be shaped like a "bell curve", and we begin to see this shape emerging above. Let's move on to 10,000 trials.

```
hist(profits(100, 10000), -40:2:40); axis tight
```

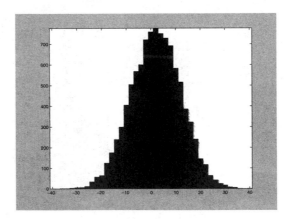

Here we see very clearly the shape of a bell curve. Though we haven't gained that much in terms of knowing how likely the house is to be behind after 100 games, and how large its net loss is likely to be in that case, we do gain confidence that our results after 1000 trials are a good depiction of the distribution of possible outcomes.

Now we consider the net profit after 1000 games. We expect on average the house to win 510 games and the player(s) to win 490, for a net profit of 20 units. Again we start with just 100 trials.

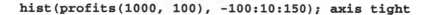

```
hist(profits(1000, 100), -100:10:150); axis tight
```

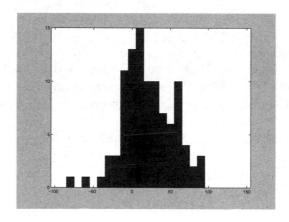

Though the range of *observed* values for the profit after 1000 games is larger than the range for 100 games, the range of *possible* values is 10 times as large, so that relatively speaking the outcomes are closer together than before. This reflects the theoretical principle (also a consequence of the *Central Limit Theorem*) that the average "spread" of outcomes after a large number of trials should be proportional to the square root of n, the number of games played in each trial. This is important for the casino, since if the spread were proportional to n, then the casino could never be too sure of making a profit. When we increase n by a factor of 10, the spread should only increase by a factor of $\sqrt{10}$, or a little more than 3.

Note that after 1000 games, the house is definitely more likely to be ahead than behind. However, the chances of being behind are still sizable. Let's repeat with 1000 trials to be more certain of our results.

```
hist(profits(1000, 1000), -100:10:150); axis tight
```

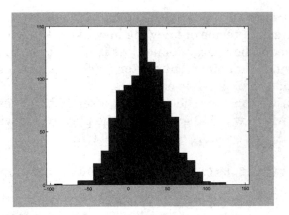

We see the bell curve shape emerging again. Though it is unlikely, the chances are not insignificant that the house is behind by more than 50 units after 1000 games. If each unit is worth $1000, then we might advise the casino to have at least $100,000 cash on hand to be prepared for this possibility. Maybe even that is not enough — to see we would have to experiment further.

Finally, let's see what happens after 10,000 games. We expect on average the house to be ahead by 200 units at this point, and based on our earlier discussion the range of values we use to make the histogram need only go up by a factor of 3 or so from the previous case. Even 100 trials will take a while to run now, but we have to start somewhere.

```
hist(profits(10000, 100), -200:25:600); axis tight
```

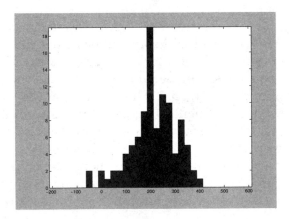

It seems that turning a profit after 10,000 games is highly likely, although with only 100 trials we do not get such a good idea of the worst-case scenario. Though it will take a good bit of time, we should certainly do 1000 trials or more if we are considering putting our money into such a venture.

```
hist(profits(10000, 1000), -200:25:600); axis tight

??? Error using ==> inlineeval
Error in inline expression ==> sum(sign(0.51 - rand(n, k)))
??? Error using ==> -
Out of memory. Type HELP MEMORY for your options.

Error in ==>
C:\MATLABR12\toolbox\matlab\funfun\@inline\subsref.m
On line 25 ==> INLINE_OUT_ = inlineeval(INLINE_INPUTS_,
INLINE_OBJ_.inputExpr, INLINE_OBJ_.expr);
```

This error message illustrates a potential hazard in using MATLAB's vector and matrix operations in place of a loop: In this case the matrix **rand(n,k)** generated within the **profits** function must fit in the memory of the computer. Since **n** is 10,000 and **k** is 1000 in our most recent attempt to run this function, we requested a matrix of 10,000,000 random numbers. Each floating point number in MATLAB takes up 8 bytes of memory, so the matrix would have required 80MB to store, which is too much for some computers. Since **k** represents a number of trials that can be done independently, a solution to the memory problem is to break the 1000 trials into 10 groups of 100, using a loop to run 100 trials 10 times and assemble the results.

```
profitvec = [];
for i = 1:10
  profitvec = [profitvec profits(10000, 100)];
end
hist(profitvec, -200:25:600); axis tight
```

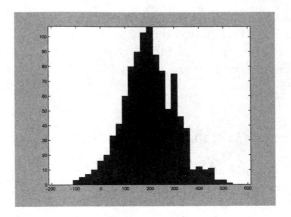

Though the chances of a loss after 10,000 games is quite small, the possibility cannot be ignored, and we might judge that the house should not rule out being behind at some point by 100 or more units. However, the overall upward trend seems clear, and we may expect that after 100,000 games the casino is overwhelmingly likely to have made a profit. Based on our previous observations of the growth of the spread of outcomes, we expect that most of the time the net profit will be within 1000 of the expected value of 2000. We show the results of 10 trials of 100,000 games below.

```
profits(100000, 10)

ans =
  Columns 1 through 6
        2294        1946        2652        2630        1872
  2078
  Columns 7 through 10
        1984        1552        2138        1852
```

Population Dynamics

We are going to look at two models for population growth of a species. The first is a standard exponential growth and decay model that describes quite well the population of a species becoming extinct, or the short-term behavior of a population growing in an unchecked fashion. The second, more realistic model, describes the growth of a species subject to constraints of space, food supply, competitors, and predators.

Exponential Growth and Decay

We assume that the species starts with an initial population P_0. The population after n times units is denoted P_n. Suppose that in each time interval, the population increases or decreases by a fixed proportion of its value at the begining of the interval. Thus $P_n = P_{n-1} + r P_{n-1}$, $n \geq 1$. The constant r represents the difference between the birth rate and the death rate. The population increases if r is positive, decreases if r is negative, and remains fixed if $r = 0$.

Here is a simple M-file that will compute the population at stage n, given the population at the previous stage and the rate r:

```
function X = itseq(f, Xinit, n, r)
% computing an iterative sequence of values
X = zeros(n + 1, 1);
X(1) = Xinit;
for i = 1:n
  X(i + 1) = f(X(i), r);
end
```

In fact, this is a simple program for computing iteratively the values of a sequence $a_n = f(a_{n-1})$, $n \geq 1$, provided you have previously entered the formula for the function f and the initial value of the sequence a_0. Note the extra parameter r built into the algorithm.

Now let's use the program to compute two populations at five-year intervals for different values of r:

```
r = 0.1; Xinit = 100; f = inline('x*(1 + r)', 'x', 'r');
X = itseq(f, Xinit, 100, r);
format long; X(1:5:101)

ans =
  1.0e+006 *
   0.00010000000000
   0.00016105100000
   0.00025937424601
   0.00041772481694
```

```
           0.00067274999493
           0.00108347059434
           0.00174494022689
           0.00281024368481
           0.00452592555682
           0.00728904836851
           0.01173908528797
           0.01890591424713
           0.03044816395414
           0.04903707252979
           0.07897469567994
           0.12718953713951
           0.20484002145855
           0.32989690295921
           0.53130226118483
           0.85566760466078
           1.37806123398224
```

```
r = -0.1; X = itseq(f, Xinit, 100, r);
X(1:5:101)
```

```
ans =
  1.0e+002  *
    1.00000000000000
    0.59049000000000
    0.34867844010000
    0.20589113209465
    0.12157665459057
    0.07178979876919
    0.04239115827522
    0.02503155504993
    0.01478088294143
    0.00872796356809
    0.00515377520732
    0.00304325272217
    0.00179701029991
    0.00106111661200
    0.00062657874822
    0.00036998848504
    0.00021847450053
```

```
0.00012900700782
0.00007617734805
0.00004498196225
0.00002656139889
```

In the first case, the population is growing rapidly; in the second, it is decaying rapidly. In fact, it is clear from the model that, for any n, the quotient $P_{n+1}/P_n = (1+r)$, and therefore it follows that $P_n = P_0(1+r)^n, n \geq 0$. This accounts for the expression *exponential growth and decay*. The model predicts a population growth without bound (for growing populations) and is therefore not realistic. Our next model allows for a check on the population caused by limited space, limited food supply, competitors and predators.

Logistic Growth

The previous model assumes that the relative change in population is constant, that is,

$$(P_{n+1} - P_n)/P_n = r.$$

Now let's build in a term that holds down the growth, namely

$$(P_{n+1} - P_n)/P_n = r - uP_n.$$

We shall simplify matters by assuming that $u = 1 + r$, so that our recursion relation becomes

$$P_{n+1} = uP_n(1 - P_n),$$

where u is a positive constant. In this model, the population P is constrained to lie between 0 and 1, and should be interpreted as a percentage of a maximum possible population in the environment in question. So let us set up the function we will use in the iterative procedure:

```
clear f; f = inline('u*x*(1 - x)', 'x', 'u');
```

Now let's compute a few examples; and use **plot** to display the results.

```
u = 0.5; Xinit = 0.5; X = itseq(f, Xinit, 20, u); plot(X)
```

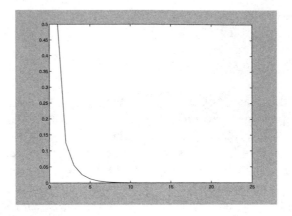

u = 1; X = itseq(f, Xinit, 20, u); plot(X)

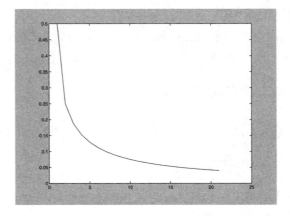

u = 1.5; X = itseq(f, Xinit, 20, u); plot(X)

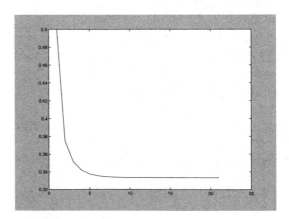

```
u = 3.4; X = itseq(f, Xinit, 20, u); plot(X)
```

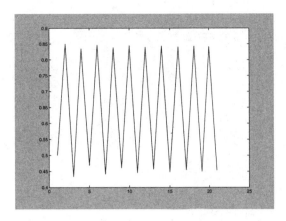

In the first computation, we have used our iterative program to compute the population density for 20 time intervals, assuming a logistic growth constant $u = 0.5$ and an initial population density of 50%. The population seems to be dying out. In the remaining examples, we kept the initial population density at 50%; the only thing we varied was the logistic growth constant. In the second example, with a growth constant $u = 1$, once again the population is dying out — although more slowly. In the third example, with a growth constant of 1.5 the population seems to be stabilizing at 33.3...%. Finally, in the last example, with a constant of 3.4 the population seems to oscillate between densities of approximately 45% and 84%.

These examples illustrate the remarkable features of the logistic population dynamics model. This model has been studied for more than 150 years, with its origins lying in an analysis by the Belgian mathematician Pierre Verhulst. Here are some of the facts associated with this model. We will corroborate some of them with MATLAB. In particular, we shall use **bar** as well as **plot** to display some of the data.

(1) The Logistic Constant Cannot Be Larger Than 4

For the model to work, the output at any point must be between 0 and 1. But the parabola $ux(1-x)$, for $0 \leq x \leq 1$, has its maximum height when $x = 1/2$, where its value is $u/4$. To keep that number between 0 and 1, we must restrict u to be at most 4. Here is what happens if u is bigger than 4:

```
u = 4.5; Xinit = 0.9; X = itseq(f, Xinit, 10, u)

X =
  1.0e+072 *
   0.00000000000000
   0.00000000000000
   0.00000000000000
  -0.00000000000000
  -0.00000000000000
  -0.00000000000000
  -0.00000000000000
  -0.00000000000000
  -0.00000000000000
  -0.00000000000000
  -3.49103403458070
```

(2) If $0 \leq u \leq 1$, the Population Density Tends to Zero for Any Initial Configuration

```
X = itseq(f, 0.99, 100, 0.8); X(101)

ans =
     1.939524024691387e-012


X = itseq(f, 0.75, 20, 1);
bar(X)
```

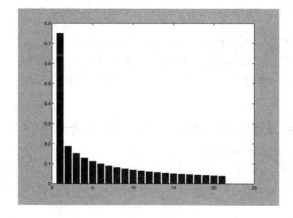

(3) If $1 < u \le 3$, the Population Will Stabilize at Density $1 - 1/u$ for Any Initial Density Other Than Zero

The third of the original four examples corroborates the assertion (with $u = 1.5$ and $1 - 1/u = 1/3$). In the following examples, we set $u = 2, 2.5$, and 3, so that $1 - 1/u$ equals 0.5, 0.6, and 0.666..., respectively. The convergence in the last computation is rather slow (as one might expect from a boundary case — or bifurcation point).

```
X = itseq(f, 0.25, 100, 2); X(101)

ans =
    0.50000000000000

X = itseq(f, 0.75, 100, 2); X(101)

ans =
    0.50000000000000

X = itseq(f, 0.5, 20, 2.5);
plot(X)
```

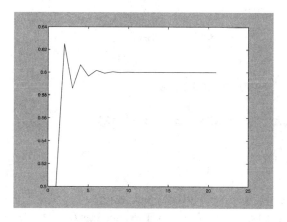

```
X = itseq(f, 0.75, 100, 3);
bar(X); axis([0 100 0 0.8])
```

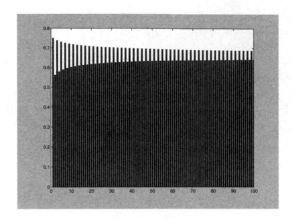

(4) If $3 < u < 3.56994\ldots$, Then There Is a Periodic Cycle

The theory is quite subtle. For a fuller explanation, the reader may consult *Encounters with Chaos*, by Denny Gulick, McGraw-Hill, 1992, Section 1.5. In fact there is a sequence

$$u_0 = 3 < u_1 = 1 + \sqrt{6} < u_2 < u_3 < \ldots < 4,$$

such that between u_0 and u_1 there is a cycle of period 2, between u_1 and u_2 there is a cycle of period 4, and in general, between u_k and u_{k+1} there is a cycle of period 2^{k+1}. One also knows that, at least for small k, one has the approximation $u_{k+1} \approx 1 + \sqrt{3 + u_k}$. So

```
u1 = 1 + sqrt(6)

u1 =
    3.44948974278318

u2approx = 1 + sqrt(3 + u1)

u2approx =
    3.53958456106175
```

This explains the oscillatory behavior we saw in the last of the original four examples (with $u_0 < u = 3.4 < u_1$). Here is the behavior for $u_1 < u = 3.5 < u_2$. The command **bar** is particularly effective here for spotting the cycle of order 4.

```
X = itseq(f, 0.75, 100, 3.5);
bar(X); axis([0 100 0 0.9])
```

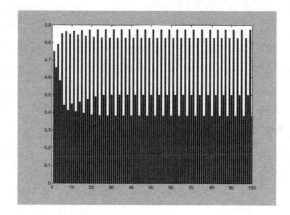

(5) There Is a Value *u* < 4 Beyond Which Chaos Ensues

It is possible to prove that the sequence u_k tends to a limit u_∞. The value of u_∞, sometimes called the *Feigenbaum parameter*, is aproximately 3.56994... . Let's see what happens if we use a value of u between the Feigenbaum parameter and 4.

```
X = itseq(f, 0.75, 100, 3.7); plot(X)
```

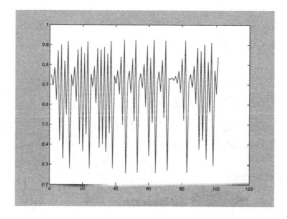

This is an example of what mathematicians call a *chaotic* phenomenon! It is not random — the sequence was generated by a precise, fixed mathematical procedure — but the results manifest no predictible pattern. Chaotic phenomena are unpredictable, but with modern methods (including computer analysis), mathematicians have been able to identify certain patterns of behavior in chaotic phenomena. For example, the last figure suggests the possibility of unstable periodic cycles and other recurring phenomena. Indeed a great deal of information is known. The aforementioned book by Gulick is a fine reference, as well as the source of an excellent bibliography on the subject.

Rerunning the Model with SIMULINK

The logistic growth model that we have been exploring lends itself particularly well to simulation using SIMULINK. Here is a simple SIMULINK model that corresponds to the above calculations:

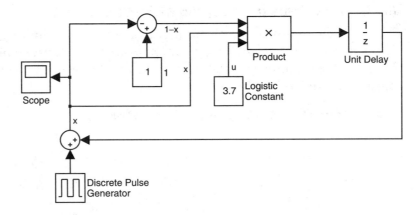

Let's briefly explain how this works. If you ignore the Discrete Pulse Generator block and the Sum block in the lower left for a moment, this model implements the equation

$$x \text{ at next time} = ux(1 - x) \text{ at old time,}$$

which is the equation for the logistic model. The Scope block displays a plot of x as a function of (discrete) time. However, we need somehow to build in the initial condition for x. The simplest way to do this is as illustrated here: We add to the right-hand side a discrete pulse that is the initial value of x at time $t = 0$ and is 0 thereafter. Since the model is discrete, you can achieve this by setting the period of the Discrete Pulse Generator block to something longer than the length of the simulation, and setting the width of the pulse to 1 and the amplitude of the pulse to the initial value of x. The outputs from the model in the two interesting cases of $u = 3.4$ and $u = 3.7$ are shown here:

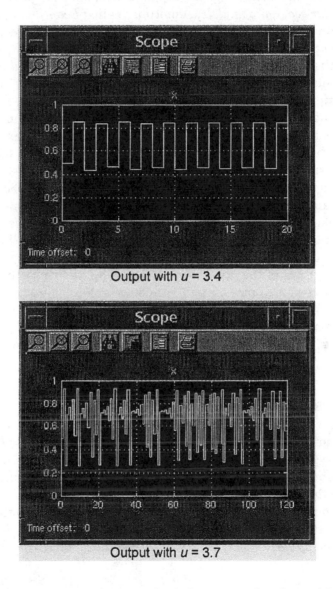

Output with $u = 3.4$

Output with $u = 3.7$

In the first case of $u = 3.4$, the periodic behavior is clearly visible. However, when $u = 3.7$, we get chaotic behavior.

Linear Economic Models

MATLAB's linear algebra capabilities make it a good vehicle for studying *linear economic models*, sometimes called *Leontief models* (after their primary developer, Nobel Prize-winning economist Wassily Leontief) or *input-output models*. We will give a few examples. The simplest such model is the *linear exchange model* or *closed Leontief model* of an economy. This model supposes that an economy is divided into, say, n sectors, such as agriculture, manufacturing, service, consumers, etc. Each sector receives input from the various sectors (including itself) and produces an output, which is divided among the various sectors. (For example, agriculture produces food for home consumption and for export, but also seeds and new livestock, which are reinvested in the agricultural sector, as well as chemicals that may be used by the manufacturing sector, and so on.) The meaning of a *closed* model is that total production is equal to total consumption. The economy is in equilibrium when each sector of the economy (at least) breaks even. For this to happen, the prices of the various outputs have to be adjusted by market forces. Let a_{ij} denote the fraction of the output of the jth sector consumed by the ith sector. Then the a_{ij} are the entries of a square matrix, called the *exchange matrix A*, each of whose columns sums to 1. Let p_i be the price of the output of the ith sector of the economy. Since each sector is to at least break even, p_i cannot be smaller than the value of the inputs consumed by the ith sector, or in other words,

$$p_i \geq \sum_j a_{ij} p_j.$$

But summing over i and using the fact that $\sum_i a_{ij} = 1$, we see that both sides must be equal. In matrix language, that means that $(I - A)p = 0$, where p is the column vector of prices. Thus p is an eigenvector of A for the eigenvalue 1, and the theory of stochastic matrices implies (assuming that A is irreducible, meaning that there is no proper subset E of the sectors of the economy such that outputs from E all stay inside E) that p is uniquely determined up to a scalar factor. In other words, *a closed irreducible linear economy has an essentially unique equilibrium state*. For example, if we have

```
A = [.3, .1, .05, .2; .1, .2, .3, .3; .3, .5, .2, .3;
.2, .45, .2]
```

```
A   =
        0.3000      0.1000      0.0500      0.2000
        0.1000      0.2000      0.3000      0.3000
        0.3000      0.5000      0.2000      0.3000
        0.3000      0.2000      0.4500      0.2000
```

then as required,

sum(A)

```
ans =
    1      1      1      1
```

That is, all the columns sum to 1, and

[V, D] = eig(A); D(1, 1)
p = V(:, 1)

```
ans =
    1.0000
p =

    0.2739
    0.4768
    0.6133
    0.5669
```

shows that 1 is an eigenvalue of A with price eigenvector p as shown.

Somewhat more realistic is the (static, linear) *open Leontief model* of an economy, which takes labor, consumption, etc., into account. Let's illustrate with an example. The following cell inputs an actual *input-output transactions table* for the economy of the United Kingdom in 1963. (This table is taken from *Input-Output Analysis and its Applications* by R. O'Connor and E. W. Henry, Hafner Press, New York, 1975.) Tables such as this one can be obtained from official government statistics. The table T is a 10×9 matrix. Units are millions of British pounds. The rows represent respectively, agriculture, industry, services, total inter-industry, imports, sales by final buyers, indirect taxes, wages and profits, total primary inputs, and total inputs. The columns represent, respectively, agriculture, industry, services, total inter-industry, consumption, capital formation, exports, total final demand, and output. Thus outputs from each sector can be read off along a row, and inputs into a sector can be read off along a column.

```
T = [277, 444, 14, 735, 1123, 35, 51, 1209, 1944; ...
587, 11148, 1884, 13619, 8174, 4497, 3934, 16605, 30224; ...
   236, 2915, 1572, 4723, 11657, 430, 1452, 13539, 18262; ...
1100, 14507, 3470, 19077, 20954, 4962, 5437, 31353, 50430; ...
   133, 2844, 676, 3653, 1770, 250, 273, 2293, 5946; ...
3, 134, 42, 179, -90, -177, 88, -179, 0; ...
  -246, 499, 442, 695, 2675, 100, 17, 2792, 3487; ...
954, 12240, 13632, 26826, 0, 0, 0, 0, 26826; ...
   844, 15717, 14792, 31353, 4355, 173, 378, 4906, 36259; ...
1944, 30224, 18262, 50430, 25309, 5135, 5815, 36259, 86689];
```

A few features of this matrix are apparent from the following:

```
T(4, :) - T(1, :) - T(2, :) - T(3, :)
T(9, :) - T(5, :) - T(6, :) - T(7, :) - T(8, :)
T(10, :) - T(4, :) - T(9, :)
T(10, 1:4) - T(1:4, 9)'

ans =
     0    0    0    0    0    0    0    0    0
ans =
     0    0    0    0    0    0    0    0    0
ans =
     0    0    0    0    0    0    0    0    0
ans =
     0    0    0    0
```

Thus the 4th row, which summarizes inter-industry inputs, is the sum of the first three rows; the 9th row, which summarizes "primary inputs," is the sum of rows 5 through 8; the 10th row, total inputs, is the sum of rows 4 and 9, and the first four entries of the last row agree with the first four entries of the last column (meaning that all output from the industrial sectors is accounted for). Also we have

```
(T(:, 4) - T(:, 1) - T(:, 2) - T(:, 3))'
(T(:, 8) - T(:, 5) - T(:, 6) - T(:, 7))'
(T(:, 9) - T(:, 4) - T(:, 8))'
```

```
ans  =
       0    0    0    0    0    0    0    0    0    0
ans  =
       0    0    0    0    0    0    0    0    0    0
ans  =
       0    0    0    0    0    0    0    0    0    0
```

So the 4th column, representing total inter-industry output, is the sum of columns 1 through 3; the 8th column, representing total "final demand," is the sum of columns 5 through 7; and the 9th column, representing total output, is the sum of columns 4 and 8. The matrix A of *inter-industry technical coefficients* is obtained by dividing the columns of T corresponding to industrial sectors (in our case there are three of these) by the corresponding total inputs. Thus we have

```
A = [T(:, 1)/T(10, 1), T(:, 2)/T(10, 2), T(:, 3)/T(10, 3)]
```

```
A  =
      0.1425    0.0147    0.0008
      0.3020    0.3688    0.1032
      0.1214    0.0964    0.0861
      0.5658    0.4800    0.1900
      0.0684    0.0941    0.0370
      0.0015    0.0044    0.0023
     -0.1265    0.0165    0.0242
      0.4907    0.4050    0.7465
      0.4342    0.5200    0.8100
      1.0000    1.0000    1.0000
```

Here the square upper block (the first three rows) is most important, so we make the replacement

```
A = A(1:3, :)
```

```
A  =
      0.1425    0.0147    0.0008
      0.3020    0.3688    0.1032
      0.1214    0.0964    0.0861
```

If the vector Y represents total final demand for the various industrial sectors, and the vector X represents total outputs for these sectors, then the fact that the last column of T is the sum of columns 4 (total inter-industry outputs) and 8 (total final demand) translates into the matrix equation $X = AX + Y$, or $Y = (1 - A)X$. Let's check this:

```
Y = T(1:3, 8); X = T(1:3, 9); Y - (eye(3) - A)*X

ans =
     0
     0
     0
```

Now one can do various numerical experiments. For example, what would be the effect on output of an increase of £10 billion (10,000 in the units of our problem) in final demand for industrial output, with no corresponding increase in demand for services or for agricultural products? Since the economy is assumed to be linear, the change ΔX in X is obtained by solving the linear equation $\Delta Y = (1 - A)\Delta X$, and

```
deltaX = (eye(3) - A) \ [0; 10000; 0]
deltaX =
  1.0e+004 *
     0.0280
     1.6265
     0.1754
```

Thus agricultural output would increase by £280 million, industrial output would increase by £16.265 billion, and service output would increase by £1.754 billion. We can illustrate the result of doing this for similar increases in demand for the other sectors with the following pie charts:

```
deltaX1 = (eye(3) - A) \ [10000; 0; 0];
deltaX2 = (eye(3) - A) \ [0; 0; 10000];
subplot(1, 3, 1), pie(deltaX1, {'Agr.', 'Ind.', 'Serv.'}),
subplot(1, 3, 2), pie(deltaX, {'Agr.', 'Ind.', 'Serv.'}),
title('Effect of increases in demand for each of the 3
sectors', 'FontSize',18),
subplot(1, 3, 3), pie(deltaX2, {'Agr.', 'Ind.', 'Serv.'});
```

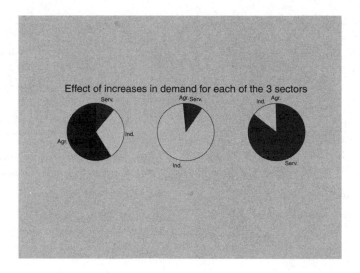

Effect of increases in demand for each of the 3 sectors

Linear Programming

MATLAB is ideally suited to handle *linear programming* problems. These are problems in which you have a quantity, depending linearly on several variables, that you want to maximize or minimize subject to several constraints that are expressed as linear inequalities in the same variables. If the number of variables and the number of constraints are small, then there are numerous mathematical techniques for solving a linear programming problem — indeed these techniques are often taught in high school or university courses in finite mathematics. But sometimes these numbers are high, or even if low, the constants in the linear inequalities or the object expression for the quantity to be optimized may be numerically complicated — in which case a software package like MATLAB is required to effect a solution. We shall illustrate the method of linear programming by means of a simple example, giving a combination graphical-numerical solution, and then solve both a slightly and a substantially more complicated problem.

Suppose a farmer has 75 acres on which to plant two crops: wheat and barley. To produce these crops, it costs the farmer (for seed, fertilizer, etc.) $120 per acre for the wheat and $210 per acre for the barley. The farmer has $15,000 available for expenses. But after the harvest, the farmer must store the crops while awaiting favorable market conditions. The farmer has storage space for 4,000 bushels. Each acre yields an average of 110 bushels of wheat or 30 bushels of barley. If the net profit per bushel of wheat (after all expenses have been subtracted) is $1.30 and for barley is $2.00, how should the farmer plant the 75 acres to maximize profit?

We begin by formulating the problem mathematically. First we express the objective, that is, the profit, and the constraints algebraically, then we graph them, and lastly we arrive at the solution by graphical inspection and a minor arithmetic calculation.

Let x denote the number of acres allotted to wheat and y the number of acres allotted to barley. Then the expression to be maximized, that is, the profit, is clearly

$$P = (110)(1.30)x + (30)(2.00)y = 143x + 60y.$$

There are three constraint inequalities, specified by the limits on expenses, storage, and acreage. They are respectively

$$120x + 210y \leq 15,000$$
$$110x + 30y \leq 4,000$$
$$x + y \leq 75.$$

Strictly speaking there are two more constraint inequalities forced by the fact that the farmer cannot plant a negative number of acres, namely,

$$x \geq 0, y \geq 0.$$

Next we graph the regions specified by the constraints. The last two say that we only need to consider the first quadrant in the x-y plane. Here's a graph delineating the triangular region in the first quadrant determined by the first inequality.

```
X = 0:125;
Y1 = (15000 - 120.*X)./210;
area(X, Y1)
```

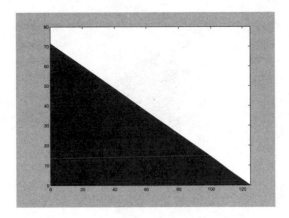

Now let's put in the other two constraint inequalities.

```
Y2 = max((4000 - 110.*X)./30, 0);
Y3 = max(75 - X, 0);
Ytop = min([Y1; Y2; Y3]);
area(X, Ytop)
```

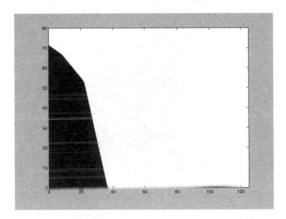

It's a little hard to see the polygonal boundary of the region clearly. Let's hone in a bit.

```
area(X, Ytop); axis([0 40 40 75])
```

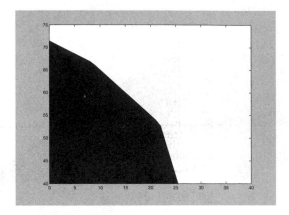

Now let's superimpose on top of this picture a contour plot of the objective function P.

```
hold on
[U V] = meshgrid(0:40, 40:75);
contour(U, V, 143.*U + 60.*V); hold off
```

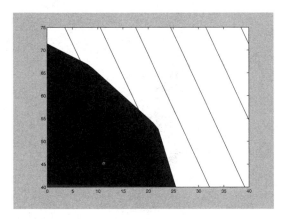

It seems apparent that the maximum value of P will occur on the level curve (that is, level line) that passes through the vertex of the polygon that lies near $(23, 53)$. In fact we can compute

```
[x, y] = solve('x + y = 75', '110*x + 30*y = 4000')
```

```
x =
175/8
```

```
y =
425/8
```

double([x, y])

```
ans =
   21.8750      53.1250
```

The acreage that results in the maximum profit is 21.875 for wheat and 53.125 for barley. In that case the profit is

P = 143*x + 60*y

```
P=
50525/8
```

format bank; double(P)

```
ans =
       6315.63
```

that is, $6,315.63.

This problem illustrates and is governed by the *Fundamental Theorem of Linear Programming*, stated here in two variables:

> A linear expression $ax + by$, defined over a closed bounded convex set
> S whose sides are line segments, takes on its maximum value at a
> vertex of S and its minimum value at a vertex of S. If S is unbounded,
> there may or may not be an optimum value, but if there is, it occurs at a
> vertex. (A *convex* set is one for which any line segment joining two
> points of the set lies entirely inside the set.)

In fact the SIMULINK toolbox has a built-in function, **simlp**, that implements the solution of a linear programming problem. The optimization toolbox has an almost identical function called **linprog**. You can learn about either one from the online help. We will use **simlp** on the above problem. After that we will use it to solve two more complicated problems involving more variables and constraints. Here is the beginning of the output from **help simlp**:

```
SIMLP Helper function for GETXO; solves linear programming
problem.
```

```
X=SIMLP(f,A,b) solves the linear programming problem:
```

$$\min_{x} f'x \qquad \text{subject to:} \qquad Ax <= b$$

So

```
f = [-143 -60];
A = [120 210; 110 30; 1 1; -1 0; 0 -1];
b = [15000; 4000; 75; 0; 0];

format short; simlp(f, A, b)

ans =
   21.8750
   53.1250
```

This is the same answer we obtained before. Note that we entered the negative of the coefficient vector for the objective function P because **simlp** searches for a *minimum* rather than a maximum. Note also that the nonnegativity constraints are accounted for in the last two rows of **A** and **b**.

Well, we could have done this problem by hand. But suppose that the farmer is dealing with a third crop, say corn, and that the corresponding data are

cost per acre	$150.75
yield per acre	125 bushels
profit per bushel	$1.56.

If we denote the number of acres allotted to corn by z, then the objective function becomes

$$P = (110)(1.30)x + (30)(2.00)y + (125)(1.56) = 143x + 60y + 195z,$$

and the constraint inequalities are

$$120x + 210y + 150.75z \le 15{,}000$$
$$110x + 30y + 125z \le 4{,}000$$
$$x + y + z \le 75$$
$$x \ge 0, y \ge 0, z \ge 0.$$

The problem is solved with **simlp** as follows:

```
clear f A b; f = [-143 -60 -195];
A = [120 210 150.75; 110 30 125; 1 1 1;...
```

```
-1 0 0; 0 -1 0; 0 0 -1];
b = [15000; 4000; 75; 0; 0; 0];

simlp(f, A, b)

ans =
    0.0000
   56.5789
   18.4211
```

So the farmer should ditch the wheat and plant 56.5789 acres of barley and 18.4211 acres of corn.

There is no practical limit on the number of variables and constraints that MATLAB can handle — certainly none that the relatively unsophisticated user will encounter. Indeed, in many true applications of the technique of linear programming, one needs to deal with many variables and constraints. The solution of such a problem by hand is not feasible, and software such as MATLAB is crucial to success. For example, in the farming problem with which we have been working, one could have more than two or three crops. (Think agribusiness instead of family farmer.) And one could have constraints that arise from other things besides expenses, storage, and acreage limitations, for example:

- Availability of seed. This might lead to constraint inequalities such as $x_j \leq k$.
- Personal preferences. Thus the farmer's spouse might have a preference for one variety or group of varieties over another, and insist on a corresponding planting, thus leading to constraint inequalities such as $x_i \leq x_j$ or $x_1 + x_2 \geq x_3$.
- Government subsidies. It may take a moment's reflection on the reader's part, but this could lead to inequalities such as $x_j \geq k$.

Below is a sequence of commands that solves exactly such a problem. You should be able to recognize the objective expression and the constraints from the data that are entered. But as an aid, you might answer the following questions:

- How many crops are under consideration?
- What are the corresponding expenses? How much money is available for expenses?
- What are the yields in each case? What is the storage capacity?
- How many acres are available?

- What crops are constrained by seed limitations? To what extent?
- What about preferences?
- What are the minimum acreages for each crop?

```
clear f A b
f = [-110*1.3 -30*2.0 -125*1.56 -75*1.8 -95*.95 -100*2.25 -
50*1.35];

A = [120 210 150.75 115 186 140 85; 110 30 125 75 95 100 50;
    1 1 1 1 1 1 1; 1 0 0 0 0 0 0; 0 0 1 0 0 0 0; 0 0 0 0 0 1 0;
1 -1 0 0 0 0 0; 0 0 1 0 -2 0 0; 0 0 0 -1 0 -1 1;
-1 0 0 0 0 0 0; 0 -1 0 0 0 0 0; 0 0 -1 0 0 0 0;
   0 0 0 -1 0 0 0; 0 0 0 0 -1 0 0; 0 0 0 0 0 -1 0;
0 0 0 0 0 0 -1];
b = [55000;40000;400;100;50;250;0;0;0;-10;-10;-10;
 -10;-20;-20;-20];

simlp(f, A, b)

ans =
   10.0000
   10.0000
   40.0000
   45.6522
   20.0000
  250.0000
   20.0000
```

Note that despite the complexity of the problem, *MATLAB* solves it almost instantaneously. It seems the farmer should bet the farm on crop number 6. We suggest you alter the expense and/or the storage limit in the problem and see what effect that has on the answer.

The 360° Pendulum

Normally we think of a pendulum as a weight suspended by a flexible string or cable, so that it may swing back and forth. Another type of pendulum consists of a weight attached by a light (but inflexible) rod to an axle, so that it can swing through larger angles, even making a 360° rotation if given enough velocity.

Though it is not precisely correct in practice, we often assume that the magnitude of the frictional forces that eventually slow the pendulum to a halt is proportional to the velocity of the pendulum. Assume also that the length of the pendulum is 1 meter, the weight at the end of the pendulum has mass 1 kg, and the coefficient of friction is 0.5. In that case, the equations of motion for the pendulum are

$$x'(t) = y(t), \, y'(t) = -0.5y(t) - 9.81\sin(x(t)),$$

where t represents time in seconds, x represents the angle of the pendulum from the vertical in radians (so that $x = 0$ is the rest position), y represents the velocity of the pendulum in radians per second, and 9.81 is approximately the acceleration due to gravity in meters per second squared. Here is a phase portrait of the solution with initial position $x(0) = 0$ and initial velocity $y(0) = 5$. This is a graph of x versus y as a function of t, on the time interval $0 \le t \le 20$.

```
g = inline('[x(2); -0.5*x(2) - 9.81*sin(x(1))]', 't', 'x');
[t, xa] = ode45(g, [0 20], [0 5]);
plot(xa(:, 1), xa(:, 2))
```

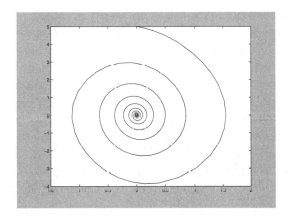

Recall that the x coordinate corresponds to the angle of the pendulum and the y coordinate corresponds to its velocity. Starting at $(0, 5)$, as t increases we follow the curve as it spirals clockwise toward $(0, 0)$. The angle oscillates back and forth, but with each swing it gets smaller until the pendulum is virtually at rest by the time $t = 20$. Meanwhile the velocity oscillates as well, taking its maximum value during each oscillation when the pendulum is in the middle of its swing (the angle is near zero) and crossing zero when the pendulum is at the end of its swing.

Next we increase the initial velocity to 10.

```
[t, xa] = ode45(g, [0 20], [0 10]);
plot(xa(:, 1), xa(:, 2))
```

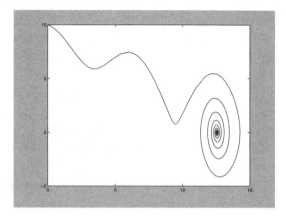

This time the angle increases to over 14 radians before the curve spirals in to a point near (12.5, 0). More precisely, it spirals toward $(4\pi, 0)$, because 4π radians represents the same position for the pendulum as 0 radians does. The pendulum has swung overhead and made two complete revolutions before beginning its damped oscillation toward its rest position. The velocity at first decreases but then rises after the angle passes through π, as the pendulum passes the upright position and gains momentum. The pendulum has just enough momentum to swing through the upright position once more at the angle 3π.

Now suppose we want to find, to within 0.1, the minimum initial velocity required to make the pendulum, starting from its rest position, swing overhead once. It will be useful to be able to see the solutions corresponding to several different initial velocities on one graph.

First we consider the integer velocities 5 to 10.

```
hold on
for a = 5:10
  [t, xa] = ode45(g, [0 20], [0 a]);
  plot(xa(:, 1), xa(:, 2))
end
hold off
```

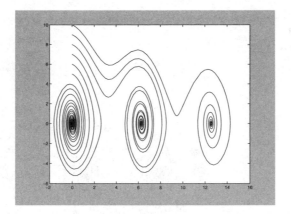

Initial velocities 5, 6, 7 are not large enough for the angle to increase past π, but initial velocities 8, 9, 10 are enough to make the pendulum swing overhead. Let's see what happens between 7 and 8.

```
hold on
for a = 7.0:0.2:8.0
  [t, xa] = ode45(g, [0 20], [0 a]);
  plot(xa(:, 1), xa(:, 2))
end
hold off
```

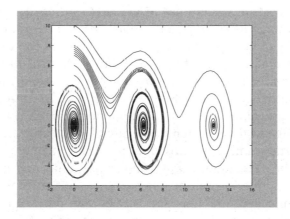

We see that the cutoff is somewhere between 7.2 and 7.4. Let's make one more refinement.

```
hold on
for a = 7.2:0.05:7.4
  [t, xa] = ode45(g, [0 20], [0 a]);
```

```
    plot(xa(:, 1), xa(:, 2))
end
hold off
```

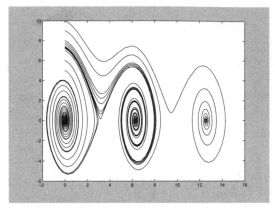

We conclude that the minimum velocity needed is somewhere between 7.25 and 7.3.

Numerical Solution of the Heat Equation

In this section we will use MATLAB to numerically solve the *heat equation* (also known as the *diffusion equation*), a partial differential equation that describes many physical processes including conductive heat flow or the diffusion of an impurity in a motionless fluid. You can picture the process of diffusion as a drop of dye spreading in a glass of water. (To a certain extent you could also picture cream in a cup of coffee, but in that case the mixing is generally complicated by the fluid motion caused by pouring the cream into the coffee and is further accelerated by stirring the coffee.) The dye consists of a large number of individual particles, each of which repeatedly bounces off of the surrounding water molecules, following an essentially random path. There are so many dye particles that their individual random motions form an essentially deterministic overall pattern as the dye spreads evenly in all directions (we ignore here the possible effect of gravity). In a similar way, you can imagine heat energy spreading through random interactions of nearby particles.

In a three-dimensional medium, the heat equation is

$$\frac{\partial u}{\partial t} = k \left(\frac{\partial^2 u}{\partial x^2} + \frac{\partial^2 u}{\partial y^2} + \frac{\partial^2 u}{\partial z^2} \right).$$

Here u is a function of t, x, y, and z that represents the temperature, or concentration of impurity in the case of diffusion, at time t at position (x, y, z) in the medium. The constant k depends on the materials involved; it is called the *thermal conductivity* in the case of heat flow and the *diffusion coefficient* in the case of diffusion. To simplify matters, let us assume that the medium is instead one-dimensional. This could represent diffusion in a thin water-filled tube or heat flow in a thin insulated rod or wire; let us think primarily of the case of heat flow. Then the partial differential equation becomes

$$\frac{\partial u}{\partial t} = k \frac{\partial^2 u}{\partial x^2},$$

where $u(x, t)$ is the temperature at time t a distance x along the wire.

A Finite Difference Solution

To solve this partial differential equation we need both *initial conditions* of the form $u(x, 0) = f(x)$, where $f(x)$ gives the temperature distribution in the wire at time 0, and *boundary conditions* at the endpoints of the wire; call them $x = a$ and $x = b$. We choose so-called Dirichlet boundary conditions $u(a, t) = T_a$ and $u(b, t) = T_b$, which correspond to the temperature being held steady at values T_a and T_b at the two endpoints. Though an exact solution is available in this scenario, let us instead illustrate the numerical method of *finite differences*.

To begin with, on the computer we can only keep track of the temperature u at a discrete set of times and a discrete set of positions x. Let the times be $0, \Delta t, 2\Delta t, \ldots, N\Delta t$, and let the positions be $a, a + \Delta x, \ldots, a + J\Delta x = b$, and let $u_j^n = u(a + j\Delta t, n\Delta t)$. Rewriting the partial differential equation in terms of finite-difference approximations to the derivatives, we get

$$\frac{u_j^{n+1} - u_j^n}{\Delta t} = k \frac{u_{j+1}^n - 2u_j^n + u_{j-1}^n}{\Delta x^2}.$$

(These are the simplest approximations we can use for the derivatives, and this method can be refined by using more accurate approximations, especially for the t derivative.) Thus if for a particular n, we know the values of u_j^n for all j, we can solve the equation above to find u_j^{n+1} for each j:

$$u_j^{n+1} = u_j^n + \frac{k\Delta t}{\Delta x^2} \left(u_{j+1}^n - 2u_j^n + u_{j-1}^n\right) = s\left(u_{j+1}^n + u_{j-1}^n\right) + (1 - 2s)u_j^n,$$

where $s = k\Delta t/(\Delta x)^2$. In other words, this equation tells us how to find the temperature distribution at time step $n + 1$ given the temperature distribution at time step n. (At the endpoints $j = 0$ and $j = J$, this equation refers to temperatures outside the prescribed range for x, but at these points we will ignore the equation above and apply the boundary conditions instead.) We can interpret this equation as saying that the temperature at a given location at the next time step is a weighted average of its temperature and the temperatures of its neighbors at the current time step. In other words, in time Δt, a given section of the wire of length Δx transfers to each of its neighbors a portion s of its heat energy and keeps the remaining portion $1 - 2s$ of its heat energy. Thus our numerical implementation of the heat equation is a discretized version of the microscopic description of diffusion we gave initially, that heat energy spreads due to random interactions between nearby particles.

The following M-file, which we have named heat.m, iterates the procedure described above:

```
function u = heat(k, x, t, init, bdry)
% solve the 1D heat equation on the rectangle described by
% vectors x and t with u(x, t(1)) = init and Dirichlet
% boundary conditions
% u(x(1), t) = bdry(1), u(x(end), t) = bdry(2).

J = length(x);
N = length(t);
dx = mean(diff(x));
dt = mean(diff(t));
s = k*dt/dx^2;

u = zeros(N,J);
u(1, :) = init;

for n = 1:N-1
  u(n+1, 2:J-1) = s*(u(n, 3:J) + u(n, 1:J-2)) +...
    (1 - 2*s)*u(n, 2:J-1);
  u(n+1, 1) = bdry(1);
  u(n+1, J) = bdry(2);
end
```

The function **heat** takes as inputs the value of k, vectors of t and x values, a vector **init** of initial values (which is assumed to have the same length as **x**), and a vector **bdry** containing a pair of boundary values. Its output is a matrix of u values. Notice that since indices of arrays in MATLAB must start at 1, not 0, we have deviated slightly from our earlier notation by letting **n=1**

represent the initial time and `j=1` represent the left endpoint. Notice also
that in the first line following the **for** statement, we compute an entire row
of **u**, except for the first and last values, in one line; each term is a vector of
length **J-2**, with the index **j** increased by 1 in the term **u(n,3:J)** and
decreased by 1 in the term **u(n,1:J-2)**.

Let's use the M-file above to solve the one-dimensional heat equation with
$k = 2$ on the interval $-5 \leq x \leq 5$ from time 0 to time 4, using boundary
temperatures 15 and 25, and initial temperature distribution of 15 for $x < 0$
and 25 for $x > 0$. You can imagine that two separate wires of length 5 with
different temperatures are joined at time 0 at position $x = 0$, and each of
their far ends remains in an environment that holds it at its initial
temperature. We must choose values for Δt and Δx; let's try $\Delta t = 0.1$ and
$\Delta x = 0.5$, so that there are 41 values of t ranging from 0 to 4 and 21 values
of x ranging from -5 to 5.

```
tvals = linspace(0, 4, 41);
xvals = linspace(-5, 5, 21);
init = 20 + 5*sign(xvals);
uvals = heat(2, xvals, tvals, init, [15 25]);
surf(xvals, tvals, uvals)
xlabel x; ylabel t; zlabel u
```

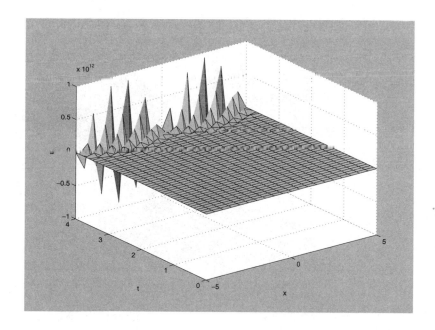

Here we used **surf** to show the entire solution $u(x, t)$. The output is clearly unrealistic; notice the scale on the u axis! The numerical solution of partial differential equations is fraught with dangers, and instability like that seen above is a common problem with finite difference schemes. For many partial differential equations a finite difference scheme will not work at all, but for the heat equation and similar equations it will work well with proper choice of Δt and Δx. One might be inclined to think that since our choice of Δx was larger, it should be reduced, but in fact this would only make matters worse. Ultimately the only parameter in the iteration we're using is the constant s, and one drawback of doing all the computations in an M-file as we did above is that we do not automatically see the intermediate quantities it computes. In this case we can easily calculate that $s = 2(0.1)/(0.5)^2 = 0.8$. Notice that this implies that the coefficient $1 - 2s$ of u_j^n in the iteration above is negative. Thus the "weighted average" we described before in our interpretation of the iterative step is not a true average; each section of wire is transferring more energy than it has at each time step!

The solution to the problem above is thus to reduce the time step Δt; for instance, if we cut it in half, then $s = 0.4$, and all coefficients in the iteration are positive.

```
tvals = linspace(0, 4, 81);
uvals = heat(2, xvals, tvals, init, [15 25]);
surf(xvals, tvals, uvals)
xlabel x; ylabel t; zlabel u
```

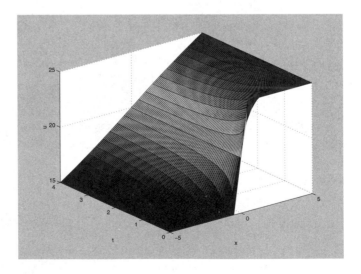

This looks much better! As time increases, the temperature distribution seems to approach a linear function of x. Indeed $u(x, t) = 20 + x$ is the limiting "steady state" for this problem; it satisfies the boundary conditions and it yields 0 on both sides of the partial differential equation.

Generally speaking, it is best to understand some of the theory of partial differential equations before attempting a numerical solution like we have done here. However, for this particular case at least, the simple rule of thumb of keeping the coefficients of the iteration positive yields realistic results. A theoretical examination of the stability of this finite difference scheme for the one-dimensional heat equation shows that indeed any value of s between 0 and 0.5 will work, and it suggests that the best value of Δt to use for a given Δx is the one that makes $s = 0.25$. (See *Partial Differential Equations: An Introduction*, by Walter A. Strauss, John Wiley and Sons, 1992.) Notice that while we can get more accurate results in this case by reducing Δx, if we reduce it by a factor of 10 we must reduce Δt by a factor of 100 to compensate, making the computation take 1000 times as long and use 1000 times the memory!

The Case of Variable Conductivity

Earlier we mentioned that the problem we solved numerically could also be solved analytically. The value of the numerical method is that it can be applied to similar partial differential equations for which an exact solution is not possible or at least not known. For example, consider the one-dimensional heat equation with a *variable coefficient*, representing an inhomogeneous material with varying thermal conductivity $k(x)$,

$$\frac{\partial u}{\partial t} = \frac{\partial}{\partial x}\left(k(x)\frac{\partial u}{\partial x}\right) = k(x)\frac{\partial^2 u}{\partial x^2} + k'(x)\frac{\partial u}{\partial x}.$$

For the first derivatives on the right-hand side, we use a symmetric finite difference approximation, so that our discrete approximation to the partial differential equations becomes

$$\frac{u_j^{n+1} - u_j^n}{\Delta t} = k_j\frac{u_{j+1}^n - 2u_j^n + u_{j-1}^n}{\Delta x^2} + \frac{k_{j+1} - k_{j-1}}{2\Delta x}\frac{u_{j+1}^n - u_{j-1}^n}{2\Delta x},$$

where $k_j = k(a + j\Delta x)$. Then the time iteration for this method is

$$u_j^{n+1} = s_j\left(u_{j+1}^n + u_{j-1}^n\right) + (1 - 2s_j)u_j^n + 0.25\left(s_{j+1} - s_{j-1}\right)\left(u_{j+1}^n - u_{j-1}^n\right),$$

where $s_j = k_j \Delta t/(\Delta x)^2$. In the following M-file, which we called `heatvc.m`, we modify our previous M-file to incorporate this iteration.

```
function u = heatvc(k, x, t, init, bdry)
% Solve the 1D heat equation with variable coefficient k on
% the rectangle described by vectors x and t with
% u(x, t(1)) = init and Dirichlet boundary conditions
% u(x(1), t) = bdry(1), u(x(end), t) = bdry(2).

J = length(x);
N = length(t);
dx = mean(diff(x));
dt = mean(diff(t));
s = k*dt/dx^2;

u = zeros(N,J);
u(1,:) = init;

for n = 1:N-1
  u(n+1, 2:J-1) = s(2:J-1).*(u(n, 3:J) + u(n, 1:J-2)) + ...
    (1 - 2*s(2:J-1)).*u(n,2:J-1) + ...
    0.25*(s(3:J) - s(1:J-2)).*(u(n, 3:J) - u(n, 1:J-2));
  u(n+1, 1) = bdry(1);
  u(n+1, J) = bdry(2);
end
```

Notice that **k** is now assumed to be a vector with the same length as **x** and that as a result so is **s**. This in turn requires that we use vectorized multiplication in the main iteration, which we have now split into three lines.

Let's use this M-file to solve the one-dimensional variable-coefficient heat equation with the same boundary and initial conditions as before, using $k(x) = 1 + (x/5)^2$. Since the maximum value of k is 2, we can use the same values of Δt and Δx as before.

```
kvals = 1 + (xvals/5).^2;
uvals = heatvc(kvals, xvals, tvals, init, [15 25]);
surf(xvals, tvals, uvals)
xlabel x; ylabel t; zlabel u
```

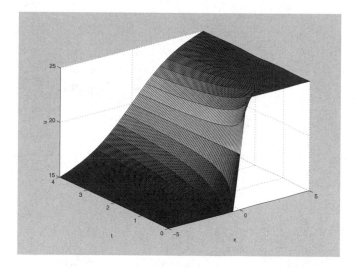

In this case the limiting temperature distribution is not linear; it has a steeper temperature gradient in the middle, where the thermal conductivity is lower. Again one could find the exact form of this limiting distribution, $u(x, t) = 20(1 + (1/\pi)\arctan(x/5))$, by setting the t derivative to zero in the original equation and solving the resulting ordinary differential equation.

You can use the method of finite differences to solve the heat equation in two or three space dimensions as well. For this and other partial differential equations with time and two space dimensions, you can also use the PDE Toolbox, which implements the more sophisticated *finite element* method.

A SIMULINK Solution

We can also solve the heat equation using SIMULINK. To do this we continue to approximate the x derivatives with finite differences, but we think of the equation as a vector-valued ordinary differential equation, with t as the independent variable. SIMULINK solves the model using MATLAB's ODE solver, **ode45**. To illustrate how to do this, let's take the same example we started with, the case where $k = 2$ on the interval $-5 \le x \le 5$ from time 0 to time 4, using boundary temperatures 15 and 25, and initial temperature distribution of 15 for $x < 0$ and 25 for $x > 0$. We replace $u(x, t)$ for fixed t by the vector **u** of values of $u(x, t)$, with, say, **x = -5:5**. Here there are 11 values of x at which we are sampling u, but since $u(x, t)$ is pre-determined at the endpoints, we can take **u** to be a 9-dimensional vector, and we just tack on the values at the endpoints when we're done. Since we're replacing $\partial^2 u / \partial x^2$ by its finite difference approximation and we've taken $\Delta x = 1$ for simplicity, our equation becomes the vector-valued ODE

$$\frac{\partial \mathbf{u}}{\partial t} = k(A\mathbf{u} + \mathbf{c}).$$

Here the right-hand side represents our approximation to $k(\partial^2 u / \partial x^2)$. The matrix A is

$$A = \begin{pmatrix} -2 & 1 & \cdots & 0 \\ 1 & -2 & \ddots & \vdots \\ \vdots & \ddots & \ddots & 1 \\ 0 & \cdots & 1 & -2 \end{pmatrix},$$

since we are replacing $\partial^2 u / \partial x^2$ at (n, t) with $u(n-1, t) - 2u(n, t) + u(n+1, t)$. We represent this matrix in MATLAB's notation by

```
-2*eye(9) + [zeros(8,1),eye(8);zeros(1,9)] +...
    [zeros(8,1),eye(8);zeros(1,9)]'
```

The vector **c** comes from the boundary conditions, and has 15 in its first entry, 25 in its last entry, and 0s in between. We represent it in MATLAB's notation as `[15;zeros(7,1);25]` The formula for **c** comes from the fact that `u(1)` represents $u(-4, t)$, and $\partial^2 u / \partial x^2$ at this point is approximated by

$$u(-5, t) - 2u(-4, t) + u(-3, t) = 15 - 2\,\mathbf{u(1)} + \mathbf{u(2)},$$

and similarly at the other endpoint. Here's a SIMULINK model representing this equation:

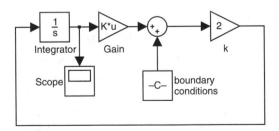

Note that one needs to specify the initial conditions for u as Block Parameters for the Integrator block, and that in the Block Parameters dialog

box for the Gain block, one needs to set the multiplication type to "Matrix".
Since **u(1)** through **u(4)** represent $u(x, t)$ at $x = -4$ through -1, and **u(6)**
through **u(9)** represent $u(x, t)$ at $x = 1$ through 4, we take the initial value
of u to be **[15*ones(4,1);20;25*ones(4,1)]**. (The value 20 is a
compromise at $x = 0$, since this is right in the middle of the regions where u
is 15 and 25.) The output from the model is displayed in the Scope block in
the form of graphs of the various entries of u as functions of t, but it's more
useful to save the output to the MATLAB Workspace and then plot it with
surf. To do this, go to the menu item **Simulation Parameters...** in the
Simulation menu of the model. Under the **Solver** tab, set the stop time to
4.0 (since we are only going out to $t = 4$), and under the **Workspace I/O** tab,
check the "States" box under "Save to workspace", like this:

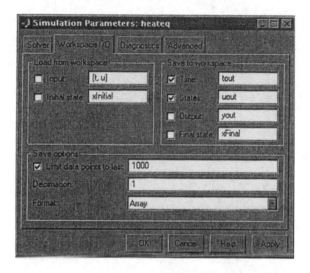

After you run the model, you will find in your Workspace a 53×1 vector
tout, plus a 53×9 matrix **uout**. Each row of these arrays corresponds to a
single time step, and each column of **uout** corresponds to one value of x. But
remember that we have to add in the values of u at the endpoints as
additional columns in **u**. So we plot the data as follows:

```
u = [15*ones(length(tout),1), uout, 25*ones(length(tout),1)];
x = -5:5;
surf(x, tout, u)
xlabel('x'), ylabel('t'), zlabel('u')
title('solution to heat equation in a rod')
```

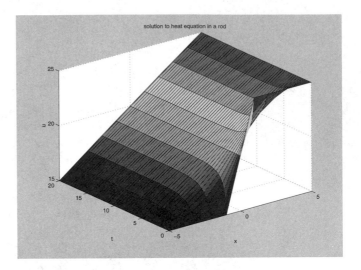

Note how similar this is to the picture obtained before. We leave it to the reader to modify the model for the case of variable heat conductivity.

Solution with pdepe

A new feature of MATLAB 6.0 is a built-in solver for partial differential equations in one space dimension (as well as time t). To find out more about it, read the online help on **pdepe**. The instructions for use of **pdepe** are quite explicit but somewhat complicated. The method it uses is somewhat similar to that used in the SIMULINK solution above; that is, it uses an ODE solver in t and finite differences in x. The following M-file solves the second problem above, the one with variable conductivity. Note the use of function handles and subfunctions.

```
function heateqex2
% Solves a sample Dirichlet problem for the heat equation in a
% rod, this time with variable conductivity, 21 mesh points

m = 0; %This simply means geometry is linear.
x = linspace(-5,5,21);
t = linspace(0,4,81);
sol = pdepe(m,@pdex,@pdexic,@pdexbc,x,t);
% Extract the first solution component as u.
u = sol(:,:,1);
% A surface plot is often a good way to study a solution.
```

```
surf(x,t,u); title(['Numerical solution',...
'computed with 21 mesh points in x.'])

xlabel('x'), ylabel('t'), zlabel('u')
% A solution profile can also be illuminating.
figure
plot(x,u(end,:))
title('Solution at t = 4')
xlabel('x'), ylabel('u(x,4)')
%-------------------------------------------------------------
function [c,f,s] = pdex(x,t,u,DuDx)
c = 1;
f = (1 + (x/5).^2)*DuDx;
% flux is variable conductivity times u_x
s = 0;
% ------------------------------------------------------------
function u0 = pdexic(x)
% initial condition at t = 0
u0 = 20+5*sign(x);
% ------------------------------------------------------------
function [pl,ql,pr,qr] = pdexbc(xl,ul,xr,ur,t)
% q's are zero since we have Dirichlet conditions
% pl = 0 at the left, pr = 0 at the right endpoint
pl = ul-15;
ql = 0;
pr = ur-25;
qr = 0;
```

Running it gives

```
heateqex2
```

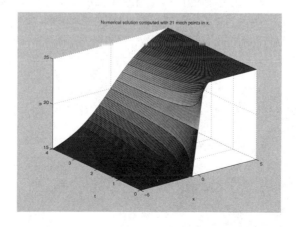

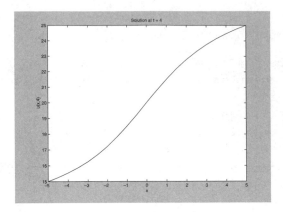

Again the results are very similar to those obtained before.

A Model of Traffic Flow

Everyone has had the experience of sitting in a traffic jam, or of seeing cars bunch up on a road for no apparent good reason. MATLAB and SIMULINK are good tools for studying models of such behavior. Our analysis here will be based on "follow-the-leader" theories of traffic flow, about which you can read more in *Kinetic Theory of Vehicular Traffic*, by Ilya Prigogine and Robert Herman, Elsevier, New York, 1971 or in *The Theory of Road Traffic Flow*, by Winifred Ashton, Methuen, London, 1966. We will analyze here an extremely simple model that already exhibits quite complicated behavior. We consider a one-lane, one-way, circular road with a number of cars on it (a very primitive model of, say, the Inner Loop of the Capital Beltway around Washington, DC, since in very dense traffic, it is hard to change lanes and each lane behaves like a one-lane road). Each driver slows down or speeds up on the basis of his or her own speed, the speed of the car directly ahead, and the distance to the car ahead. But human drivers have a finite *reaction time*. In other words, it takes them a certain amount of time (usually about a second) to observe what is going on around them and to press the gas pedal or the brake, as appropriate. The standard "follow-the-leader" theory supposes that

$$\ddot{u}_n(t + T) = \lambda(\dot{u}_{n-1}(t) - \dot{u}_n(t)), \qquad (*)$$

where t is time; T is the reaction time; u_n is the position of the nth car; and the "sensitivity coefficient" λ may depend on $u_{n-1}(t) - u_n(t)$, the spacing between cars, and/or $\dot{u}_n(t)$, the speed of the nth car. The idea behind this equation is this. Drivers will tend to decelerate if they are going faster than the car in front of them, or if they are close to the car in front of them, and will tend to accelerate if they are going slower than the car in front of them. In addition, drivers (especially in light traffic) may tend to speed up or slow down depending on whether they are going slower or faster (respectively) than a "reasonable" speed for the road (often, but not always, equal to the posted speed limit). Since our road is circular, in this equation u_0 is interpreted as u_N, where N is the total number of cars.

The simplest version of the model is the one where the "sensitivity coefficient" λ is a (positive) constant. Then we have a homogeneous linear differential-difference equation with constant coefficients for the velocities $\dot{u}_n(t)$. Obviously there is a "steady state" solution when all the velocities are equal and constant (i.e., traffic is flowing at a uniform speed), but what we are interested in is the stability of the flow, or the question of what effect is produced by small differences in the velocities of the cars. The solution of (*) will be a superposition of exponential solutions of the form $\dot{u}_n(t) = \exp(\alpha t)v_n$, where the v_ns and α are (complex) constants, and the system will be unstable if the velocities are unbounded; that is, there are any solutions where the real part of α is positive. Using vector notation, we have

$$\dot{u}(t) = \exp(\alpha\, t)v, \quad \ddot{u}(t + T) = \alpha \exp(\alpha\, T)\exp(\alpha\, t)v.$$

Substituting back in (*), we get the equation

$$\alpha \exp(\alpha\, T)\exp(\alpha\, t)v = \lambda(S - I)\exp(\alpha\, t)v,$$

where

$$S = \begin{pmatrix} 0 & \cdot & \cdot & \cdot & 0 & 1 \\ 1 & 0 & \cdot & \cdot & \cdot & 0 \\ 0 & 1 & \cdot & \cdot & \cdot & \cdot \\ \cdot & \cdot & \cdot & \cdot & \cdot & \cdot \\ \cdot & \cdot & \cdot & 1 & 0 & \cdot \\ \cdot & \cdot & \cdot & 0 & 1 & 0 \end{pmatrix}$$

is the "shift" matrix that, when it multiplies a vector on the left, cyclically permutes the entries of the vector. We can cancel the $\exp(\alpha\, t)$ on each side to get

$$\alpha \exp(\alpha\, T)v = \lambda(S - I)v, \text{ or } \{S - [1 + (\alpha/\lambda)\exp(\alpha\, T)]I\}v = 0, \quad (**)$$

which says that v is an eigenvector for S with eigenvalue $1 + (\alpha/\lambda)e^{\alpha T}$. Since the eigenvalues of S are the Nth roots of unity, which are evenly spaced around the unit circle in the complex plane, and closely spaced together for large N, there is potential instability whenever $1 + (\alpha/\lambda)e^{\alpha T}$ has absolute value 1 for some α with positive real part: that is, whenever $(\alpha T/\lambda T)e^{\alpha T}$ can be of the form $e^{i\theta} - 1$ for some αT with positive real part. Whether instability occurs or not depends on the value of the product λT. We can see this by plotting values of $z \exp(z)$ for $z = \alpha T = iy$ a complex number on the critical line Re $z = 0$, and comparing with plots of $\lambda T(e^{i\theta} - 1)$ for various values of the parameter λT.

```
syms y; expand(i*y*(cos(y) + i*sin(y)))

ans =
i*y*cos(y)-y*sin(y)

ezplot(-y*sin(y), y*cos(y), [-2*pi, 2*pi]); hold on
theta = 0:0.05*pi:2*pi;
plot((1/2)*(cos(theta) - 1), (1/2)*sin(theta), '-');
plot(cos(theta) - 1, sin(theta), ':')
plot(2*(cos(theta) - 1), 2*sin(theta), '--');
title('iye^{iy} and circles \lambda T(e^{i\theta}-1)');
hold off
```

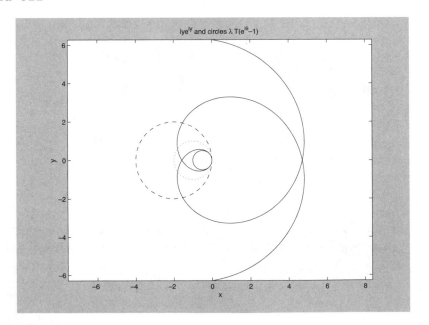

Here the small solid circle corresponds to $\lambda T = 1/2$, and we are just at the limit of stability, since this circle does not cross the spiral produced by $z \exp(z)$ for z a complex number on the critical line Re $z = 0$, though it "hugs" the spiral closely. The dotted and dashed circles, corresponding to $\lambda T = 1$ or 2, do cross the spiral, so they correspond to unstable traffic flow.

We can check these theoretical predictions with a simulation using SIMULINK. We'll give a picture of the SIMULINK model and then explain it.

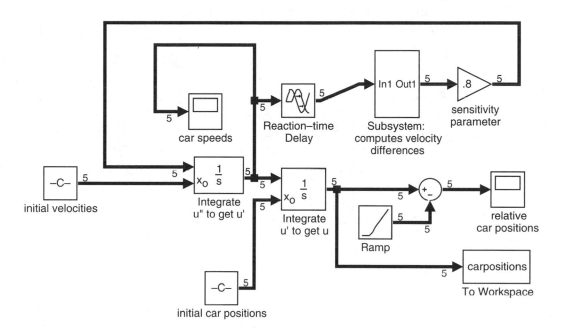

Here the subsystem, which corresponds to multiplication by $S - I$, looks like this:

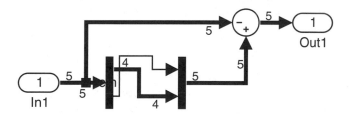

Here are some words of explanation. First, we are showing the model using the options **Wide nonscalar lines** and **Signal dimensions** in the **Format**

menu of the SIMULINK model, to distinguish quantities that are vectors from those that are scalars. The dimension 5 on most of the lines is the value of N, the number of cars. Most of the model is like the example in Chapter 8, except that our unknown function (called u), representing the car positions, is vector-valued and not scalar-valued. The major exceptions are these:

1. We need to incorporate the reaction-time delay, so we've inserted a Transport Delay block from the **Continuous** block library.
2. The parameter λ shows up as the value of the gain in the sensitivity parameter Gain block in the upper right.
3. Plotting car positions by themselves is not terribly useful, since only the relative positions matter. So before outputting the car positions to the Scope block labeled "relative car positions," we've subtracted off a constant linear function (corresponding to uniform motion at the average car speed) created by the Ramp block from the **Sources** block library.
4. We've made use of the option in the Integrator blocks to input the initial conditions, instead of having them built into the block. This makes the logical structure a little clearer.
5. We've used the *subsystem* feature of SIMULINK. If you enclose a bunch of blocks with the mouse and then click on "Create subsystem" in the model's **Edit** menu, SIMULINK will package them as a subsystem. This is helpful if your model is large or if there is some combination of blocks that you expect to use more than once. Our subsystem sends a vector v to $(S - I)v = Sv - v$. A Sum block (with one of the signs changed to a $-$) is used for vector subtraction. To model the action of S, we've used the Demux and Mux blocks from the **Signals and Systems** block library. The Demux block, with "number of outputs" parameter set to [4, 1], splits a five-dimensional vector into a pair consisting of a four-dimensional vector and a scalar (corresponding to the last car). Then we reverse the order and put them back together with the Mux block, with "number of inputs" parameter set to [1, 4].

Once the model is assembled, it can be run with various inputs. The following pictures show the two scope windows with a set of conditions corresponding to stable flow (though, to be honest, we've let two cars cross through each other briefly!):

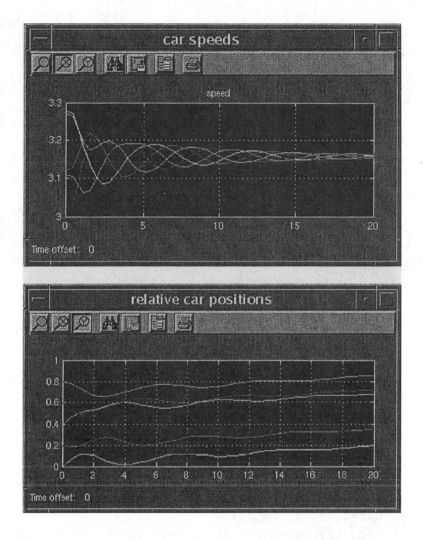

As you can see, the speeds fluctuate but eventually converge to a single value, and the separations between cars eventually stabilize.

In contrast, if λ is increased by changing the "sensitivity parameter" in the Gain block in the upper right, say from 0.8 to 2.0, one gets this sort of output, typical of instability:

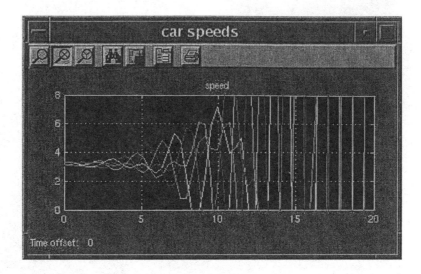

We encourage you to go back and tinker with the model (for instance using a sensitivity parameter that is also inversely proportional to the spacing between cars) and study the results. We should mention that the To Workspace block in the lower right has been put in to make it possible to create a movie of the moving cars. This block sends the car positions to a variable called **carpositions**. This variable is what is called a *structure array*. To make use of it, you can create a movie with the following script M-file:

```
theta = 0:0.025*pi:2*pi;
for j = 1:length(tout)
plot(cos(carpositions.signals.values(j, :)*2*pi), ...
sin(carpositions.signals.values(j, :)*2*pi), 'o');
axis([-1, 1, -1, 1]);
hold on; plot(cos(theta), sin(theta), 'r'); hold off;
axis equal;
M(j) = getframe;
end
```

The idea here is that we have taken the circular road to have radius 1 (in suitable units), so that the command **plot(cos(theta),sin(theta),'r')** draws a red circle (representing the road) in each frame of the movie, and on top of that the cars are shown with moving little circles. The vector **tout** is a list of all the values of t at which the model computes the values of the vector

$u(t)$, and at the jth time, the car positions are stored in the jth row of the matrix **carpositions.signals.values**. Try the program!

We should mention here one fine point needed to create a realistic movie. Namely, we need the values of **tout** to be equally spaced — otherwise the cars will appear to be moving faster when the time steps are large and will appear to be moving slower when the time steps are small. In its *default* mode of operation, SIMULINK uses a variable-step differential equation solver based on MATLAB's command **ode45**, and so the entries of **tout** will *not* be equally spaced. To fix this, open the **Simulation Parameters...** dialog box using the **Edit** menu in the model window, choose the **Solver** tab, and change the **Output options** box to read: Produce specified output only, chosen to be something such as [0:0.5:20]. Then the model will output the car positions only at multiples of $t = 0.5$, and the MATLAB program above will produce a 41-frame movie.

Practice Set C

Developing Your MATLAB Skills

Remarks. Problem 7 is a bit more advanced than the others. Problem 11a requires the Symbolic Math Toolbox; the others do not. SIMULINK is needed for Problems 12 and 13.

1. Captain Picard is hiding in a square arena, 50 meters on a side, which is protected by a level-5 force field. Unfortunately, the Cardassians, who are firing on the arena, have a death ray that can penetrate the force field. The point of impact of the death ray is exposed to 10,000 *illumatons* of lethal radiation. It requires only 50 illumatons to dispatch the Captain; anything less has no effect. The amount of illumatons that arrive at point (x, y) when the death ray strikes one meter above ground at point (x_0, y_0) is governed by an inverse square law, namely

$$\frac{10,000}{4\pi((x - x_0)^2 + (y - y_0)^2 + 1)}.$$

   The Cardassian sensors cannot locate Picard's exact position, so they fire at a random point in the arena.

   (a) Use **contour** to display the arena after five random bursts of the death ray. The half-life of the radiation is very short, so one can assume it disappears almost immediately; only its initial burst has any effect. Nevertheless include all five bursts in your picture, like a time-lapse photo. Where in the arena do you think Captain Picard should hide?

   (b) Suppose Picard stands in the center of the arena. Moreover, suppose the Cardassians fire the death ray 100 times, each shot landing at a random point in the arena. Is Picard killed?

   (c) Rerun the "experiment" in part (b) 100 times, and approximate the probability that Captain Picard can survive an attack of 100 shots.

(d) Redo part (c) but place the Captain halfway to one side (that is, at $x = 37.5$, $y = 25$ if the coordinates of the arena are $0 \le x \le 50$, $0 \le y \le 50$).

(e) Redo the simulation with the Captain completely to one side, and finally in a corner. What self-evident fact is reinforced for you?

2. Consider an account that has M dollars in it and pays monthly interest J. Suppose beginning at a certain point an amount S is deposited monthly and no withdrawals are made.

(a) Assume first that $S = 0$. Using the *Mortgage Payments* application in Chapter 9 as a model, derive an equation relating J, M, the number n of months elapsed, and the total T in the account after n months. Assume that the interest is credited on the last day of the month and that the total T is computed on the last day after the interest is credited.

(b) Now assume that $M = 0$, that S is deposited on the first day of the month, that as before interest is credited on the last day of the month, and that the total T is computed on the last day after the interest is credited. Once again, using the mortgage application as a model, derive an equation relating J, S, the number n of months elapsed, and the total T in the account after n months.

(c) By combining the last two models derive an equation relating all of M, S, J, n, and T, now of course assuming there is an initial amount in the account (M) as well as a monthly deposit (S).

(d) If the annual interest rate is 5%, and no monthly deposits are made, how many years does it take to double your initial stash of money? What if the annual interest rate is 10%?

(e) In this and the next part, there is no initial stash. Assume an annual interest rate of 8%. How much do you have to deposit monthly to be a millionaire in 35 years (a career)?

(f) If the interest rate remains as in (e) and you can only afford to deposit $300 each month, how long do you have to work to retire a millionaire?

(g) You hit the lottery and win $100,000. You have two choices: Take the money, pay the taxes, and invest what's left; or receive $100,000/240 monthly for 20 years, depositing what's left after taxes. Assume a $100,000 windfall costs you $35,000 in federal and state taxes, but that the smaller monthly payoff only causes a 20% tax liability. In which way are you better off 20 years later? Assume a 5% annual interest rate here.

(h) Banks pay roughly 5%, the stock market returns 8% on average over a 10-year period. So parts (e) and (f) relate more to investing than to saving. But suppose the market in a 5-year period returns 13%, 15%, -3%, 5%, and 10% in five successive years, and then repeats the cycle. (Note that the [arithmetic] average is 8%, though a geometric mean would be more relevant here.) Assume $50,000 is invested at the start of a 5-year market period. How much does it grow to in 5 years? Now recompute four more times, assuming you enter the cycle at the beginning of the second year, the third year, etc. Which choice yields the best/worst results? Can you explain why? Compare the results with a bank account paying 8%. Assume simple annual interest. Redo the five investment computations, assuming $10,000 is invested at the start of each year. Again analyze the results.

3. In the late 1990s, Tony Gwynn had a lifetime batting average of .339. This means that for every 1000 at bats he had 339 hits. (For this exercise, we shall ignore walks, hit batsmen, sacrifices, and other plate appearances that do not result in an official at bat.) In an average year he amassed 500 official at bats.

 (a) Design a Monte Carlo simulation of a year in Tony's career. Run it. What is his batting average?
 (b) Now simulate a 20-year career. Assume 500 official at bats every year. What is his best batting average in his career? What is his worst? What is his lifetime average?
 (c) Now run the 20-year career simulation four more times. Answer the questions in part (b) for each of the four simulations.
 (d) Compute the average of the five lifetime averages you computed in parts (b) and (c). What do you think would happen if you ran the 20-year simulation 100 times and took the average of the lifetime averages for all 100 simulations?

The next four problems illustrate some basic MATLAB programming skills.

4. For a positive integer n, let $A(n)$ be the $n \times n$ matrix with entries $a_{ij} = 1/(i + j - 1)$. For example,

$$A(3) = \begin{pmatrix} 1 & \frac{1}{2} & \frac{1}{3} \\ \frac{1}{2} & \frac{1}{3} & \frac{1}{4} \\ \frac{1}{3} & \frac{1}{4} & \frac{1}{5} \end{pmatrix}.$$

The eigenvalues of $A(n)$ are all real numbers. Write a script M-file that prints the largest eigenvalue of $A(500)$, without any extraneous output. (*Hint*: The M-file may take a while to run if you use a loop within a loop to define A. Try to avoid this!)

5. Write a script M-file that draws a bulls-eye pattern with a central circle colored red, surrounded by alternating circular strips (annuli) of white and black, say ten of each. Make sure the final display shows circles, not ellipses. (*Hint*: One way to color the region between two circles black is to color the entire inside of the outer circle black and then color the inside of the inner circle white.)

6. MATLAB has a function `lcm` that finds the least common multiple of two numbers. Write a function M-file `mylcm.m` that finds the least common multiple of an arbitrary number of positive integers, which may be given as separate arguments or in a vector. For example, `mylcm(4, 5, 6)` and `mylcm([4 5 6])` should both produce the answer 60. The program should produce a helpful error message if any of the inputs are not positive integers. (*Hint*: For three numbers you could use `lcm` to find the least common multiple m of the first two numbers and then use `lcm` again to find the least common multiple of m and the third number. Your M-file can generalize this approach.)

7. ⋆ Write a function M-file that takes as input a string containing the name of a text file and produces a histogram of the number of occurrences of each letter from A to Z in the file. Try to label the figure and axes as usefully as you can.

8. Consider the following linear programming problem. Jane Doe is running for County Commissioner. She wants to personally canvass voters in the four main cities in the county: Gotham, Metropolis, Oz, and River City. She needs to figure out how many residences (private homes, apartments, etc.) to visit in each city. The constraints are as follows:

   (i) She intends to leave a campaign pamphlet at each residence; she only has 50,000 available.

   (ii) The travel costs she incurs for each residence are: $0.50 in each of Gotham and Metropolis, $1 in Oz, and $2 in River City; she has $40,000 available.

   (iii) The number of minutes (on average) that her visits to each residence require are: 2 minutes in Gotham, 3 minutes in Metropolis, 1 minute in Oz, and 4 minutes in River City; she has 300 hours available.

   (iv) Because of political profiles Jane knows that she should not visit any more residences in Gotham than she does in Metropolis and that however many residences she visits in Metropolis and Oz, the total of the two should not exceed the number she visits in River City;

   (v) Jane expects to receive, during her visits, on average, campaign contributions of: one dollar from each residence in Gotham, a quarter from those in Metropolis, a half-dollar from the Oz residents, and three bucks from the folks in River City. She must raise at least $10,000 from her entire canvass.

Jane's goal is to maximize the number of supporters (those likely to vote for her). She estimates that for each residence she visits in Gotham the odds are 0.6 that she picks up a supporter, and the corresponding probabilities in Metropolis, Oz, and River City are, respectively, 0.6, 0.5, and 0.3.

(a) How many residences should she visit in each of the four cities?

(b) Suppose she can double the time she can allot to visits. Now what is the profile for visits?

(c) But suppose that the extra time (in part (b)) also mandates that she double the contributions she receives. What is the profile now?

9. Consider the following linear programming problem. The famous football coach Nerv Turnip is trying to decide how many hours to spend with each component of his offensive unit during the coming week — that is, the quarterback, the running backs, the receivers, and the linemen. The constraints are as follows:

(i) The number of hours available to Nerv during the week is 50.

(ii) Nerv figures he needs 20 points to win the next game. He estimates that for each hour he spends with the quarterback, he can expect a point return of 0.5. The corresponding numbers for the running backs, receivers, and linemen are 0.3, 0.4, and 0.1, respectively.

(iii) In spite of their enormous size, the players have a relatively thin skin. Each hour with the quarterback is likely to require Nerv to criticize him once. The corresponding number of criticisms per hour for the other three groups are 2 for running backs, 3 for receivers, and 0.5 for linemen. Nerv figures he can only bleat out 75 criticisms in a week before he loses control.

(iv) Finally, the players are *prima donnas* who engage in rivalries. Because of that, he must spend the exact same number of hours with the running backs as he does with the receivers, at least as many hours with the quarterback as he does with the runners and receivers combined, and at least as many hours with the receivers as with the linemen.

Nerv figures he's going to be fired at the end of the season regardless of the outcome of the game, so his goal is to maximize his pleasure during the week. (The team's owner should only know.) He estimates that, on a sliding scale from 0 to 1, he gets 0.2 units of personal satisfaction for each

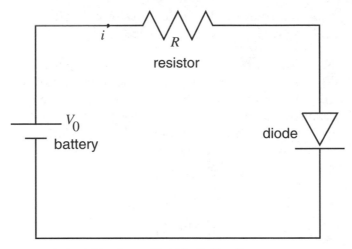

Figure C-1: A Nonlinear Electrical Circuit

hour with the quarterback. The corresponding numbers for the runners, receivers and linemen are 0.4, 0.3, and 0.6, respectively.
(a) How many hours should Nerv spend with each group?
(b) Suppose he only needs 15 points to win; then how many?
(c) Finally suppose, despite needing only 15 points, that the troops are getting restless and he can only dish out 70 criticisms this week. Is Nerv getting the most out of his week?

10. This problem, suggested to us by our colleague Tom Antonsen, concerns an electrical circuit, one of whose components does not behave linearly. Consider the circuit in Figure C-1.

Unlike the resistor, the diode is a nonlinear element — it does not obey Ohm's Law. In fact its behavior is specified by the formula

$$i - I_0 \exp(V_D/V_T), \tag{1}$$

where i is the current in the diode (which is the same as in the resistor by Kirchhoff's Current Law), V_D is the voltage across the diode, I_0 is the leakage current of the diode, and $V_T = kT/e$, where k is Boltzmann's constant, T is the temperature of the diode, and e is the electrical charge.

By Ohm's Law applied to the resistor, we also know that $V_R = iR$, where V_R is the voltage across the resistor and R is its resistance. But by Kirchhoff's Voltage Law, we also have $V_R = V_0 - V_D$. This gives a second equation relating the diode current and voltage, namely

$$i = (V_0 - V_D)/R. \tag{2}$$

Note now that (2) says that i is a decreasing linear function of V_D with value V_0/R when V_D is zero. At the same time (1) says that i is an exponentially growing function of V_D starting out at I_0. Since typically, $RI_0 < V_0$, the two resulting curves (for i as a function of V_D) must cross once. Eliminating i from the two equations, we see that the voltage in the diode must satisfy the transcendental equation

$$(V_0 - V_D)/R = I_0 \exp(V_D/V_T),$$

or

$$V_D = V_0 - RI_0 \exp(V_D/V_T).$$

(a) Reasonable values for the electrical constants are: $V_0 = 1.5$ volts, $R = 1000$ ohms, $I_0 = 10^{-5}$ amperes, and $V_T = .0025$ volts. Use **fzero** to find the voltage V_D and current i in the circuit.

(b) In the remainder of the problem, we assume the voltage in the battery V_0 and the resistance of the resistor R are unchanged. But suppose we have some freedom to alter the electrical characteristics of the diode. For example, suppose that I_0 is halved. What happens to the voltage?

(c) Suppose instead of halving I_0, we halve V_T. Then what is the effect on V_D?

(d) Suppose both I_0 and V_T are cut in half. What then?

(e) Finally, we want to examine the behavior of the voltage if both I_0 and V_T are decreased toward zero. For definitiveness, assume that we set $I_0 = 10^{-5}u$ and $V_T = .0025u$, and let $u \to 0$. Specifically, compute the solution for $u = 10^{-j}$, $j = 0, \ldots, 5$. Then, display a **loglog** plot of the solution values, for the voltage as a function of I_0. What do you conclude?

11. This problem is based on both the *Population Dynamics* and *360° Pendulum* applications from Chapter 9. The growth of a species was modeled in the former by a *difference equation*. In this problem we will model population growth by a *differential equation*, akin to the second application mentioned above. In fact we can give a differential equation model for the logistic growth of a population x as a function of time t by the equation

$$\dot{x} = x(1 - x) = x - x^2, \tag{3}$$

where $\dot{x}$ denotes the derivative of x with respect to t. We think of x as a fraction of some maximal possible population. One advantage of this continuous model over the discrete model in Chapter 9 is that we can get a "reading" of the population at any point in time (not just on integer intervals).

(a) The differential equation (3) is solved in any beginning course in ordinary differential equations, but you can do it easily with the MATLAB command **dsolve**. (Look up the syntax via online help.)

(b) Now find the solution assuming an initial value $x_0 = x(0)$ of x. Use the values $x_0 = 0, 0.25, \ldots, 2.0$. Graph the solutions and use your picture to justify the statement: "Regardless of $x_0 > 0$, the solution of (3) tends to the constant solution $x(t) \equiv 1$ in the long term."
The logistic model presumes two underlying features of population growth: (i) that ideally the population expands at a rate proportional to its current total (that is, exponential growth — this corresponds to the x term on the right side of (3)) and (ii) because of interactions between members of the species and natural limits to growth, unfettered exponential growth is held in check by the logistic term, given by the $-x^2$ expression in (3). Now assume there are two species $x(t)$ and $y(t)$, competing for the same resources to survive. Then there will be another negative term in the differential equation that reflects the interaction between the species. The usual model presumes it to be proportional to the product of the two populations, and the larger the constant of proportionality, the more severe the interaction, as well as the resulting check on population growth.

(c) Here is a typical pair of differential equations that model the growth in population of two competing species $x(t)$ and $y(t)$:

$$\begin{aligned} \dot{x}(t) &= x - x^2 - 0.5xy \\ \dot{y}(t) &= y - y^2 - 0.5xy. \end{aligned} \qquad (4)$$

The command **dsolve** can solve many pairs of ordinary differential equations — especially linear ones. But the mixture of quadratic terms in (4) makes it unsolvable symbolically, and so we need to use a numerical ODE solver as we did in the pendulum application. Using the commands in that application as a template, graph numerical solution curves to the system (4) for initial data

$$x(0) = 0 : 1/12 : 13/12$$
$$y(0) = 0 : 1/12 : 13/12.$$

(*Hint*: Use **axis** to limit your view to the square $0 \leq x, y \leq 13/12$.)

(d) The picture you drew is called a *phase portrait* of the system. Interpret it. Explain the long-term behavior of any population distribution that starts with only one species present. Relate it to part (b). What happens in the long term if both populations are present initially? Is there an initial population distribution that remains undisturbed? What is it? Relate those numbers to the model (4).

(e) Now replace 0.5 in the model by 2; that is, consider the new model

$$\dot{x}(t) = x - x^2 - 2xy$$
$$\dot{y}(t) = y - y^2 - 2xy. \tag{5}$$

Draw the phase portrait. (Use the same initial data and viewing square.) Answer the same questions as in part (d). Do you see a special solution trajectory that emanates from near the origin and proceeds to the special fixed point? And another trajectory from the upper right to the fixed point? What happens to all population distributions that do not start on these trajectories?

(f) Explain why model (4) is called "peaceful coexistence" and model (5) is called "doomsday." Now explain heuristically why the coefficient change from 0.5 to 2 converts coexistence into doomsday.

12. Build a SIMULINK model corresponding to the pendulum equation

$$\ddot{x}(t) = -0.5\dot{x}(t) - 9.81\sin(x(t)) \tag{6}$$

from *The 360° Pendulum* in Chapter 9. You will need the Trigonometric Function block from the Math library. Use your model to redraw some of the phase portraits.

13. As you know, Galileo and Newton discovered that all bodies near the earth's surface fall with the same acceleration g due to gravity, approximately 32.2 ft/sec^2. However, real bodies are also subjected to forces due to air resistance. If we take both gravity and air resistance into account, a moving ball can be modeled by the differential equation

$$\ddot{\mathbf{x}} = [0, -g] - c \, \|\dot{\mathbf{x}}\| \, \dot{\mathbf{x}}. \tag{7}$$

Here $\mathbf{x}$, a function of the time t, is the vector giving the position of the ball (the first coordinate is measured horizontally, the second one vertically), $\dot{\mathbf{x}}$ is the velocity vector of the ball, $\ddot{\mathbf{x}}$ is the acceleration of the ball, $\|\dot{\mathbf{x}}\|$

is the magnitude of the velocity, that is, the speed, and c is a constant depending on the shape and mass of the ball and the density of the air. (We are neglecting the lift force that comes from the ball's rotation, which can also play a major role in some situations, for instance in analyzing the path of a curve ball, as well as forces due to wind currents.) For a baseball, the constant c turns out to be approximately 0.0017, assuming distances are measured in feet and time is measured in seconds. (See, for example, Chapter 18, "Balls and Strikes and Home Runs," in *Towing Icebergs, Falling Dominoes, and Other Adventures in Applied Mathematics*, by Robert Banks, Princeton University Press, 1998.) Build a SIMULINK model corresponding to Equation (7), and use it to study the trajectory of a batted baseball. Here are a few hints. Represent $\ddot{\mathbf{x}}$, $\dot{\mathbf{x}}$, and $\mathbf{x}$ as vector signals, joined by two Integrator blocks. The quantity $\ddot{\mathbf{x}}$, according to (7), should be computed from a Sum block with two vector inputs. One should be a Constant block with the vector value $[0, -32.2]$, representing gravity, and the other should represent the drag term on the right of Equation (7), computed from the value of $\dot{\mathbf{x}}$. You should be able to change one of the parameters to study what happens both with and without air resistance (the cases of $c = 0.0017$ and $c = 0$, respectively). Attach the output to an XY Graph block, with the parameters x-min = 0, y-min = 0, x-max = 500, y-max = 150, so that you can see the path of the ball out to a distance of 500 feet from home plate and up to a height of 150 feet.

(a) Let $\mathbf{x}(0) = [0, 4]$, $\dot{\mathbf{x}}(0) = [80, 80]$. (This corresponds to the ball starting at $t = 0$ from home plate, 4 feet off the ground, with the horizontal and vertical components of its velocity both equal to 80 ft/sec. This corresponds to a speed off the bat of about 77 mph, which is not unrealistic.) How far (approximately — you can read this off your XY Graph output) will the ball travel before it hits the ground, both with and without air resistance? About how long will it take the ball to hit the ground, and how fast will the ball be traveling at that time (again, both with and without air resistance)? (The last parts of the question are relevant for outfielders.)

(b) Suppose a game is played in Denver, Colorado, where because of thinning of the atmosphere due to the high altitude, c is only 0.0014. How far will the ball travel now (given the same initial velocity as in (a))?

(c) (This is not a MATLAB problem.) Estimate from a comparison of your answers to (a) and (b) what effect altitude might have on the team batting average of the Colorado Rockies.

Chapter 10

MATLAB and the Internet

In this chapter, we discuss a number of interrelated subjects: how to use the Internet to get additional help with MATLAB and to find MATLAB programs for certain specific applications, how to disseminate MATLAB programs over the Internet, and how to use MATLAB to prepare documents for posting on the World Wide Web.

MATLAB Help on the Internet

For answers to a variety of questions about MATLAB, it pays to visit the web site for The MathWorks,

```
http://www.mathworks.com
```

(In MATLAB 6, the **Web** menu on the Desktop menu bar can take you there automatically.) Since files on this site are moved around periodically, we won't tell you precisely what is located where, but we will point out a few things to look for. First, you can find complete documentation sets for MATLAB and all the toolboxes. This is particularly useful if you didn't install all the documentation locally in order to save space. Second, there are lists of frequently asked questions about MATLAB, bug reports and bug fixes, etc. Third, there is an index of MATLAB-based books (including this one), with descriptions and ordering information. And finally, there are libraries of M-files, developed both by The MathWorks and by various MATLAB users, which you can download for free. These are especially useful if you need to do a standard sort of calculation for which there are established algorithms but for which MATLAB has no built-in M-file; in all probability, someone has written an M-file for it and made it available. You can also find M-files and MATLAB help elsewhere on the Internet; a search on "MATLAB" will turn up dozens of MATLAB tutorials and help pages at all levels, many based at various universities. One of these is the web site associated with this book,

```
http://www.math.umd.edu/schol/matlab
```

where you can find nearly all of the MATLAB code used in this book.

Posting MATLAB Programs and Output

To post your own MATLAB programs or output on the Web, you have a number of options, each with different advantages and disadvantages.

M-Files, M-Books, Reports, and HTML Files

First, since M-files (either script M-files or function M-files) are simply plain text files, you can post them, as is, on a web site, for interested parties to download. This is the simplest option, and if you've written a MATLAB program that you'd like to share with the world, this is the way to do it. It's more likely, however, that you want to incorporate MATLAB graphics into a web page. If this is the case, there are basically three options:

1. You can prepare your document as an M-book in Microsoft Word. After debugging and executing your M-book, you have two options. You can simply post the M-book on your web site, allowing viewers with a Word installation to read it, and allowing viewers with both a Word and a MATLAB installation to execute it. Or you can click on **File : Save As...**, and when the dialog box appears, under "Save as type", select "Web Page (∗.htm, ∗.html)". This will store your entire document in HTML (HyperText Markup Language) format for posting on the web, and will automatically convert all of the graphics to the correct format. Once your web document is created, you can modify it with any HTML editor (including Word itself).

2. If you've installed the MATLAB Report Generator, it can take your MATLAB programs and convert them into an HTML report with embedded graphics.

3. Finally, you can create your web document with your favorite HTML editor and add links to your MATLAB graphics. For this to work, you need to save your graphics in a convenient format. The simplest way to do this is to select **File : Export...** in your figure window. Under "Save as type" in the dialog box that appears, you can for instance select "JPEG images (∗.jpg)", and the resulting JPEG file can be incorporated into the document with a

tag such as `<img src=sphere.jpg>`. If you are not happy with the size of the resulting image, you can modify it with any image editor. (Almost any PC these days comes with one; in UNIX you can use ImageMagick©, xv©, or many other programs.) If you are planning to modify the image before posting it, it may be preferable to have MATLAB store the figure in TIFF format instead; that way no resolution is lost before you begin the editing process.

✓ If you are an advanced MATLAB user and you want to use MATLAB as an engine to power an *interactive* web site, then you might want to purchase the MATLAB Web Server, which is designed exactly for this purpose. You can see samples of what it can do at

http://www.mathworks.com/products/demos/webserver/

Configuring Your Web Browser

In this section, we explain how to configure the most popular Web browsers to display M-files in the M-file editor or to launch M-books automatically.

Microsoft Internet Explorer

If MATLAB and Word are installed on your Windows computer then Internet Explorer® should automatically know how to open M-books. With M-files, it may give you a choice of downloading the file or "opening" it; if you choose the latter, it will appear in the M-file editor, a slightly stripped-down version of the Editor/Debugger.

Netscape Navigator

The situation with Netscape Navigator® is slightly more complicated. If you click on an M-file (with the .m extension), it will probably appear as a plain text file. You can save the file and then open it if you wish with the M-file editor. On a PC (but not in UNIX) you can open the M-file editor without launching MATLAB; look for it in the MATLAB group under **Start : Programs**, or else look for the executable file meditor.exe (in MATLAB 5.3 and earlier, Medit.exe). If you click on an M-book (with the .doc extension), your browser will probably offer you a choice of opening it or saving it, unless you have preconfigured Netscape to open it without prompting. (This depends also on your security settings.) What program Netscape uses to open

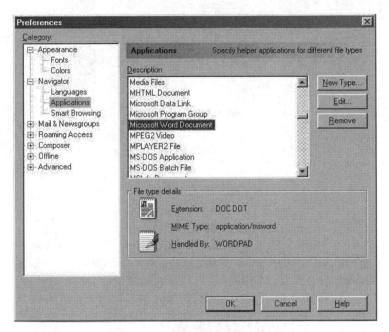

Figure 10-1: The Netscape Preferences Panel.

a file is controlled by your Preferences. To make changes, select **Edit** : **Preferences** in the Netscape menu bar, find the **Navigator** section, and look for the "Applications" subsection. You will see a panel that looks something like Figure 10-1. (Its exact appearance depends on what version of Netscape you are using and your operating system.) Look for the "Microsoft Word Document" file type (with file extension .doc) and, if necessary, change the program used to open such files. Typical choices would be Word or Wordpad® in Windows and StarOffice® or PC File Viewer® in UNIX. Choices other than Word will only allow you to view, not to execute, M-books.

Chapter 11

Troubleshooting

In this chapter, we offer advice for dealing with some common problems that you may encounter. We also list and describe the most common mistakes that MATLAB users make. Finally, we offer some simple but useful techniques for debugging your M-files.

Common Problems

Problems manifest themselves in various ways: Totally unexpected or plainly wrong output appears; MATLAB produces an error message (or at least a warning); MATLAB refuses to process an input line; something that worked earlier stops working; or, worst of all, the computer freezes. Fortunately, these problems are often caused by several easily identifiable and correctable mistakes. What follows is a description of some common problems, together with a presentation of likely causes, suggested solutions, and illustrative examples. We also refer to places in the book where related issues are discussed.

Here is a list of the problems:

- wrong or unexpected output,
- syntax error,
- spelling error,
- error messages when plotting,
- a previously saved M-file evaluates differently, and
- computer won't respond.

Wrong or Unexpected Output

There are many possible causes for this problem, but they are likely to be among the following:

CAUSE: Forgetting to clear or reset variables.

SOLUTION: **Clear or initialize variables before using them, especially in a long session.**

☞ *See* Variables and Assignments *in Chapter 2.*

CAUSE: Conflicting definitions.

SOLUTION: **Do not use the same name for two different functions or variables, and in particular, try not to overwrite the names of any of MATLAB's built-in functions.**

You can accidentally mask one of MATLAB's built-in M-files either with your own M-file of the same name or with a variable (including, perhaps, an inline function). When unexpected output occurs and you think this might be the cause, it helps to use **which** to find out what M-file is actually being referenced.

Here is perhaps an extreme example.

EXAMPLE:

```
>> plot = gcf;
>> x = -2:0.1:2;
>> plot(x, x.^2)
Warning: Subscript indices must be integer values.
??? Index into matrix is negative or zero. See release
notes on changes to logical indices.
```

What's wrong, of course, is that **plot** has been masked by a variable with the same name. You could detect this with

```
>> which plot
plot is a variable.
```

If you type **clear plot** and execute the **plot** command again, the problem will go away and you'll get a picture of the desired parabola. A more subtle example could occur if you did this on purpose, not thinking you would use **plot**, and then called some other graphics script M-file that uses it indirectly.

CAUSE: Not keeping track of **ans**.

SOLUTION: **Assign variable names to any output that you intend to use.**

If you decide at some point in a session that you wish to refer to prior output that was unnamed, then give the output a name, and execute the command again. (The UP-ARROW key or Command History window is useful for recalling the command to edit it.) Do not rely on **ans** as it is likely to be overwritten before you execute the command that references the prior output.

CAUSE: Improper use of built-in functions.

SOLUTION: **Always use the names of built-in functions exactly as MATLAB specifies them; always enclose inputs in parentheses, not brackets and not braces; always list the inputs in the required order.**

☞ *See* Managing Variables *and* Online Help *in Chapter 2.*

CAUSE: Inattention to precedence of arithmetic operations.

SOLUTION: **Use parentheses liberally and correctly when entering arithmetic or algebraic expressions.**

EXAMPLE:

MATLAB, like any calculator, first exponentiates, then divides and multiplies, and finally adds and subtracts, unless a different order is specified by using parentheses. So if you attempt to compute $5^{2/3} - 25/(2*3)$ by typing

```
>> 5^2/3 - 25/2*3
```

```
ans =
     -29.1667
```

the answer MATLAB produces is not what you intended because **5** is raised to the power **2** before the division by **3**, and **25** is divided by **2** before the multiplication by **3**. Here is the correct calculation:

```
>> 5^(2/3) - 25/(2*3)
```

```
ans =
     -1.2426
```

Syntax Error

CAUSE: Mismatched parentheses, quote marks, braces, or brackets.

SOLUTION: **Look carefully at the input line to find a missing or an extra delimiter.**

MATLAB usually catches this kind of mistake. In addition, the MATLAB 6 Desktop automatically highlights matching delimiters as you type and color-codes strings (expressions enclosed in single quotes) so that you can see where they begin and end. In the Command Window of MATLAB 5 and earlier versions, however, you have to hunt for matching delimiters by hand.

CAUSE: Wrong delimiters: Using parentheses in place of brackets, or vice versa, and so on.

SOLUTION: **Remember the basic rules about delimiters in MATLAB.**

Parentheses are used both for grouping arithmetic expressions and for enclosing inputs to a MATLAB command, an M-file, or an inline function. They are also used for referring to an entry in a matrix. *Square brackets* are used for defining vectors or matrices. *Single quote marks* are used for defining strings.

EXAMPLE:

The following illustrates what can happen if you don't follow these rules:

```
>> X = -1:.01:1;
>> X[1]
??? X[1]
       |
Error: Missing operator, comma, or semicolon.
>> A=(0,1,2)
???   A=(0,1,2)
            |
Error: Error: ")" expected, "," found.
```

These examples are fairly straightforward to understand; in the first case, **X(1)** was intended, and in the second case, **A=[0,1,2]** was intended. But here's a trickier example:

```
>> sin 3

ans =
     0.6702
```

Here there's no error message, but if one looks closely, one discovers that MATLAB has printed out the sine of 51 radians, not of 3 radians!! The explanation is as follows: Any time a MATLAB command is followed by a space and then an argument to the command (as in the construct **clear x**), the argument is always interpreted as a string. Thus MATLAB has interpreted **3** not as the number 3, but as the string **'3'**! And sure enough, one discovers:

```
>> char(51)

ans =
3
```

In other words, in MATLAB's encoding scheme, the string **'3'** is stored as the number **51**, which is why **sin 3** (or also **sin('3')**) produces as output the sine of 51 radians.

Braces or *curly brackets* are used less often than either parentheses or square brackets and are usually not needed by beginners. Their main use is with cell arrays. One example to keep in mind is that if you want an M-file to take a variable number of inputs or produce a variable number of outputs, then these are stored in the cell arrays **varargin** and **varargout**, and braces are used to refer to the cells of these arrays. Similarly, **case** is sometimes used with braces in the middle of a **switch** construct. If you want to construct a vector of strings, then it has to be done with braces, since brackets when applied to strings are interpreted as concatenation.

EXAMPLE:

```
>> {'a', 'b'}

ans =
    'a'      'b'
>> ['a', 'b']

ans =
ab
```

CAUSE: Improper use of arithmetic symbols.

SOLUTION: **When you encounter a syntax error, review your input line carefully for mistakes in typing.**

EXAMPLE:

If the user, intending to compute 2 times −4, inadvertently switches the symbols, the result is

```
>> 2 - * 4
???   2 - * 4
          |
Error:  Expected a variable, function, or constant,
found "*".
```

Here the vertical bar highlights the place where MATLAB believes the error is located. In this case, the actual error is earlier in the input line.

Spelling Error

CAUSE: Using uppercase instead of lowercase letters in MATLAB commands, or misspelling the command.

SOLUTION: **Fix the spelling.**

For example, the UNIX version of MATLAB does not recognize **Fzero** or **FZERO** (in spite of the convention that the **help** lines in MATLAB's M-files always refer to *capitalized* function names); the correct command is **fzero**.

EXAMPLE:

```
>> Fzero(inline('x^2 - 3'), 1)
???  Undefined function or variable 'Fzero'.
>> FZERO(inline('x^2 - 3'), 1)
???  Undefined function or variable 'FZERO'.
>> text = help('fzero'); text(1:38)

ans =
 FZERO  Scalar nonlinear zero finding.
>> fzero(inline('x^2 - 3'), 1)

ans =
    1.7321
```

Error Messages When Plotting

CAUSE: There are several possible explanations, but usually the problem is the wrong type of input for the plotting command chosen.

SOLUTION: **Carefully follow the examples in the help lines of the plotting command, and pay attention to the error messages.**

EXAMPLE:

```
>> [X,Y] = meshgrid(-1:.1:1, -1:.1:1);
>> mesh(X, Y, sqrt(1 - X.^2 - Y.^2))
???  Error using ==> surface
X, Y, Z, and C cannot be complex.
```

```
Error in ==> /usr/matlabr12/toolbox/matlab/graph3d/mesh.m
On line 68 ==> hh = surface(x,'FaceColor',fc,'EdgeColor',
'flat', 'FaceLighting', 'none', 'EdgeLighting', 'flat');
```

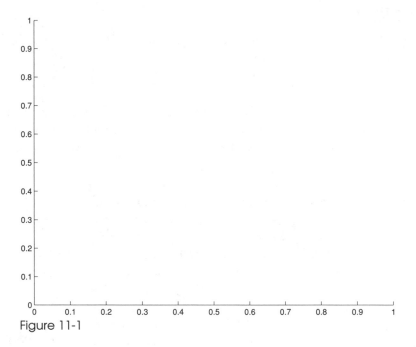

Figure 11-1

These error messages indicate that you have tried to plot the wrong kind of object, and that's why the figure window (Figure 11-1) is blank. What's wrong in this case is evident from the first error message. While you might think you can plot the hemisphere $z = \sqrt{1 - x^2 - y^2}$ this way, there are points in the domain $-1 \leq x, y \leq 1$ where $1 - x^2 - y^2$ is negative and thus the square root is imaginary. But **mesh** can't handle complex inputs; the coordinates need to be real. One can get around this by redefining the function at the points where it's not real, like this:

```
>> [X,Y] = meshgrid(-1:.1:1, -1:.1:1);
>> mesh(X, Y, sqrt(max(1 - X.^2 - Y.^2, 0)))
```

The output is shown in Figure 11-2.

A Previously Saved M-File Evaluates Differently

One of the most frustrating problems you may encounter occurs when a previously saved M-file, one that you are sure is in good shape, won't evaluate or evaluates incorrectly, when opened in a new session.

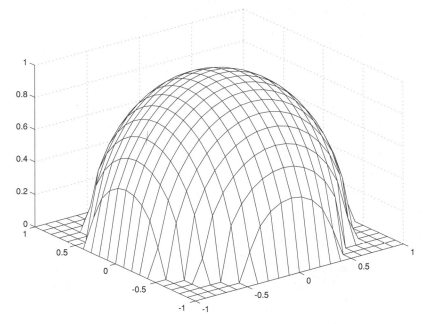

Figure 11-2

CAUSE: Change in the sequence of evaluation, or failure to clear variables.

CAUSE: Differences between the Professional and Student Versions

EXAMPLE:

Some commands that work correctly in the Professional Version of MATLAB may not work in the Student Version. Here is an example from MATLAB Release 11:

```
>> syms p t
>> ezsurf(sin(p)*cos(t), sin(p)*sin(t), cos(p), ···
[0, pi, 0, 2*pi]); axis equal
```

This correctly plots a sphere (using spherical coordinates) in the Professional Version, but in the Student Version you get strange error messages such as

```
???  The 'maple' function is restricted in the
Student Edition.
Error in ==> C:\MATLAB_SR11\toolbox\symbolic\maplemex.dll
Error in ==> C:\MATLAB_SR11\toolbox\symbolic\maple.m
On line 116 ==> [result,status] = maplemex(statement);
Error in ==> C:\MATLAB_SR11\toolbox\symbolic\@sym\ezsurf.m
(symfind)
On line 104 ==> vars = maple([ vars ' minus ' 'pi' ]);
```

```
Error in ==> C:\MATLAB_SR11\toolbox\symbolic\@sym\ezsurf.m
(makeinline)
On line 73 ==> vars = symfind(f);
Error in ==> C:\MATLAB_SR11\toolbox\symbolic\@sym\ezsurf.m
On line 60 ==> F = makeinline(f);
```

since **ezsurf** in the Student Version is not equipped to accept symbolic inputs; it requires string inputs instead. You can easily fix this by typing

```
>> ezsurf('sin(p)*cos(t)', 'sin(p)*sin(t)', 'cos(p)', ...
[0, pi, 0, 2*pi]); axis equal
```

or else by using **char** to convert symbolic expressions to strings.

Computer Won't Respond

CAUSE: MATLAB is caught in a very large calculation, or some other calamity has occurred that has caused it to fail to respond. Perhaps you are using an array that is too large for your computer memory to handle.

SOLUTION: **Abort the calculation with** CTRL+C.

If overuse of computer memory is the problem, try to redo your calculation using smaller arrays, for example, by using fewer grid points in a 3D plot, or by breaking a large vectorized calculation into smaller pieces using a loop. Clearing large arrays from your Workspace may help too.

EXAMPLE:

You'll know it when you see it!

The Most Common Mistakes

The most common mistakes are all accounted for in the causes of the problems described earlier. But to help you prevent these mistakes, we compile them here in a single list to which you can refer periodically. Doing so will help you to establish "good MATLAB habits". The most common mistakes are

- forgetting to clear values,
- improperly using built-in functions,
- not paying attention to the order of precedence of arithmetic operations,
- improperly using arithmetic symbols,
- mismatching delimiters,
- using the wrong delimiters,

- plotting the wrong kind of object, and
- using uppercase instead of lowercase letters in MATLAB commands, or misspelling commands.

Debugging Techniques

Now that we have discussed the most common mistakes, it's time to discuss how to debug your M-files, and how to locate and fix those pesky problems that don't fit into the neat categories above.

If one of your M-files is not working the way you expected, perhaps the easiest thing you can do to debug it is to insert the command **keyboard** somewhere in the middle. This temporarily suspends (but does not stop) execution and returns command to the keyboard, where you are given a special prompt with a **K** in it. You can execute whatever commands you want at this point (for instance, to examine some of the variables). To return to execution of the M-file, type **return** or **dbcont**, short for "debug continue."

A more systematic way to debug M-files is to use the MATLAB M-file debugger to insert "breakpoints" in the file. Usually you would do this with the **Breakpoints** menu or with the "Set/clear breakpoint" icon at the top of the Editor/Debugger window, but you can also do this from the command line with the command **dbstop**. Once a breakpoint is inserted in the M-file, you will see a little red dot next to the appropriate line in the Editor/Debugger. (An example is illustrated in Figure 11-8 below.) Then when you call the M-file, execution will stop at the breakpoint, and just as in the case of **keyboard**, control will return to the Command Window, where you will be given a special prompt with a **K** in it. Again, when you are ready to resume execution of the M-file, type **dbcont**. When you are done with the debugging process, **dbclear** "clears" the breakpoint from the M-file.

Let's illustrate these techniques with a real example. Suppose you want to construct a function M-file that takes as input two expressions f and g (given either as symbolic expressions or as strings) and two numbers a and b, plots the functions f and g between $x = a$ and $x = b$, and shades the region in between them. As a first try, you might start with the nine-line function M-file shadecurves.m given as follows:

```
function shadecurves(f, g, a, b)
%SHADECURVES Draws the region between two curves
% SHADECURVES(f, g, a, b) takes strings or expressions f
% and g, interprets them as functions, plots them between
% x = a and x = b, and shades the region in between.
```

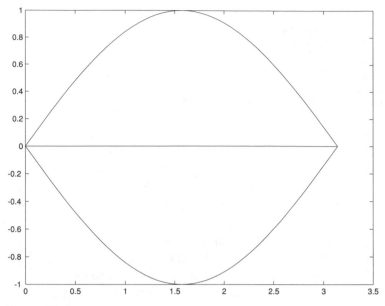

Figure 11-3

```
% Example: shadecurves('sin(x)', '-sin(x)', 0, pi)
ffun = inline(vectorize(f)); gfun = inline(vectorize(g));
xvals = a:(b - a)/50:b;
plot([xvals, xvals], [ffun(xvals), gfun(xvals)])
```

Trying this M-file out with the example specified in the help lines, that is, executing

```
>> shadecurves('sin(x)', '-sin(x)', 0, pi)
```

or

```
>> syms x; shadecurves(sin(x), -sin(x), 0, pi)
```

gives the output shown in Figure 11-3.

This is not really what we wanted; the figure we seek is shown in Figure 11-4. To begin to determine what went wrong, let's try a different example, say

```
>> shadecurves('x^2', 'sqrt(x)', 0, 1)
>> axis square
```

or

```
>> syms x; shadecurves(x^2, sqrt(x), 0, 1)
>> axis square
```

Now we get the output shown in Figure 11-5.

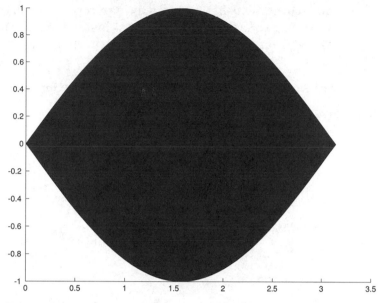

Figure 11-4

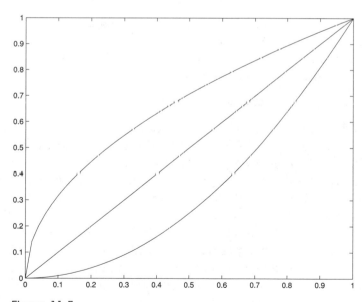

Figure 11-5

It's not too hard to figure out why our regions aren't shaded; that's because we used **plot** (which plots curves) instead of **patch** (which plots *filled* patches). So that suggests we should try changing the last line of the M-file to

```
patch([xvals, xvals], [ffun(xvals), gfun(xvals)])
```

That gives the error message

```
???  Error using ==> patch
Not enough input arguments.

Error in ==> shadecurves.m
On line 9 ==> patch([xvals, xvals], [ffun(xvals),
gfun(xvals)])
```

So we go back and try

```
>> help patch
```

to see if we can get the syntax right. The help lines indicate that **patch** requires a third argument, the color (in RGB coordinates) with which our patch is to be filled. So we change our final line to, for instance,

```
patch([xvals,xvals], [ffun(xvals),gfun(xvals)], [.2,0,.8])
```

That gives us now as output to **shadecurves(x^2, sqrt(x), 0, 1);** **axis square** the picture shown in Figure 11-6.

That's better, but still not quite right, because we can see a mysterious diagonal line down the middle. Not only that, but if we try

```
>> syms x; shadecurves(x^2, x^4, -1.5, 1.5)
```

we now get the bizarre picture shown in Figure 11-7.

There aren't a lot of lines in the M-file, and lines 7 and 8 seem OK, so the problem must be with the last line. We need to reread the online help for **patch**. It indicates that **patch** draws a filled 2D polygon defined by the vectors X and Y, which are its first two inputs. A way to see how this is working is to change the "50" in line 9 of the M-file to something much smaller, say 5, and then insert a breakpoint in the M-file before line 9. At this point, our M-file in the Editor/Debugger window now looks like Figure 11-8. Note the large dot to the left of the last line, indicating the breakpoint. When we run the M-file with the same input, we now obtain in the Command Window a **K>>** prompt. At this point, it is logical to try to list the coordinates of the points that are the vertices of our filled polygon, so we try

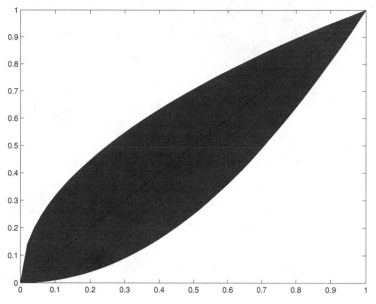

Figure 11-6

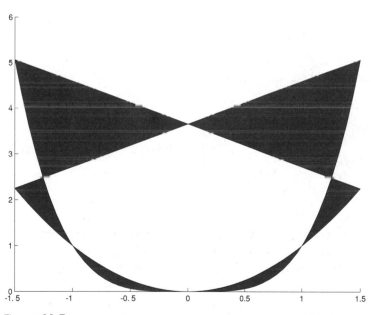

Figure 11-7

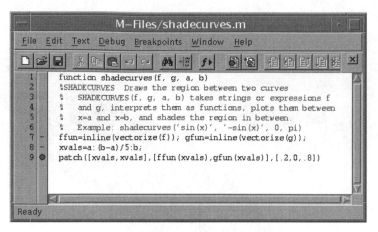

Figure 11-8: The Editor/Debugger.

```
K>> [[xvals, xvals]', [ffun(xvals), gfun(xvals)]']
```

```
ans =
    -1.5000 2.2500
    -0.9000 0.8100
    -0.3000 0.0900
     0.3000 0.0900
     0.9000 0.8100
     1.5000 2.2500
    -1.5000 5.0625
    -0.9000 0.6561
    -0.3000 0.0081
     0.3000 0.0081
     0.9000 0.6561
     1.5000 5.0625
```

If we now type

```
K>> dbcont
```

we see in the figure window what is shown in Figure 11-9 below.

Finally we can understand what is going on; MATLAB has "connected the dots" using the points whose coordinates were just printed out, in the order it encountered them. In particular, MATLAB has drawn a line from the point (1.5, 2.25) to the point (−1.5, 5.0625). This is not what we wanted; we wanted MATLAB to join the point (1.5, 2.25) on the curve $y = x^2$ to the point (1.5, 5.0625) on the curve $y = x^4$. We can fix this by reversing the order of the

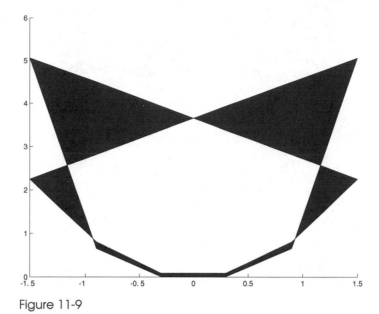

Figure 11-9

x coordinates at which we evaluate the second function g. So letting **slavx** denote **xvals** reversed, we correct our M-file to read

```
function shadecurves(f, g, a, b)
%SHADECURVES Draws the region between two curves
% SHADECURVES(f, g, a, b) takes strings or expressions f
% and g, interprets them as functions, plots them between
% x = a and x = b, and shades the region in between.
% Example: shadecurves('sin(x)', '-sin(x)', 0, pi)
ffun = inline(vectorize(f)); gfun = inline(vectorize(g));
xvals = a:(b - a)/50:b; slavx = b:(a - b)/50:a;
patch([xvals,slavx], [ffun(xvals),gfun(slavx)], [.2,0,.8])
```

Now it works properly. Sample output from this M-file is shown in Figure 11-4. Try it out on the other examples we have discussed, or on others of your choice.

Solutions to the Practice Sets

Practice Set A

■ Problem 1

(a)

```
1111 - 345
```

```
ans =
   766
```

(b)

```
format long; [exp(14), 382801*pi]
```

```
ans =
  1.0e+006 *
   1.20260428416478   1.20260480938683
```

The second number is bigger.

(c)

```
[2709/1024, 10583/4000, 2024/765, sqrt(7)]
```

```
ans =
   2.64550781250000   2.64575000000000   2.64575163398693
2.64575131106459
```

The third, that is, 2024/765, is the best approximation.

■ Problem 2

(a)

```
cosh(0.1)
```

```
ans =
    1.00500416805580
```

(b)

```
log(2)
```

```
ans =
    0.69314718055995
```

(c)

```
atan(1/2)
```

```
ans =
    0.46364760900081
```

```
format short
```

■ Problem 3

```
[x, y, z] = solve('3*x + 4*y + 5*z = 2', '2*x - 3*y + 7*z = -
1', 'x - 6*y + z = 3', 'x', 'y', 'z')
```

```
x =
241/92
y =
-21/92
z =
-91/92
```

Now we'll check the answer.

```
A = [3, 4, 5; 2, -3, 7; 1, -6, 1]; A*[x; y; z]
```

```
ans =
[   2]
```

```
[  -1]
[   3]
```

It checks!

■ Problem 4

```
[x, y, z] = solve('3*x - 9*y + 8*z = 2', '2*x - 3*y + 7*z = -
1', 'x - 6*y + z = 3', 'x', 'y', 'z')

x =
39/5*y+22/5
y =
y
z =
-9/5*y-7/5
```

We get a one-parameter family of answers depending on the variable y. In fact the three planes determined by the three linear equations are not independent, because the first equation is the sum of the second and third. The locus of points that satisfy the three equations is not a point, the intersection of three independent planes, but rather a line, the intersection of two distinct planes. Once again we check.

```
   B = [3, -9, 8; 2, -3, 7; 1, -6, 1]; B*[x; y; z]

ans =
[   2]
[  -1]
[   3]
```

■ Problem 5

```
syms x y; factor(x^4 - y^4)

ans =
(x-y)*(x+y)*(x^2+y^2)
```

■ Problem 6

(a)

```
simplify(1/(1 + 1/(1 + 1/x)))
```

```
ans =
(x+1)/(2*x+1)
```

(b)

```
simplify(cos(x)^2 - sin(x)^2)
```

```
ans =
2*cos(x)^2-1
```

Let's try **simple** instead.

```
[better, how] = simple(cos(x)^2 - sin(x)^2)
```

```
better =
cos(2*x)
how =
combine
```

■ Problem 7

```
3^301
```

```
ans =
  4.1067e+143
```

```
sym('3')^301
```

```
ans =
41067443717576512797397808214626494789939108687601230941444057
02351069915324972297814006184670668241647514533217939821284405
3819829297087323698003
```

But note the following:
```
sym('3^301')
```

```
ans =
3^301
```

This does not work because **sym**, by itself, does not cause an evaluation.

■ Problem 8

(a)

```
solve('8*x + 3 = 0', 'x')

ans =
-3/8
```

(b)

```
vpa(ans, 15)

ans =
-.375000000000000
```

(c)

```
syms p q; solve('x^3 + p*x + q = 0', 'x')

ans =
[
1/6*(-108*q+12*(12*p^3+81*q^2)^(1/2))^(1/3)-2*p/(-
108*q+12*(12*p^3+81*q^2)^(1/2))^(1/3)]
[ -1/12*(-108*q+12*(12*p^3+81*q^2)^(1/2))^(1/3)+p/(-
108*q+12*(12*p^3+81*q^2)^(1/2))^(1/3)+1/2*i*3^(1/2)*(1/6*(-
108*q+12*(12*p^3+81*q^2)^(1/2))^(1/3)+2*p/(-
108*q+12*(12*p^3+81*q^2)^(1/2))^(1/3))]
[ -1/12*(-108*q+12*(12*p^3+81*q^2)^(1/2))^(1/3)+p/(-
108*q+12*(12*p^3+81*q^2)^(1/2))^(1/3)-1/2*i*3^(1/2)*(1/6*(-
108*q+12*(12*p^3+81*q^2)^(1/2))^(1/3)+2*p/(-
108*q+12*(12*p^3+81*q^2)^(1/2))^(1/3))]
```

(d)

```
ezplot('exp(x)'); hold on; ezplot('8*x - 4'); hold off
```

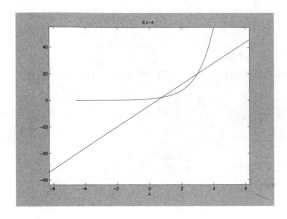

```
fzero(inline('exp(x) - 8*x + 4'), 1)
```

```
ans =
    0.7700
```

```
fzero(inline('exp(x) - 8*x + 4'), 3)
```

```
ans =
    2.9929
```

■ Problem 9

(a)

```
ezplot('x^3 - x', [-4 4])
```

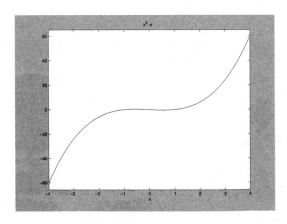

(b)

```
ezplot('sin(1/x^2)', [-2 2])
```

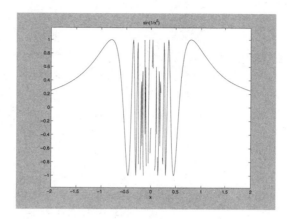

```
X = -2:0.1:2;
plot(X, sin(1./X.^2))
```

```
Warning: Divide by zero.
```

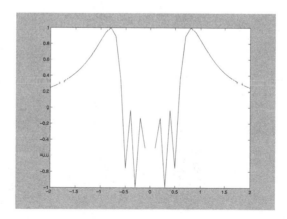

This picture is incomplete. Let's see what happens if we refine the mesh.

```
X = -2:0.01:2; plot(X, sin(1./X.^2))
```

```
Warning: Divide by zero.
```

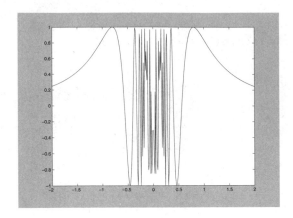

Because of the wild oscillation near $x = 0$, neither **plot** nor **ezplot** gives a totally accurate graph of the function.

(c)

```
ezplot('tan(x/2)', [-pi pi]); axis([-pi, pi, -10, 10])
```

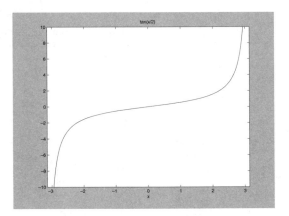

(d)

```
X = -2:0.05:2;
plot(X, exp(-X.^2), X, X.^4 - X.^2)
```

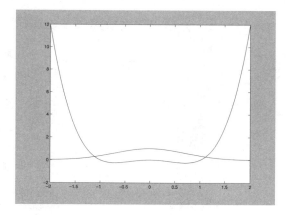

■ Problem 10

Let's plot 2^x and x^4 and look for points of intersection. We plot them first with **ezplot** just to get a feel for the graph.

```
ezplot('x^4'); hold on; ezplot('2^x'); hold off
```

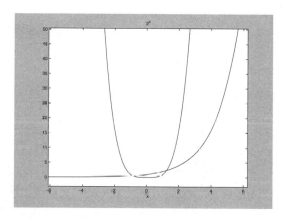

Note the large vertical range. We learn from the plot that there are no points of intersection between 2 and 6 or −6 and −2; but there are apparently two points of intersection between −2 and 2. Let's change to **plot** now and focus on the interval between −2 and 2. We'll plot the monomial dashed.

```
X = -2:0.1:2; plot(X, 2.^X); hold on; plot(X, X.^4, '--');
hold off
```

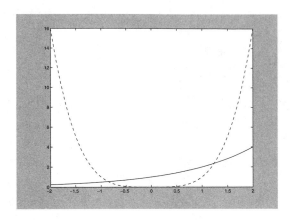

We see that there are points of intersection near -0.9 and 1.2. Are there any other points of intersection? To the left of 0, 2^x is always less than 1, whereas x^4 goes to infinity as x goes to $-\infty$. However, both x^4 and 2^x go to infinity as x goes to ∞, so the graphs may cross again to the right of 6. Let's check.

```
X = 6:0.1:20; plot(X, 2.^X); hold on; plot(X, X.^4, '--');
hold off
```

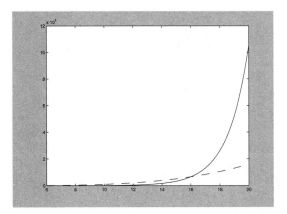

We see that they do cross again, near $x = 16$. If you know a little calculus, you can show that the graphs never cross again (by taking logarithms, for example), so we have found all the points of intersection. Now let's use **fzero** to find these points of intersection numerically. This command looks for a solution near a given starting point. To find the three different points of intersection we will have to use three different starting points. The graphical analysis above suggests appropriate starting points.

```
r1 = fzero(inline('2^x - x^4'), -0.9)
r2 = fzero(inline('2^x - x^4'), 1.2)
r3 = fzero(inline('2^x - x^4'), 16)

r1 =
   -0.8613
r2 =
    1.2396
r3 =
    16
```

Let's check that these "solutions" satisfy the equation.

```
subs('2^x - x^4', 'x', r1)
subs('2^x - x^4', 'x', r2)
subs('2^x - x^4', 'x', r3)

ans =
  2.2204e-016
ans =
 -8.8818e-016
ans =
  0
```

So **r1** and **r2** very nearly satisfy the equation, and **r3** satisfies it exactly. It is easily seen that 16 is a solution. It is also interesting to try **solve** on this equation.

```
symroots = solve('2^x - x^4 = 0')

symroots =
[    -4*lambertw(-1/4*log(2))/log(2)]
[                                 16]
[ -4*lambertw(-1/4*i*log(2))/log(2)]
```

```
[    -4*lambertw(1/4*log(2))/log(2)]
[  -4*lambertw(1/4*i*log(2))/log(2)]
```

In fact we get the three real solutions already found and two complex solutions.

double(symroots)

```
ans =
   1.2396
  16.0000
  -0.1609 + 0.9591i
  -0.8613
  -0.1609 - 0.9591i
```

Only the real solutions correspond to points where the graphs intersect.

Practice Set B

■ Problem 1

(a)

```
[X, Y] = meshgrid(-1:0.1:1, -1:0.1:1); contour(X, Y, 3*Y +
Y.^3 - X.^3, 'k')
```

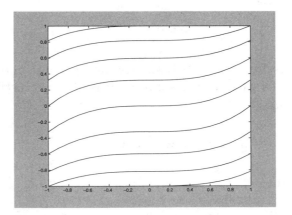

```
[X, Y] = meshgrid(-10:0.1:10, -10:0.1:10); contour(X, Y, 3*Y
+ Y.^3 - X.^3, 'k')
```

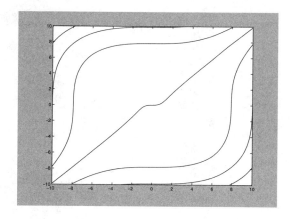

Here is a plot with more level curves.

```
[X, Y] = meshgrid(-10:0.1:10, -10:0.1:10); contour(X, Y, 3*Y
+ Y.^3 - X.^3, 30, 'k')
```

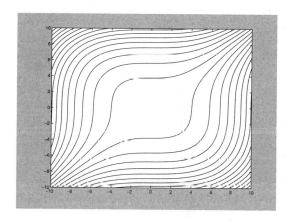

(b)

Now we plot the level curve through 5.

```
[X, Y] = meshgrid(-5:0.1:5, -5:0.1:5); contour(X, Y, 3.*Y +
Y.^3 - X.^3, [5 5], 'k')
```

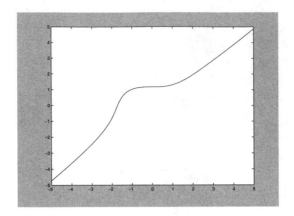

(c)

We note that $f(1, 1) = 0$, so the appropriate command to plot the level curve of f through the point $(1, 1)$ is

```
[X, Y] = meshgrid(0:0.1:2, 0:0.1:2); contour(X, Y, Y.*log(X)
+ X.*log(Y), [0 0], 'k')
```

```
Warning: Log of zero.
Warning: Log of zero.
```

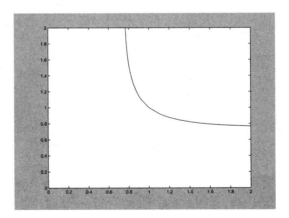

■ Problem 2

We find the derivatives of the given functions:

```
syms x r
```

(a)

```
diff(6*x^3 - 5*x^2 + 2*x - 3, x)

ans =
18*x^2-10*x+2
```

(b)

```
diff((2*x - 1)/(x^2 + 1), x)

ans =
2/(x^2+1)-2*(2*x-1)/(x^2+1)^2*x

simplify(ans)

ans =
-2*(x^2-1-x)/(x^2+1)^2
```

(c)

```
diff(sin(3*x^2 + 2), x)

ans =
6*cos(3*x^2+2)*x
```

(d)

```
diff(asin(2*x + 3), x)

ans =
1/(-2-x^2-3*x)^(1/2)
```

(e)

```
diff(sqrt(1 + x^4), x)

ans =
2/(1+x^4)^(1/2)*x^3
```

(f)

```
diff(x^r, x)

ans =
x^r*r/x
```

(g)

```
diff(atan(x^2 + 1), x)
```

```
ans =
2*x/(1+(x^2+1)^2)
```

■ Problem 3

We compute the following integrals.

(a)

```
int(cos(x), x, 0, pi/2)
```

```
ans =
1
```
(b)

```
int(x*sin(x^2), x)
```

```
ans =
-1/2*cos(x^2)
```

To check the indefinite integral, we just differentiate.

```
diff(-cos(x^2)/2, x)
```

```
ans =
x*sin(x^2)
```
(c)

```
int(sin(3*x)*sqrt(1 - cos(3*x)), x)
```

```
ans =
2/9*(1-cos(3*x))^(3/2)
```

```
diff(ans, x)
```

```
ans =
sin(3*x)*(1-cos(3*x))^(1/2)
```
(d)

```
int(x^2*sqrt(x + 4), x)
```

```
ans =
2/7*(x+4)^(7/2)-16/5*(x+4)^(5/2)+32/3*(x+4)^(3/2)
```

```
diff(ans, x)

ans =
(x+4)^(5/2)-8*(x+4)^(3/2)+16*(x+4)^(1/2)

simplify(ans)

ans =
x^2*(x+4)^(1/2)
```

(e)

```
int(exp(-x^2), x, -Inf, Inf)

ans =
pi^(1/2)
```

■ Problem 4

(a)

```
int(exp(sin(x)), x, 0, pi)

Warning: Explicit integral could not be found.
> In C:\MATLABR12\toolbox\symbolic\@sym\int.m at line 58
ans =
int(exp(sin(x)),x = 0 .. pi)

format long; quadl('exp(sin(x))', 0, pi)

ans -
   6.2087580358484585
```

(b)

```
quadl('sqrt(x.^3 + 1)', 0, 1)

ans =
   1.11144798484585
```

(c)

MATLAB integrated this one exactly in 4(e) above; let's integrate it numerically and compare answers. Unfortunately, the range is infinite, so to use **quadl** we have to approximate the interval. Note that for

$|x| > 35$, the integrand is much smaller than

```
exp(-35)

ans =
    6.305116760146989e-016
```

which is close to the standard floating point accuracy, so:

```
quadl('exp(-x.^2)', -35, 35)

ans =
    1.77245385102263
```

```
sqrt(pi)

ans =
    1.77245385090552
```

The answers agree to 9 digits.

■ Problem 5

(a)

```
limit(sin(x)/x, x, 0)

ans =
1
```

(b)

```
limit((1 + cos(x))/(x + pi), x, -pi)

ans =
0
```

(c)

```
limit(x^2*exp(-x), x, Inf)

ans =
0
```

(d)

```
limit(1/(x - 1), x, 1, 'left')

ans =
-inf
```

(e)

```
limit(sin(1/x), x, 0, 'right')

ans =
-1 .. 1
```

This means that every real number in the interval between -1 and $+1$ is a "limit point" of $\sin(1/x)$ as x tends to zero. You can see why if you plot $\sin(1/x)$ on the interval $(0, 1]$.

```
ezplot(sin(1/x), [0 1])
```

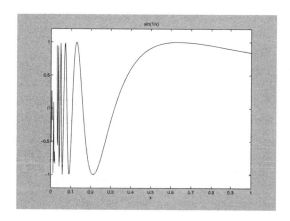

■ Problem 6

(a)

```
syms k n r x z

symsum(k^2, k, 0, n)

ans =
1/3*(n+1)^3-1/2*(n+1)^2+1/6*n+1/6
```

```
simplify(ans)
```

```
ans =
1/3*n^3+1/2*n^2+1/6*n
```

(b)

```
symsum(r^k, k, 0, n)
```

```
ans =
r^(n+1)/(r-1)-1/(r-1)
```

```
pretty(ans)
```

$$
\frac{r^{(n + 1)}}{r - 1} - \frac{1}{r - 1}
$$

(c)

```
symsum(x^k/factorial(k), k, 0, Inf)
```

```
??? Error using ==> fix
Function 'fix' not defined for variables of class 'sym'.
```

```
Error in ==> C:\MATLABR12\toolbox\matlab\specfun\factorial.m
On line 14 ==> if (length(n)~=1) | (fix(n)~= n) | (n < 0)
```

Here are two ways around this difficulty. The second method will not work with the Student Version.

```
symsum(x^k/gamma(k + 1), k, 0, Inf)
```

```
ans =
exp(x)
```

```
symsum(x^k/maple('factorial', k), k, 0, Inf)
```

```
ans =
exp(x)
```

(d)

```
symsum(1/(z - k)^2, k, -Inf, Inf)
```

```
ans =
pi^2+pi^2*cot(pi*z)^2
```

■ Problem 7

(a)

```
taylor(exp(x), 7, 0)
```

```
ans =
1+x+1/2*x^2+1/6*x^3+1/24*x^4+1/120*x^5+1/720*x^6
```
(b)

```
taylor(sin(x), 5, 0)
```

```
ans =
x-1/6*x^3
```

```
taylor(sin(x), 6, 0)
```

```
ans =
x-1/6*x^3+1/120*x^5
```
(c)

```
taylor(sin(x), 6, 2)
```

```
ans =
sin(2)+cos(2)*(x-2)-1/2*sin(2)*(x-2)^2-1/6*cos(2)*(x-
2)^3+1/24*sin(2)*(x-2)^4+1/120*cos(2)*(x-2)^5
```
(d)

```
taylor(tan(x), 7, 0)
```

```
ans =
x+1/3*x^3+2/15*x^5
```
(e)

```
taylor(log(x), 5, 1)
```

```
ans =
x-1-1/2*(x-1)^2+1/3*(x-1)^3-1/4*(x-1)^4
```
(f)

```
taylor(erf(x), 9, 0)
```

```
ans =
2/pi^(1/2)*x-2/3/pi^(1/2)*x^3+1/5/pi^(1/2)*x^5-
1/21/pi^(1/2)*x^7
```

■ Problem 8

(a)

```
syms x y; ezsurf(sin(x)*sin(y), [-3*pi 3*pi -3*pi 3*pi])
```

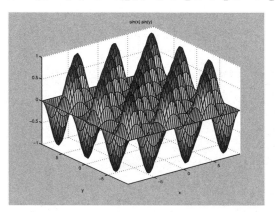

(b)

```
ezsurf((x^2 + y^2)*cos(x^2 + y^2), [-1 1 -1 1])
```

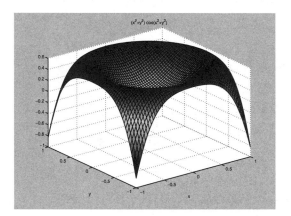

■ Problem 9

You can't do animations in an M-book. But from the Command Window, you can type:

```
T = 0:0.01:1;
for j = 0:16
    fill(4*cos(j*pi/8) + (1/2)*cos(2*pi*T), ...
      4*sin(j*pi/8) + (1/2)*sin(2*pi*T), 'r');
    axis equal; axis([-5 5 -5 5]);
    M(j + 1) = getframe;
end
movie(M)
```

■ Problem 10

(a)

```
A1 = [3 4 5; 2 -3 7; 1 -6 1]; b = [2; -1; 3];

format short; x = A1\b

x =
    2.6196
   -0.2283
   -0.9891

A1*x

ans =
    2.0000
   -1.0000
    3.0000
```

(b)

```
A2 = [3 -9 8; 2 -3 7; 1 -6 1]; b = [2; -1; 3];

x = A2\b

Warning: Matrix is close to singular or badly scaled.
        Results may be inaccurate. RCOND = 4.189521e-018.
x =
   -6.000
   -1.333
    1.000
```

The matrix **A2** is singular. In fact

```
det(A2)

ans =
     0
```

(c)

```
A3 = [1 3 -2 4; -2 3 4 -1; -4 -3 1 2; 2 3 -4 1]; b3 = [1; 1;
1; 1];
x = A3\b3

x =
   -0.5714
    0.3333
   -0.2857
   -0.0000

 A3*x

ans =
    1.0000
    1.0000
    1.0000
    1.0000
```

(d)

```
syms a b c d x y u v;
A4 = [a b; c d]; A4\[u; v]

ans =
[ -(b*v-u*d)/(a*d-c*b)]
[  (a*v-c*u)/(a*d-c*b)]

det(A4)

ans =
a*d-c*b
```

The determinant of the coefficient matrix is the denominator in the answer. So the answer is valid only if the coefficient matrix is non singular.

■ Problem 11

(a)

```
rank(A1)

ans =
     3

rank(A2)

ans =
     2

rank(A3)

ans =
     4

rank(A4)

ans =
2
```

MATLAB implicitly assumes $ad - bc \neq 0$ here.

(b)

Only the second one computed is singular.

(c)

```
det(A1)
inv(A1)

ans =
    92
ans =
     0.4239    -0.3696     0.4674
     0.0543    -0.0217    -0.1196
    -0.0978     0.2391    -0.1848

det(A2)
```

```
ans =
    0
```

The matrix **A2** does not have an inverse.

det(A3)
inv(A3)

```
ans =
    294
ans =
    0.1837   -0.1531   -0.2857   -0.3163
    0.0000    0.1667   -0.0000    0.1667
    0.1633    0.0306   -0.1429   -0.3367
    0.2857   -0.0714        0     -0.2143
```

det(A4)
inv(A4)

```
ans =
a*d-c*b
ans =
[  d/(a*d-c*b),  -b/(a*d-c*b)]
[ -c/(a*d-c*b),   a/(a*d-c*b)]
```

■ Problem 12

(a)

[U1, R1] = eig(A1)

```
U1 =
  -0.9749          0.6036              0.6036
  -0.2003          0.0624 + 0.5401i    0.0624 - 0.5401i
   0.0977         -0.5522 + 0.1877i   -0.5522 - 0.1877i
R1 =
   3.3206              0                   0
        0         -1.1603 + 5.1342i        0
        0               0             -1.1603 - 5.1342i
```

A1*U1 - U1*R1

```
ans =
  1.0e-014 *
   0.3109              0.2554 - 0.3553i     0.2554 + 0.3553i
  -0.0333             -0.1776 - 0.3220i    -0.1776 + 0.3220i
  -0.0833             -0.1721 - 0.0444i    -0.1721 + 0.0444i
```

This is essentially zero. Notice the "e-014".

[U2, R2] = eig(A2)

```
U2 =
   0.9669    0.7405              0.7405
   0.1240    0.4574 - 0.2848i    0.4574 + 0.2848i
  -0.2231    0.2831 + 0.2848i    0.2831 - 0.2848i
R2 =
  -0.0000            0                  0
        0    0.5000 + 6.5383i           0
        0            0          0.5000 - 6.5383i
```

A2*U2 - U2*R2

```
ans =
  1.0e-014 *
  -0.3154             -0.3331 - 0.4441i    -0.3331 + 0.4441i
  -0.2423              0.0888 + 0.3109i     0.0888 - 0.3109i
  -0.1140             -0.0222 + 0.2665i    -0.0222 - 0.2665i
```

This is essentially zero as well.

[U3, R3] = eig(A3)

```
U3 =
  -0.2446 - 0.4647i -0.2446 + 0.4647i 0.5621 - 0.1062i
0.5621 + 0.1062i
   0.6254             0.6254              -0.1982 - 0.0654i -
0.1982 + 0.0654i
   0.0025 + 0.3017i 0.0025 - 0.3017i 0.5833
```

```
0.5833
  -0.1736 - 0.4603i -0.1736 + 0.4603i  0.2215 + 0.4898i
0.2215 - 0.4898i
R3 =
    4.0755 + 4.1517i           0                  0
0
          0             4.0755 - 4.1517i          0
0
          0                    0          -1.0755 + 2.7440i
0
          0                    0                  0          -
1.0755 - 2.7440i
```

A3*U3 - U3*R3

```
ans =
  1.0e-014 *
  -0.2998 - 0.4885i -0.2998 + 0.4885i  0.0944 + 0.3553i
0.0944 - 0.3553i
   0.1776 + 0.3109i  0.1776 - 0.3109i  0.0111 - 0.1055i
0.0111 + 0.1055i
   0.0444 + 0.0888i  0.0444 - 0.0888i -0.0666 - 0.0666i -
0.0666 + 0.0666i
  -0.1110 - 0.3109i -0.1110 + 0.3109i -0.1776 + 0.2970i -
0.1776 - 0.2970i
```

Again, with the `e-014` term this is essentially zero.

[U4, R4] = eig(A4)

```
U4 =
[                                                        1,
1]
[ -(-1/2*d+1/2*a-1/2*(d^2-2*a*d+a^2+4*c*b)^(1/2))/b, -(-
1/2*d+1/2*a+1/2*(d^2-2*a*d+a^2+4*c*b)^(1/2))/b]
R4 =
[ 1/2*d+1/2*a+1/2*(d^2-2*a*d+a^2+4*c*b)^(1/2),
0]
```

```
[                                                    0, 1/2*d+1/2*a-
1/2*(d^2-2*a*d+a^2+4*c*b)^(1/2)]
```

A4*U4 - U4*R4

```
ans =
[
0,
0]
[c-d*(-1/2*d+1/2*a-1/2*(d^2-2*a*d+a^2+4*c*b)^(1/2))/b+(-
1/2*d+1/2*a-1/2*(d^2-
2*a*d+a^2+4*c*b)^(1/2))/b*(1/2*d+1/2*a+1/2*(d^2-
2*a*d+a^2+4*c*b)^(1/2)), c-d*(-1/2*d+1/2*a+1/2*(d^2-
2*a*d+a^2+4*c*b)^(1/2))/b+(-1/2*d+1/2*a+1/2*(d^2-
2*a*d+a^2+4*c*b)^(1/2))/b*(1/2*d+1/2*a-1/2*(d^2-
2*a*d+a^2+4*c*b)^(1/2))]
```

simplify(ans)

```
ans =
[ 0, 0]
[ 0, 0]
```

(b)

```
A = [1 0 2; -1 0 4; -1 -1 5];
clear U1 U2 R1 R2
[U1, R1] = eig(A)
```

```
U1 =
   -0.8165    0.5774    0.7071
   -0.4082    0.5774   -0.7071
   -0.4082    0.5774    0.0000
R1 =
   2.0000         0         0
        0    3.0000         0
        0         0    1.0000
```

```
B = [5 2 -8; 3 6 -10; 3 3 -7];
[U2, R2] = eig(B)
```

```
U2 =
     0.8165     -0.5774      0.7071
     0.4082     -0.5774     -0.7071
     0.4082     -0.5774     -0.0000
R2 =
     2.0000          0           0
          0    -1.0000           0
          0          0      3.0000
```

We observe that the columns of **U1** are negatives of the corresponding columns of **U2**. Finally,

A*B - B*A

```
ans =
     0     0     0
     0     0     0
     0     0     0
```

■ Problem 13

(a)

If we set X_n to be the column matrix with entries x_n, y_n, z_n, and M the square matrix with entries 1, 1/4, 0; 0, 1/2, 0; 0, 1/4, 1 then $X_{n+1} = MX_n$.

(b)

We have $X_n = MX_{n-1} = M^2X_{n-2} = \ldots = M^nX_0$.

(c)

```
M = [1, 1/4, 0; 0, 1/2, 0; 0, 1/4, 1];
[U,R] = eig(M)

U =
     1.0000          0     -0.4082
          0          0      0.8165
          0     1.0000     -0.4082
R =
     1.0000          0           0
          0     1.0000           0
          0          0      0.5000
```

(d)

M should be URU^{-1}. Let's check:

```
M - U*R*inv(U)

ans =
        0      0      0
        0      0      0
        0      0      0
```

It is evident that R_∞ is the diagonal matrix with entries 1, 1, 0. Since $M_\infty = UR_\infty U^{-1}$, we have:

```
Minf = U*diag([1, 1, 0])*inv(U)

Minf =
    1.0000      0.5000           0
         0           0           0
         0      0.5000      1.0000
```

(e)

```
syms x0 y0 z0; X0 = [x0; y0; z0]; Minf*X0

ans =
[  x0+1/2*y0]
[         0]
[  1/2*y0+z0]
```

Half of the mixed genotype migrates to the dominant genotype and the other half of the mixed genotype migrates to the recessive genotype. These are added to the two original pure types, whose proportions are preserved.

(f)

```
M^5*X0

ans =
[  x0+31/64*y0]
[      1/32*y0]
[  31/64*y0+z0]
```

```
M^10*X0
```

```
ans =
[  x0+1023/2048*y0]
[         1/1024*y0]
[ 1023/2048*y0+z0]
```

(g)

If you use the suggested alternate model, then only the first three columns of the table are relevant, the transition matrix M becomes $M =$ [1 1/2 0; 0 1/2 1; 0 0 0], and we leave it to you to compute that the eventual population distribution is [1; 0; 0], independent of the initial population.

Practice Set C

■ Problem 1

(a)

```
radiation = inline(vectorize('10000/(4*pi*((x - x0)^2 + (y -
y0)^2 + 1))'), 'x', 'y', 'x0', 'y0')
```

```
radiation =
     Inline function:
     radiation(x,y,x0,y0) = 10000./(4.*pi.*((x-x0).^2 + (y-
y0).^2 + 1))
```

```
x = zeros(1, 5); y = zeros(1, 5);
for j = 1:5
  x(j) = 50*rand;
  y(j) = 50*rand;
end
[X, Y] = meshgrid(0:0.1:50, 0:0.1:50);
contourf(X, Y, radiation(X, Y, x(1), y(1)) + radiation(X, Y,
x(2), y(2)) + radiation(X, Y, x(3), y(3)) + radiation(X, Y,
x(4), y(4)) + radiation(X, Y, x(5), y(5)), 20);
colormap('gray')
```

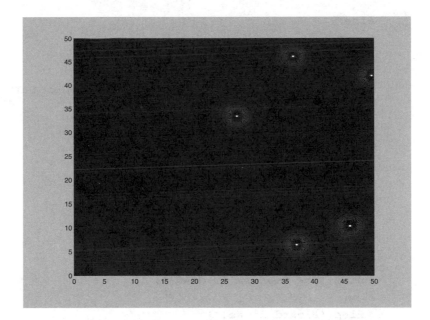

It is not so clear from the picture where to hide, although it looks like the Captain has a pretty good chance of surviving a small number of shots. But 100 shots may be enough to find him. Intuition says he ought to stay close to the boundary.

(b)

Below is a series of commands that places Picard at the center of the arena, fires the death ray 100 times, and then determines the health of Picard. It uses the function **lifeordeath**, which computes the fate of the Captain after a single shot.

```
function r = lifeordeath(x1, y1, x0, y0)
%This file computes the number of illuminatons.
%that arrive at the point (x1, y1), assuming the death,
%ray strikes 1 meter above the point (x0, y0).
%If that number exceeds 50, a "1" is returned in the
%variable "r"; otherwise a "0" is returned for "r".
dosage = 10000/(4*pi*((x1 - x0)^2 + (y1 - y0)^2 + 1));
if dosage > 50
    r = 1;
```

```
else
    r = 0;
end
```

Here is the series of commands to test the Captain's survival possibilities:

```
x1 = 25; y1 = 25; h = 0;
for n = 1:100
    x0 = 50*rand;
    y0 = 50*rand;
    r = lifeordeath(x1, y1, x0, y0);
    h = h + r;
end
if h > 0
  disp('The Captain is dead!')
else
  disp('Picard lives!')
end
```

```
The Captain is dead!
```

In fact if you run this sequence of commands multiple times, you will see the Captain die far more often than he lives.

(c)

So let's do a Monte Carlo simulation to see what his odds are:

```
x1 = 25; y1 = 25; c = 0;
for k = 1:100
  h = 0;
  for n = 1:100
    x0 = 50*rand;
    y0 = 50*rand;
    r = lifeordeath(x1, y1, x0, y0);
    h = h + r;
  end
  if h > 0
    c = c;
```

```
    else
       c = c + 1;
    end
end
disp(['The chances of Picard surviving are = ', ...
num2str(c/100)])
```

```
The chances of Picard surviving are = 0.16
```

We ran this a few times and saw survival chances ranging from 9 to 16%.

(d)

```
x1 = 37.5; y1 = 25; c = 0;
for k = 1:100
  h = 0;
  for n = 1:100
    x0 = 50*rand;
    y0 = 50*rand;
    r = lifeordeath(x1, y1, x0, y0);
    h = h + r;
  end
  if h > 0
    c = c;
  else
    c = c + 1;
  end
end
disp(['The chances of Picard surviving are = ',...
num2str(c/100)])
```

```
The chances of Picard surviving are = 0.17
```

This time the numbers were between 10 and 18%. Let's keep moving him toward the periphery.

(e)

```
x1 = 50; y1 = 25; c = 0;
for k = 1:100
  h = 0;
```

```
    for n = 1:100
      x0 = 50*rand;
      y0 = 50*rand;
      r = lifeordeath(x1, y1, x0, y0);
      h = h + r;
    end
    if h > 0
      c = c;
    else
      c = c + 1;
    end
end
disp(['The chances of Picard surviving are = ',...
num2str(c/100)])
```

```
The chances of Picard surviving are = 0.44
```

The numbers now hover between 36 and 47% upon multiple runnings of this scenario; so finally, suppose he cowers in the corner.

```
x1 = 50; y1 = 50; c = 0;
for k = 1:100
  h = 0;
  for n = 1:100
    x0 = 50*rand;
    y0 = 50*rand;
    r = lifeordeath(x1, y1, x0, y0);
    h = h + r;
  end
  if h > 0
    c = c;
  else
    c = c + 1;
  end
end
disp(['The chances of Picard surviving are = ',...
num2str(c/100)])
```

```
The chances of Picard surviving are = 0.64
```

We saw numbers between 56 and 64%.

They say a brave man dies but a single time, but a coward dies a thousand deaths. But the person who said that probably never encountered a Cardassian. Long live Picard!

■ Problem 2

(a)

Consider the status of the account on the last day of each month. At the end of the first month, the account has $M + M \times J = M(1 + J)$ dollars. Then at the end of the second month the account contains $[M(1 + J)](1 + J) = M(1 + J)^2$ dollars. Similarly, at the end of n months, the account will hold $M(1 + J)^n$ dollars. Therefore, our formula is

$$T = M(1 + J)^n.$$

(b)

Now we take $M = 0$ and S dollars deposited monthly. At the end of the first month the account has $S + S \times J = S(1 + J)$ dollars. S dollars are added to that sum the next day, and then at the end of the second month the account contains $[S(1 + J) + S](1 + J) = S[(1 + J)^2 + (1 + J)]$ dollars. Similarly, at the end of n months, the account will hold

$$S[(1 + J)^n + \cdots + (1 + J)]$$

dollars. We recognize the geometric series — with the constant term "1" missing, so the amount T in the account after n months will equal

$$T = S[((1 + J)^{n+1} - 1)/((1 + J) - 1) - 1] = S[((1 + J)^{n+1} - 1)/J - 1].$$

(c)

By combining the two models it is clear that in an account with an initial balance M and monthly deposits S, the amount of money T after n months is given by

$$T = M(1 + J)^n + S[((1 + J)^{n+1} - 1)/J - 1].$$

(d)

We are asked to solve the equation

$$(1 + J)^n = 2$$

with the values $J = 0.05/12$ and $J = 0.1/12$.

```
months = solve('(1 + (0.05)/12)^n = 2')
years = months/12
```

```
months =
166.70165674865177999568182581405
years =
13.891804729054314999640152151171
```

```
months = solve('(1 + (0.1)/12)^n = 2')
years = months/12
```

```
months =
83.523755900375880189555262964714
years =
6.9603129916799900157962719137262
```

If you double the interest rate, you roughly halve the time to achieve the goal.

(e)

```
solve('1000000 = S*((((1 + (0.08/12))^(35*12 + 1) -
1)/(0.08/12)) - 1)')
```

```
ans =
433.05508895308253849797798306477
```

You need to deposit $433.06 every month.

(f)

```
solve('1000000 = 300*((((1 + (0.08/12))^(n + 1) -
1)/(0.08/12)) - 1)')
```

```
ans =
472.38046393034711345013989217261
```

```
ans/12
```

```
ans =
39.365038660862259454178324347717
```

You have to work nearly 5 more years.

(g)

First, taking the whole bundle at once, after 20 years the $65,000 left after taxes generates

```
format bank; option1 = 65000*(1 + (.05/12))^(12*20)
```

```
option1 =
    176321.62
```

The stash grows to about $176,322. The second option yields

```
S = .8*(100000/240)
```

```
S =
      333.33
```

```
option2 = S*((1/(.05/12))*(((1 + (.05/12))^241) - 1) - 1)
```

```
option2 =
    137582.10
```

You only accumulate $137,582 this way. Taking the lump sum up front is clearly the better strategy.

(h)

```
rates = [.13, .15, -.03, .05, .10, .13, .15, -.03, .05];

clear T
for k = 0:4
  T = 50000;
  for j = 1:5
    T = T*(1 + rates(k + j));
  end
  disp([k + 1,T])
end
```

```
        1.00        72794.74
        2.00        72794.74
```

```
3.00          72794.74
4.00          72794.74
5.00          72794.74
```

The results are all the same; you wind up with \$72,795 regardless of where you enter in the cycle, because the product $\prod_{1 \le j \le 5}(1 + \textbf{rates}(j))$ is independent of the order in which you place the factors. If you put the \$50,000 in a bank account paying 8%, you get

```
50000*(1.08)^5

ans =
    73466.40
```

that is, \$73,466 — better than the market. The market's volatility hurts you compared to the bank's stability. But of course that assumes you can find a bank that will pay 8%. Now let's see what happens with no stash, but an annual investment instead. The analysis is more subtle here. Set $S = 10, 000$ (which now represents a yearly deposit). At the end of one year, the account contains $S(1 + r_1)$; then at the end of the second year $(S(1 + r_1) + S)(1 + r_2)$, where we have written r_j for $\textbf{rates}(j)$. So at the end of 5 years, the amount in the account will be the product of S and the number

$$\Pi_{j \ge 1}(1 + r_j) + \Pi_{j \ge 2}(1 + r_j) + \Pi_{j \ge 3}(1 + r_j) + \Pi_{j \ge 4}(1 + r_j) + (1 + r_5).$$

If you enter at a different year in the business cycle the terms get cycled appropriately. So now we can compute

```
format short
for k = 0:4
  T = ones(1, 5);
  for j = 1:5
    TT = 1;
    for m = j:5
      TT = TT*(1 + rates(k + m));
    end
    T(j) = TT;
  end
```

```
    disp([k + 1, sum(T)])
end
```

```
    1.0000    6.1196
    2.0000    6.4000
    3.0000    6.8358
    4.0000    6.1885
    5.0000    6.0192
```

Multiplying each of these by $10,000 gives the portfolio amounts for the five scenarios. Not surprisingly, all are less than what one obtains by investing the original $50,000 all at once. But in this model it matters where you enter the business cycle. It's clearly best to start your investment program when a recession is in force and end in a boom. Incidentally, the bank model yields in this case

```
(1/.08)*(((1.08)^6) - 1) - 1
```

```
ans =
    6.3359
```

which is better than the results of some of the previous investment models and worse than others.

■ Problem 3

(a)

First we define an expression that computes whether Tony gets a hit or not during a single at bat, based on a random number chosen between 0 and 1. If the random number is less than or equal to 0.339, Tony is credited with a hit, whereas if the number exceeds 0.339, he is retired by the opposition.

Here is an M-file, called **atbat.m**, which computes the outcome of a single at bat:

```
%This file simulates a single at bat.
%The variable r contains a "1" if Tony gets a hit,
%that is, if rand <= 0.339; and it contains a "0"
%if Tony fails to hit safely, that is, if rand > 0.339.
s = rand;
```

```
if s <= 0.339
    r = 1;
else
    r = 0;
end
```

We can simulate a year in Tony's career by evaluating the script M-file `atbat` 500 times. The following program does exactly that. Then it computes his average by adding up the number of hits and dividing by the number of at bats, that is, 500. We build in a variable that allows for a varying number of at bats in a year, although we shall only use 500.

```
function y = yearbattingaverage(n)
%This function file computes Tony's batting average for
%a single year, by simulating n at bats, adding up the
%number of hits, and then dividing by n.
X = zeros(1, n);
for i = 1:n
    atbat;
    X(i) = r;
end
y = sum(X)/n;

yearbattingaverage(500)

ans =
    0.3200
```

(b)

Now let's write a function M-file that simulates a 20-year career. As with the number of at bats in a year, we'll allow for a varying length career.

```
function y = career(n,k)
%This function file computes the batting average for each
%year in a k-year career, asuming n at bats in each year.
%Then it lists the maximum, minimum, and lifetime average.
Y = zeros(1, k);
for j = 1:k
    Y(j) = yearbattingaverage(n);
end
```

```
disp(['Best avg: ', num2str(max(Y))])
disp(['Worst average: ', num2str(min(Y))])
disp(['Lifetime avg: ', num2str(sum(Y)/k)])

career(500, 20)
```

```
Best avg: 0.376
Worst average: 0.316
Lifetime avg: 0.3439
```

(c)

Now we run the simulation four more times:

```
career(500, 20)
```

```
Best avg: 0.366
Worst average: 0.31
Lifetime avg: 0.3393
```

```
career(500, 20)
```

```
Best avg: 0.38
Worst average: 0.288
Lifetime avg: 0.3381
```

```
career(500, 20)
```

```
Best avg: 0.378
Worst average: 0.312
Lifetime avg: 0.3428
```

```
career(500, 20)
```

```
Best avg: 0.364
Worst average: 0.284
Lifetime avg: 0.3311
```

(d)

The average for the five different 20-year careers is:

```
(.3439 + .3393 + .3381 + .3428 + .3311)/5
```

```
ans =
    0.33904000000000
```

How about that!

If we ran the simulation 100 times and took the average it would likely be extremely close to .339 — even closer than the previous number.

■ Problem 4

Our solution and its output are below. First we set **n** to 500 to save typing in the following lines and make it easier to change this value later. Then we set up a row vector **j** and a zero matrix **A** of the appropriate sizes and begin a loop that successively defines each row of the matrix. Notice that on the line defining **A(i,j)**, **i** is a scalar and **j** is a vector. Finally, we extract the maximum value from the list of eigenvalues of **A**.

```
n = 500;
j = 1:n;
A = zeros(n);
for i = 1:n
  A(i,j) = 1./(i + j - 1);
end
max(eig(A))
```

```
ans =
    2.3769
```

■ Problem 5

Again we display below our solution and its output. First we define a vector **t** of values between 0 and 2π, in order to later represent circles parametrically as $x = r \cos t$, $y = r \sin t$. Then we clear any previous figure that might exist and prepare to create the figure in several steps. Let's say the red circle will have radius 1; then the first black ring should have inner radius 2 and outer radius 3, and thus the tenth black ring should have inner radius 20 and outer radius 21. We start drawing from the outside in because the idea is to fill the largest circle in black, then fill the next largest circle in white leaving only a ring of black, then fill the next largest circle in black leaving a ring of white, etc. The **if** statement tests true when **r** is odd and false when it is even. We stop the alternation of black and white at a radius of 2 to make the last circle red instead of black; then we adjust the axes to make the circles appear round.

```
t = linspace(0, 2*pi, 100);
cla reset; hold on
for r = 21:-1:2
  if mod(r, 2)
    fill(r*cos(t), r*sin(t), 'k')
  else
    fill(r*cos(t), r*sin(t), 'w')
  end
end
fill(cos(t), sin(t), 'r')
axis equal; hold off
```

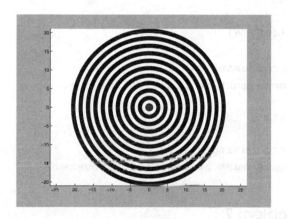

■ Problem 6

Here are the contents of our solution M-file:

```
function m = mylcm(varargin)
nums = [varargin{:}];
if ~isnumeric(nums) | any(nums ~= round(real(nums))) | ...
    any(nums <= 0)
```

```
      error('Arguments must be positive integers.')
end

for k = 2:length(nums);
  nums(k) = lcm(nums(k), nums(k - 1));
end
m = nums(end);
```

Here are some examples:

```
mylcm([4 5 6])
```

```
ans =
    60
```

```
mylcm(6, 7, 12, 15)
```

```
ans =
    420
```

```
mylcm(4.5, 6)
```

```
??? Error using ==> mylcm
Arguments must be positive integers.
```

```
mylcm('a', 'b', 'c')
```

```
??? Error using ==> mylcm
Arguments must be positive integers.
```

■ Problem 7

Here is our solution M-file:

```
function letcount(file)
if isunix
  [stat, str] = unix(['cat ' file]);
else
  [stat, str] = dos(['type ' file]);
end
```

```
letters = 'abcdefghijklmnopqrstuvwxyz';
caps = 'ABCDEFGHIJKLMNOPQRSTUVWXYZ';
for n = 1:26
  count(n) = sum(str == letters(n)) + sum(str == caps(n));
end
bar(count)
ylabel 'Number of occurrences'
title(['Letter frequencies in ' file])
set(gca, 'XLim', [0 27], 'XTick', 1:26, 'XTickLabel', ...
  letters')
```

Here is the result of running this M-file on itself:

```
letcount('letcount.m')
```

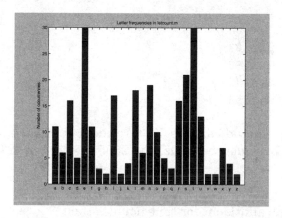

■ Problem 8

We let w, x, y, and z, denote the number of residences canvassed in the four cities Gotham, Metropolis, Oz, and River City, respectively. Then the linear inequalities specified by the given data are as follows:

Nonnegative data: $w \geq 0, x \geq 0, y \geq 0, z \geq 0$;

Pamphlets: $w + x + y + z \leq 50{,}000$;

Travel cost: $0.5w + 0.5x + y + 2z \leq 40{,}000$;

Time available: $2w + 3x + y + 4z \leq 18{,}000$;

Preferences: $w \leq x, x + y \leq z$;

Contributions: $w + 0.25x + 0.5y + 3z \geq 10,000$.
The quantity to be maximized is:
Voter support: $0.6w + 0.6x + 0.5y + 0.3z$.

(a)

This enables us to set up and solve the linear programming problem in MATLAB as follows:

```
f = [-0.6 -0.6 -0.5 -0.3];
A = [1 1 1 1; 0.5 0.5 1 2; 2 3 1 4; 1 -1 0 0; 0 1 1 -1; -1 -
0.25 -0.5 -3; -1 0 0 0; 0 -1 0 0; 0 0 -1 0; 0 0 0 -1];
b = [50000; 40000; 18000; 0; 0; -10000; 0; 0; 0; 0];
```

simlp(f, A, b)

```
Optimization terminated successfully.
ans =
   1.0e+003 *
   1.2683
   1.2683
   1.3171
   2.5854
```

Jane should canvass 1268 residences in each of Gothan and Metropolis, 1317 residences in Oz, and 2585 residences in River City.

(b)

If the allotment for time doubles then

b = [50000; 40000; 36000; 0; 0; -10000; 0; 0; 0; 0];

simlp(f, A, b)

```
Optimization terminated successfully.
ans =
   1.0e+003 *
   4.0000
   4.0000
   0.0000
   4.0000
```

Jane should canvass 4000 residences in each of Gotham, Metropolis, and River City and ignore Oz.

(c)

Finally, if in addition she needs to raise $20,000 in contributions, then

```
b = [50000; 40000; 36000; 0; 0; -20000; 0; 0; 0; 0];

simlp(f, A, b)

Optimization terminated successfully.
ans =
  1.0e+003 *
    2.5366
    2.5366
    2.6341
    5.1707
```

Jane needs to canvass 2537 residences in each of Gotham and Metropolis, 2634 residences in Oz, and 5171 in River City.

■ Problem 9

We let w, x, y, and z, denote the number of hours that Nerv spends with the quarterback, the running backs, the receivers, and the linemen, respectively. Then the linear inequalities specified by the given data are as follows:
Nonnegative data: $w \geq 0, x \geq 0, y \geq 0, z \geq 0$;
Time available: $w + x + y + z \leq 50$;
Point production: $0.5w + 0.3x + 0.4y + 0.1z \geq 20$;
Criticisms: $w + 2x + 3y + 0.5z \leq 75$;
Prima Donna status: $x = y, w \geq x + y, x \geq z$.

The quantity to be maximized is:
Personal satisfaction: $0.2w + 0.4x + 0.3y + 0.6z$.

(a)

This enables us to set up and solve the linear programming problem in MATLAB as follows:

```
f = [-0.2 -0.4 -0.3 -0.6];
A = [1 1 1 1; -0.5 -0.3 -0.4 -0.1; 1 2 3 0.5; 0 -1 1 0; ...
```

```
      0 1 -1 0; -1 1 1 0; 0 -1 0 1; -1 0 0 0; 0 -1 0 0; ...
      0 0 -1 0; 0 0 0 -1];
  b = [50; -20; 75; 0; 0; 0; 0; 0; 0; 0; 0];
```

simlp(f, A, b)

```
Optimization terminated successfully.
ans =
    25.9259
     9.2593
     9.2593
     5.5556
```

Nerv should spend 7.5 hours each with the running backs and receivers; 6.9 hours with the linemen; and the majority of his time, 28.1 hours, with the quarterback.

(b)

If the team only needs 15 points to win, then

b = [50; -15; 75; 0; 0; 0; 0; 0; 0; 0; 0];

simlp(f, A, b)

```
Optimization terminated successfully.
ans =
    20.0000
    10.0000
    10.0000
    10.0000
```

Nerv can spread his time more evenly, 10 hours each with the running backs, receivers, and linemen; but still the biggest chunk of his time, 20 hours, should be spent with the quarterback.

(c)

Finally if in addition the number of criticisms is reduced to 70, then

b = [50; -15; 70; 0; 0; 0; 0; 0; 0; 0; 0];

simlp(f, A, b)

```
Optimization terminated successfully.
ans =
    18.6667
     9.3333
     9.3333
     9.3333
```

Nerv must spend $18\frac{2}{3}$ hours with the quarterback and $9\frac{1}{3}$ hours with each of the other three groups. Note that the total is less than 50, leaving Nerv some free time to look for a job for next year.

■ Problem 10

```
syms V0 R I0 VT x

f = x - V0 + R*I0*exp(x/VT)

f =
x-V0+R*I0*exp(x/VT)
```

(a)

```
VD = fzero(char(subs(f, [V0, R, I0, VT], [1.5, 1000, 10^(-5),
.0025])), [0, 1.5])

VD =
    0.0125
```

That's the voltage; the current is therefore

```
I = (1.5 - VD)/1000

I =
    0.0015
```

(b)

```
g = subs(f, [V0, R], [1.5, 1000])

g =
x-3/2+1000*I0*exp(x/VT)
```

```
fzero(char(subs(g, [I0, VT], [(1/2)*10^(-5), .0025])),
[0, 1.5])
```

```
ans =
    0.0142
```

Not surprisingly, the voltage goes up slightly.

(c)

```
fzero(char(subs(g, [I0, VT], [10^(-5), .0025/2])), [0, 1.5])
```

```
??? Error using ==> fzero
Function values at interval endpoints must be finite and
real.
```

The problem is that the values of the exponential are too big at the right-hand endpoint of the test interval. We have to specify an interval big enough to catch the solution, but small enough to prevent the exponential from blowing up too drastically at the right endpoint. This will be the case even more dramatically in part (e) below.

```
fzero(char(subs(g, [I0, VT], [10^(-5), .0025/2])), [0, 0.5])
```

```
ans =
    0.0063
```

This time the voltage goes down.

(d)

Next we halve both:

```
fzero(char(subs(g, [I0, VT], [(1/2)*10^(-5), .0025/2])), [0,
0.5])
```

```
ans =
    0.0071
```

The voltage is less than in part (b) but more than in part (c).

(e)

```
syms u
h = subs(g, [I0, VT], [10^(-5)*u, 0.0025*u])
```

```
h =
x-3/2+1/100*u*exp(400*x/u)

X = zeros(6);
I = zeros(6);
for j = 0:5
  X(j + 1) = fzero(char(subs(h, u, 10^(-j))), ...
     [0, 10^(-j-1)]);
  I(j + 1) = 10^(-j-5);
end

loglog(I, X)
```

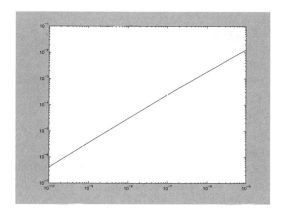

The **loglog** plot has a slope of approximately 1, reflecting a linear dependence.

■ Problem 11

(u)

```
dsolve('Dx = x - x^2')

ans =
1/(1+exp(-t)*C1)

syms x0; sol = dsolve('Dx = x - x^2', 'x(0) = x0')
```

```
sol =
1/(1-exp(-t)*(-1+x0)/x0)
```

Note that this includes the zero solution; indeed

bettersol = simplify(sol)

```
bettersol =
-x0/(-x0-exp(-t)+exp(-t)*x0)
```

subs(bettersol, x0, 0)

```
ans =
0
```

(b)

T = 0:0.1:5;

```
hold on
solcurves = inline(vectorize(bettersol), 't', 'x0');
for initval = 0:0.25:2.0
  plot(T, solcurves(T, initval))
end
axis tight
title 'Solutions of Dx = x - x^2, with x(0) = 0, 0.25,..., 2'
xlabel 't'
ylabel 'x'
hold off
```

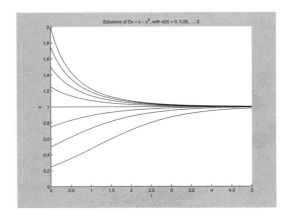

The graphical evidence suggests that: The solution that starts at zero stays there; all the others tend toward the constant solution 1.

(c)

```
clear all; close all; hold on
f = inline('[x(1) - x(1)^2 - 0.5*x(1)*x(2); x(2) - x(2)^2 -
0.5*x(1)*x(2)]', 't', 'x');
for a = 0:1/12:13/12
  for b = 0:1/12:13/12
     [t, xa] = ode45(f, [0 3], [a,b]);
     plot(xa(:, 1), xa(:, 2))
     echo off
  end
end
axis([0 13/12 0 13/12])
```

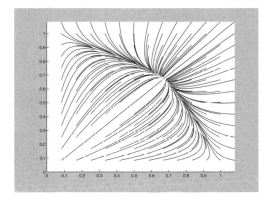

(d)

The endpoints on the curves are the start points. So clearly any curve that starts out inside the first quadrant, that is, one that corresponds to a situation in which both populations are present at the outset, tends toward a unique point — which from the graph appears to be about (2/3,2/3). In fact if $x = y = 2/3$, then the right sides of both equations in (4) vanish, so the derivatives are zero and the values of $x(t)$ and $y(t)$ remain constant — they don't depend on t. If only one species is present at the outset, that is, you start out on one of the axes, then the solution tends toward either (1,0) or (0,1) depending on whether x or y is the species present. That is precisely the behavior we saw in part (b).

(e)

```
close all; hold on
f = inline('[x(1) - x(1)^2 - 2*x(1)*x(2); x(2) - x(2)^2 -
2*x(1)*x(2)]', 't', 'x');
for a = 0:1/12:13/12
  for b = 0:1/12:13/12
     [t, xa] = ode45(f, [0 3], [a,b]);
     plot(xa(:, 1), xa(:, 2))
     echo off
  end
end
axis([0 13/12 0 13/12])
```

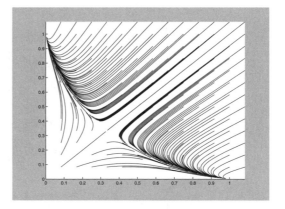

This time most of the curves seem to be tending toward one of the points (1,0) or (0,1) — in particular, any solution curve that starts on one of the axes (corresponding to no initial poulation for the other species) does so. It seems that whichever species has a greater population at the outset will eventually take over all the population — the other will die out. But there is a delicate balance in the middle — it appears that if the two populations are about equal at the outset, then they tend to the unique population distribution at which, if you start there, nothing happens. That value looks like (1/3,1/3). In fact this is the value that renders both sides of (5) zero and its role is analogous to that played by (2/3,2/3) in part (d).

(f)

It makes sense to refer to the model (4) as "peaceful coexistence", since whatever initial populations you have — provided both are present — you wind up with equal populations eventually. "Doomsday" is an appropriate name for model (5), since if you start out with unequal populations, then the smaller group becomes extinct. The lower coefficient 0.5 means relatively small interaction between the species, allowing for coexistence. The larger coefficient 2 means stronger interaction and competition, precluding the survival of both.

■ Problem 12

Here is a SIMULINK model for redoing the pendulum application from Chapter 9:

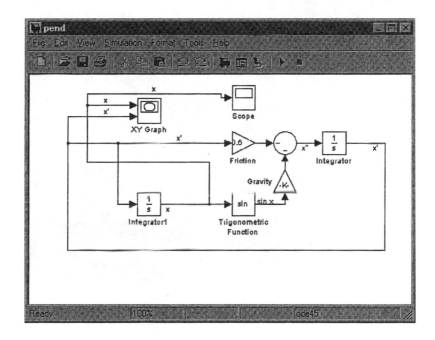

With the initial conditions $x(0) = 0$, $\dot{x}(0) = 10$, the XY Graph block shows the following phase portrait:

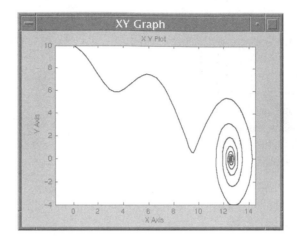

Meanwhile, the Scope block gives the following graph of x as a function of t:

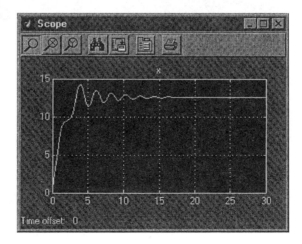

■ Problem 13

Here is a SIMULINK model for studying the equation of motion of a baseball:

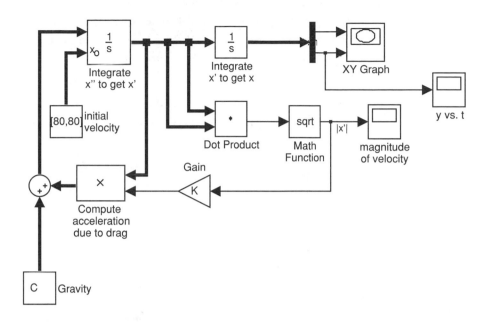

The way this works is fairly straightforward. The Integrator block in the upper left integrates the acceleration (a vector quantity) to get the velocity (also a vector — we have chosen the option, from the **Format** menu, of indicating vector quantities with thicker arrows). This block requires the initial value of the velocity as an initial condition; we define it in the "initial velocity" Constant block. Output from the first Integrator goes into the second Integrator, which integrates the velocity to get the position (also a vector). The initial condition for the position, [0, 4], is stored in the parameters of this second Integrator. The position vector is fed into a Demux block, which splits off the horizontal and vertical components of the position. These are fed into the XY Graph block, and also the vertical component is fed into a scope block so that we can see the height of the ball as a function of time. The hardest part is the computation of the acceleration:

$$\ddot{\mathbf{x}} = [0, -g] - c\|\dot{\mathbf{x}}\|\dot{\mathbf{x}}.$$

This is computed by adding the two terms on the right with the Sum block near the lower left. The value of $[0, -g]$ is stored in the "gravity" Constant block. The second term on the right is computed in the Product block labeled "Compute acceleration due to drag", which multiplies the velocity (a vector) by $-c$ times the speed (a scalar). We compute the speed by taking the dot product of the velocity with itself and then taking the square root; then we multiply by $-c$ in the Gain block in the middle bottom of the model. The Scope block in the lower right plots the ball's speed as a function of time.

(a)

With c set to 0 (no air resistance) and the initial velocity set to [80, 80], the ball follows a familiar parabolic trajectory, as seen in the following picture:

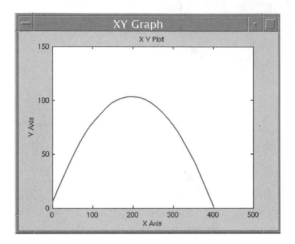

Note that the ball travels about 400 feet before hitting the ground, and so the trajectory is just about what is required for a home run in most ballparks. We can read off the flight time and final speed from the other two scopes:

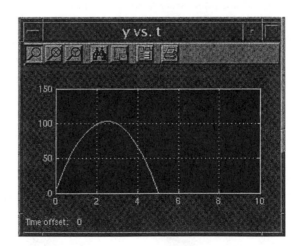

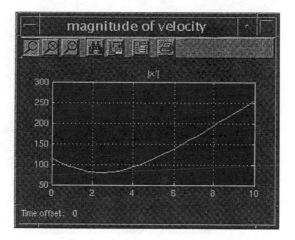

Thus the ball stays in the air about 5 seconds and is traveling about 115 ft/sec when it hits the ground.

Now let's see what happens when we factor in air resistance, again with the initial velocity set to [80, 80]. First we take c = 0.0017. The trajectory now looks like this:

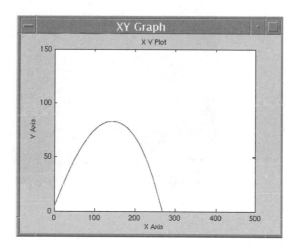

Note the enormous difference air resistance makes; the ball only travels about 270 feet. We can also investigate the flight time and speed with the other two scopes:

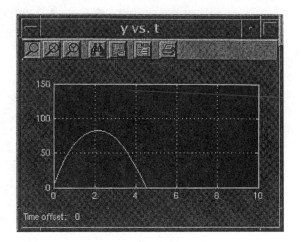

So the ball is about 80 feet high at its peak, and hits the ground in about $4\frac{1}{2}$ seconds. Its final speed can be read off from the picture:

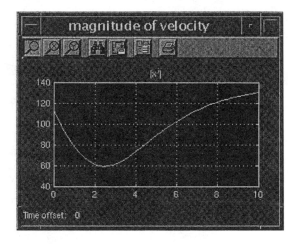

So the final speed is only about 80 ft/sec, which is much gentler on the hands of the outfielder than in the no-air-resistance case.

(b)

Let's now redo exactly the same calculation with $c = 0.0014$ (corresponding to playing in Denver). The ball's trajectory is now:

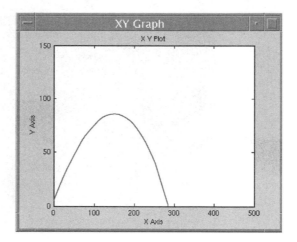

The ball goes about 285 feet, or about 15 feet further than when playing at sea level. This particular ball is probably an easy play, but with some hard-hit balls, those extra 15 feet could mean the difference between an out and a home run. If we look at the height scope for the Denver calculation, we see:

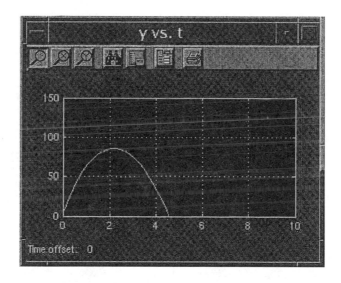

So there is a very small increase in the flight time. Similarly, if we look at the speed scope for the Denver calculation, we see:

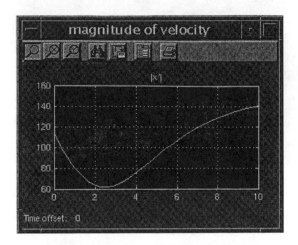

and so the final speed is a bit faster, about 83 ft/sec.

(c)

One would expect that batting averages would be higher in Denver, as indeed is the case according to Major League Baseball statistics.

Glossary

We present here the most commonly used MATLAB objects in six categories: operators, built-in constants, built-in functions, commands, graphics commands, and MATLAB programming constructs. Though MATLAB does not distinguish between commands and functions, it is convenient to think of a MATLAB function as we normally think of mathematical functions. A MATLAB function is something that can be evaluated or plotted; a command is something that manipulates data or expressions or that initiates a process.

We list each operator, function, and command together with a short description of its effect, followed by one or more examples. Many MATLAB commands can appear in a number of different forms, because you can apply them to different kinds of objects. In our examples, we have illustrated the most commonly used forms of the commands. Many commands also have numerous optional arguments; in this glossary, we have only included some very common options. You can find a full description of all forms of a command, and get a more complete accounting of all the optional arguments available for it, by reading the help text — which you can access either by typing **help <commandname>** or by invoking the Help Browser, shown in Figure G-1.

This glossary does not contain a comprehensive list of MATLAB commands. We have selected the commands that we feel are most important. You can find a comprehensive list in the Help Browser. The Help Browser is accessible from the Command Window by typing **helpdesk** or **helpwin**, or from the Launch Pad window in your Desktop under **MATLAB : Help.** Exactly what commands are covered in your documentation depends on your installation, in particular which *toolboxes* and what parts of the overall documentation files you installed.

☞ *See* Online Help *in Chapter 2 for a detailed description of the Help Browser.*

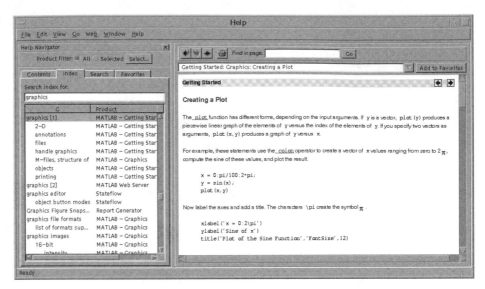

Figure G-1: The Help Browser, Opened to "Graphics".

MATLAB Operators

\   Left matrix division. **X = A\B** is the solution of the equation **A*X = B**. Type **help slash** for more information.

```
A = [1 0; 2 1]; B = [3; 5];
A\B
```

/   Ordinary scalar division, or right matrix division. For matrices, **A/B** is essentially equivalent to **A*inv(B)**. Type **help slash** for more information.

*   Scalar or matrix multiplication. See the online help for **mtimes**.

.   Not a true MATLAB operator. Used in conjunction with arithmetic operators to force element-by-element operations on arrays. Also used to access fields of a structure array.

```
a = [1 2 3]; b = [4 -6 8];
a.*b
syms x y; solve(x + y - 2, x - y); ans.x
```

.*   Element-by-element multiplication of arrays. See the previous entry and the online help for **times**.

^   Scalar or matrix powers. See the online help for **mpower**.

.^   Element-by-element powers. See the online help for **power**.

: Range operator, used for defining vectors and matrices. Type **help colon** for more information.

' Complex conjugate transpose of a matrix. See **ctranspose**. Also delimits the beginning and end of a string.

; Suppresses output of a MATLAB command, and can be used to separate commands on a command line. Also used to separate the rows of a matrix or column vector.

```
X = 0:0.1:30;
[1; 2; 3]
```

, Separates elements of a row of a matrix, or arguments to a command. Can also be used to separate commands on a command line.

.' Transpose of a matrix. See **transpose**.

... Line continuation operator. Cannot be used inside quoted strings. Type **help punct** for more information.

```
1 + 3 + 5 + 7 + 9 + 11 ...
  + 13 + 15 + 17
['This is a way to create very long strings ', ...
'that span more than one line. Note the square brackets.']
```

! Run command from operating system.

```
!C:\Programs\program.bat
```

% Comment. MATLAB will ignore the rest of the same line.

@ Creates a function handle.

```
fminbnd(@cos, 0, 2*pi)
```

Built-in Constants

eps Roughly the size of the computer's floating point round-off error; on most computers it is around 2×10^{-16}.

exp(1) $e = 2.71828\ldots$. Note that **e** has no special meaning.

i $i = \sqrt{-1}$. This assignment can be overridden, for example, if you want to use **i** as an index in a **for** loop. In that case **j** can be used for the imaginary unit.

Inf ∞. Also **inf** (in lower-case letters).

NaN Not a number. Used for indeterminate expressions such as $0/0$.

pi $\pi = 3.14159\ldots$.

Built-in Functions

abs $|x|$.

acos $\arccos x$.

asin $\arcsin x$.

atan $\arctan x$. Use **atan2** instead if you want the angular coordinate θ of the point (x, y).

bessel   Bessel functions; **besselj(n, x)** and **bessely(n, x)** are linearly independent solutions of Bessel's equation of order n.

conj   Gives the complex conjugate of a complex number.

   `conj(1 - 5*i)`

cos $\cos x$.

cosh $\cosh x$.

cot $\cot x$.

erf   The error function $\operatorname{erf}(x) = (2/\sqrt{\pi}) \int_0^x e^{-t^2}\, dt$.

exp e^x.

expm   Matrix exponential.

gamma   The gamma function $\Gamma(x) = \int_0^\infty e^{-t} t^{x-1} dt$ (when Re $x > 0$). The property $\Gamma(k+1) = k!$, for nonnegative integers k, is sometimes useful.

imag   imag(z), the imaginary part of a complex number.

log   The natural logarithm $\ln x = \log_e x$.

real   real(z), the real part of a complex number.

sec $\sec x$.

sech $\operatorname{sech} x$.

sign   Returns -1, 0, or 1, depending on whether the argument is negative, zero, or positive.

sin $\sin x$.

sinh $\sinh x$.

sqrt $\sqrt{x}$.

tan $\tan x$.

tanh $\tanh x$.

MATLAB Commands

addpath   Adds the specified directory to MATLAB's file search path.

```
addpath C:\my_mfiles
```

ans   A variable holding the value of the most recent unassigned output.

cd   Makes the specified directory the current (working) directory.

```
cd C:\mydocs\mfiles
```

char   Converts a symbolic expression to a string. Useful for defining inline functions.

```
syms x y
f = inline(char(sin(x)*sin(y)))
```

clear   Clears values and definitions for variables and functions. If you specify one or more variables, then only those variables are cleared.

```
clear
clear f g
```

collect   Collects coefficients of powers of the specified symbolic variable in a given symbolic expression.

```
syms x y
collect(x^2 - 2*x^2 + 3*x + x*y, x)
```

compose   Composition of functions.

```
syms x y; f = exp(x); g = sin(y); h = compose(f, g)
```

ctranspose   Conjugate transpose of a matrix. Usually invoked with the ' operator. Equivalent to **transpose** for real matrices.

```
A = [1 3 i]
A'
```

D   Not a true MATLAB command. Used in **dsolve** to denote differentiation. See **diff**.

```
dsolve('x*Dy + y = sin(x)', 'x')
```

delete   Deletes a file.

```
delete <filename>
```

det   The determinant of a matrix.

```
det([1 3; 4 5])
```

diag   Gives a square matrix with a prescribed diagonal vector, or picks out the diagonal in a square matrix.

```
V = [2 3 4 5]; diag(V)
X = [2 3; 4 5]; diag(X)
```

diary Writes a transcript of a MATLAB session to a file.

```
diary <filename>
diary off
```

diff Symbolic differentiation operator (also difference operator).

```
syms x; diff(x^3)
diff('x*y^2', 'y')
```

dir Lists the files in the current working directory. Similar to **ls**.

disp Displays output without first giving its name.

```
x = 5.6; disp(x)
syms x; disp(x^2)
disp('This will print without quotes.')
```

double Gives a double-precision value for either a numeric or symbolic quantity. Applied to a string, **double** returns a vector of ASCII codes for the characters in the string.

```
z = sym('pi'); double(z)
double('think')
```

dsolve Symbolic ODE solver. By default, the independent variable is t, but a different variable can be specified as the last argument.

```
dsolve('D2y - x*y = 0', 'x')
dsolve('Dy + y^2 = 0', 'y(0) = 1', 'x')
[x, y] = dsolve('Dx = 2x + y', 'Dy = - x')
```

echo Turns on or off the echoing of commands inside script M-files.

edit Opens the specified M-file in the Editor/Debugger.

```
edit mymfile
```

eig Computes eigenvalues and eigenvectors of a square matrix.

```
eig([2, 3; 4, 5])
[e, v] = eig([1, 0, 0; 1, 1, 1; 1, 2, 4])
```

end Last entry of a vector. Also a programming command.

```
v(end)
v(3:end)
```

eval Used for evaluating strings as MATLAB expressions. Useful in M-files.

```
eval('cos(x)')
```

expand Expands an algebraic expression.

```
syms x y; expand((x - y)^2)
```

eye The identity matrix of the specified size.

```
eye(5)
```

factor Factors a polynomial.

```
syms x y; factor(x^4 - y^4)
```

feval Evaluates a function specified by a string. Useful in function M-files.

```
feval('exp', 1)
```

find Finds the indices of nonzero elements of a vector or matrix.

```
X = [2 0 5]; find(X)
```

fminbnd Finds the smallest (approximate) value of a function over an interval.

```
fminbnd('x^4 - x^2 + 1', 0, 1)
f = inline('x^3 - 7*x^2 - 5*x + 2', 'x'); fminbnd(f, 4, 6)
```

format Specifies the output format for numerical variables.

```
format long
```

fzero Tries to find a zero of the specified function near a given starting point or on a specified interval.

```
fzero(inline('cos(x) - x'), 1)
fzero(@cos, [-pi 0])
```

guide Opens the GUI Design Environment.

```
guide mygui
```

help Asks for documentation for a MATLAB command. See also **lookfor**.

```
help factor
```

inline Constructs a MATLAB inline function from a string expression.

```
f = inline('x^5 - x'); f(3)
sol = dsolve('Dy = x^2 + y', 'y(0) = 2', 'x');
fsol = inline(vectorize(sol), 'x')
```

int Integration operator for both definite and indefinite integrals.

```
int('1/(1 + x^2)', 'x')
syms x; int(exp(-x), x, 0, Inf)
```

inv Inverse of a square matrix.

```
inv([1 2; 3 5])
```

jacobian Computes the Jacobian matrix, or for a scalar function, the symbolic gradient.

```
syms x y; f = x^2*y^3; jacobian(f)
```

length   Returns the number of elements in a vector or string.

```
length('abcde')
```

limit   Finds a two-sided limit, if it exists. Use **'right'** or **'left'** for one-sided limits.

```
syms x; limit(sin(x)/x, x, 0)
syms x; limit(1/x, x, Inf, 'left')
```

linspace   Generates a vector of linearly spaced points.

```
linspace(0, 2*pi, 30)
```

load   Loads Workspace variables from a disk file.

```
load filename
```

lookfor   Searches for a specified string in the first line of all M-files found in the MATLAB path.

```
lookfor ode
```

ls   Lists files in the current working directory. Similar to **dir**.

maple   String access to the Maple kernel; generally is used in the form **maple('function', 'arg')**. Not available in the Student Version.

```
maple('help', 'csgn')
```

max   Computes the arithmetic maximum of the entries of a vector.

```
X = [3 5 1 -6 23 -56 100]; max(X)
```

mean   Computes the arithmetic average of the entries of a vector.

```
X = [3 5 1 -6 23 -56 100]; mean(X)
syms x y z; X = [x y z]; mean(X)
```

median   Computes the arithmetic median of the entries of a vector.

```
X = [3 5 1 -6 23 -56 100]; median(X)
```

min   Computes the arithmetic minimum of the entries of a vector.

```
X = [3 5 1 -6 23 -56 100]; min(X)
```

more   Turns on (or off) page-by-page scrolling of MATLAB output. Use the SPACE BAR to advance to the next page, the RETURN key to advance line-by-line, and Q to abort the output.

```
more on
more off
```

notebook   Opens an M-book (Windows only).

```
notebook problem1.doc
notebook -setup
```

num2str Converts a number to a string. Useful in programming.

```
constant = ['a' num2str(1)]
```

ode45 Numerical ODE solver for first-order equations. See MATLAB's online help for **ode45** for a list of other MATLAB ODE solvers.

```
f = inline('t^2 + y', 't', 'y')
[x, y] = ode45(f, [0 10], 1);
plot(x, y)
```

ones Creates a matrix of ones.

```
ones(3)
ones(3, 1)
```

open Opens a file. The way this is done depends on the filename extension.

```
open myfigure.fig
```

path Without an argument, displays the search path. With an argument, sets the search path. Type **help path** for details.

pretty Displays a symbolic expression in a more readable format.

```
syms x y; expr = x/(x - 3)/(x + 2/y)
pretty(expr)
```

prod Computes the product of the entries of a vector.

```
X = [3 5 1 -6 23 -56 100]; prod(X)
```

pwd Shows the name of the current (working) directory.

quadl Numerical integration command. In MATLAB 5.3 or earlier, use **quad8** instead.

```
format long; quadl('sin(exp(x))', 0, 1)
g = inline('sin(exp(x))'); quad8(g, 0, 1)
```

quit Terminates a MATLAB session.

rand Random number generator; gives a random number between 0 and 1.

rank Gives the rank of a matrix.

```
A = [2 3 5; 4 6 8]; rank(A)
```

roots Finds the roots of a polynomial whose coefficients are given by the elements of the vector argument of **roots**.

```
roots([1 2 2])
```

round Rounds a number to the nearest integer.

save Saves Workspace variables to a specified file. See also **diary** and **load**.

```
save filename
```

sim   Runs a SIMULINK model.

```
sim('model')
```

simple   Attempts to simplify an expression using multiple methods.

```
syms x y; [expression, how] = simple(sin(x)*cos(y) + cos(x)*sin(y))
```

simplify   Attempts to simplify an expression symbolically.

```
syms x; simplify(1/(1 + x)^2 - 1/(1 - x)^2)
```

simulink   Opens the SIMULINK library.

size   Returns the number of rows and the number of columns in a matrix.

```
A = [1 3 2; 4 1 5]
[r, c] = size(A)
```

solve   Solves an equation or set of equations. If the right-hand side of the equation is omitted, '0' is assumed.

```
solve('2*x^2 - 3*x + 6')
[x, y] = solve('x + 3*y = 4', '-x - 5*y = 3', 'x', 'y')
```

sound   Plays a vector through the computer speakers.

```
sound(sin(0:0.1*pi:1000*pi))
```

strcat   Concatenates two or more strings.

```
strcat('This ', 'is ', 'a ', 'long ', 'string.')
```

str2num   Converts a string to a number. Useful in programming.

```
constant = 'a7'
index = str2num(constant(2))
```

subs   Substitutes for parts of an expression.

```
subs('x^3 - 4*x + 1', 'x', 2)
subs('sin(x)^2 + cos(x)', 'sin(x)', 'z')
```

sum   Sums a vector, or sums the columns of a matrix.

```
k = 1:10; sum(k)
```

sym   Creates a symbolic variable or number.

```
sym pi
x = sym('x')
constant = sym('1/2')
```

syms   Shortcut for creating symbolic variables. The command **syms x** is equivalent to **x = sym('x')**.

```
syms x y z
```

symsum Performs a symbolic summation of a vector, possibly with infinitely many entries.

```
syms x k n; symsum(x^k, k, 0, n)
syms n; symsum(n^(-2), n, 1, Inf)
```

taylor Gives a Taylor polynomial approximation of a specified order (the default is 5) at a specified point (default is 0).

```
syms x; taylor(cos(x), 8, 0)
taylor(exp(1/x), 10, Inf)
```

transpose Transpose of a matrix (compare **ctranspose**). Converts a column vector to a row vector, and vice versa. Usually invoked with the **.'** operator.

```
A = [1 3 4]
A.'
```

type Displays the contents of a specified file.

```
type myfile.m
```

vectorize Vectorizes a symbolic expression. Useful in defining inline functions.

```
f = inline(vectorize('x^2 - 1/x'))
```

vpa Evaluates an expression to the specified degree of accuracy using variable precision arithmetic.

```
vpa('1/3', 20)
```

whos Lists current information on all the variables in the Workspace.

zeros Creates a matrix of zeros.

```
zeros(10)
zeros(3, 1)
```

Graphics Commands

area Produces a shaded graph of the area between the x axis and a curve.

```
X = 0:0.1:4*pi; Y = sin(X); area(X, Y)
```

axes Creates an empty figure window.

axis Sets axis scaling and appearance.

```
axis([xmin xmax ymin ymax]) — sets ranges for the axes.
axis tight — sets the axis limits to the full range of the data.
axis equal — makes the horizontal and vertical scales equal.
axis square — makes the axis box square.
axis off — hides the axes and tick marks.
```

bar   Draws a bar graph.

```
bar([2, 7, 1.5, 6])
```

cla   Clear axes.

close   Closes the current figure window; **close all** closes all figure windows.

colormap   Sets the colormap features of the current figure; type **help graph3d** to see examples of colormaps.

```
X = 0:0.1:4*pi; Y = sin(X); colormap cool
```

comet   Displays an animated parametric plot.

```
t = 0:0.1:4*pi; comet(t.*cos(t), t.*sin(t))
```

contour   Plots the level curves of a function of two variables; usually used with **meshgrid**.

```
[X, Y] = meshgrid(-3:0.1:3, -3:0.1:3);
contour(X, Y, X.^2 - Y.^2)
```

contourf   Filled contour plot. Often used with **colormap**.

```
[X,Y] = meshgrid(-2:0.1:2, -2:0.1:2); contourf(X, Y, X.^2 - Y.^3);
colormap autumn
```

ezcontour   Easy plot command for contour or level curves.

```
ezcontour('x^2 - y^2')
syms x y; ezcontour(x - y^2)
```

ezmesh   Easy plot command for mesh view of surfaces.

```
ezmesh('x^2 + y^2')
syms x y; ezmesh(x*y)
```

ezplot   Easy plot command for symbolic expressions.

```
ezplot('exp(-x^2)', [-5, 5])
syms x; ezplot(sin(x))
```

ezplot3   Easy plot command for 3D parametric curves.

```
ezplot3('cos(t)', 'sin(t)', 't')
syms t; ezplot3(1 - cos(t), t - sin(t), t, [0 4*pi])
```

ezsurf   Easy plot command for standard shaded view of surfaces.

```
ezsurf('(x^2 + y^2)*exp(-(x^2 + y^2))')
syms x y; ezsurf(sin(x*y), [-pi pi -pi pi])
```

figure   Creates a new figure window.

fill   Creates a filled polygon. See also **patch**.

```
fill([0 1 1 0], [0 0 1 1], 'b'); axis equal tight
```

findobj   Finds graphics objects with specified property values.

```
findobj('Type', 'Line')
```

gca   Gets current axes.

gcf   Gets current figure.

get   Gets properties of a figure.

```
get(gcf)
```

getframe   Command to get the frames of a movie or animation.

```
T = 0:0.1:2*pi;
for j = 1:12
    plot(5*cos(j*pi/6) + cos(T), 5*sin(j*pi/6) + sin(T));
    axis([-6 6 -6 6]);
    M(j) = getframe;
end
movie(M)
```

ginput   Gathers coordinates from a figure using the mouse (press the RETURN key to finish).

```
[X, Y] = ginput
```

grid   Puts a grid on a figure.

gtext   Places a text label using the mouse.

```
gtext('Region of instability')
```

hist   Draws a histogram.

```
for j = 1:100
    Y(j) = rand;
end
hist(Y)
```

hold   Holds the current graph. Superimposes any new graphics generated by MATLAB on top of the current figure.

```
hold on
hold off
```

legend   Creates a legend for a figure.

```
t = 0:0.1:2*pi;
plot(t, cos(t), t, sin(t))
legend('cos(t)', 'sin(t)')
```

loglog   Creates a log-log plot.

```
x = 0.0001:0.1:12; loglog(x, x.^5)
```

mesh   Draws a mesh surface.

```
[X,Y] = meshgrid(-2:.1:2, -2:.1:2);
mesh(X, Y, sin(pi*X).*cos(pi*Y))
```

meshgrid   Creates a vector array that can be used as input to a graphics command, for example, **contour, quiver,** or **surf.**

```
[X, Y] = meshgrid(0:0.1:1, 0:0.1:2)
contour(X, Y, X.^2 + Y.^2)
```

movie   Plays back a movie. See the entry for **getframe.**

patch   Creates a filled polygon or colored surface patch. See also **fill.**

```
t = (0:1:5)*2*pi/5; patch(cos(t), sin(t), 'r'); axis equal
```

pie   Draws a pie plot of the data in the input vector.

```
Z = [34 5 32 6]; pie(Z)
```

plot   Plots vectors of data.

```
X = [0:0.1:2];
plot(X, X.^3)
```

plot3   Plots curves in 3D space.

```
t = [0:0.1:30];
plot3(t, t.*cos(t), t.*sin(t))
```

polar   Polar coordinate plot command.

```
theta = 0:0.1:2*pi; rho = theta; polar(theta, rho)
```

print   Sends the contents of the current figure window to the printer or to a file.

```
print
print -deps picture.eps
```

quiver   Plots a (numerical) vector field in the plane.

```
[x, y] = meshgrid(-4:0.5:4, -4:0.5:4);
quiver(x, y, x.*(y - 2), y.*x); axis tight
```

semilogy   Creates a semilog plot, with logarithmic scale along the vertical axis.

```
x = 0:0.1:12; semilogy(x, exp(x))
```

set   Set properties of a figure.

```
set(gcf, 'Color', [0, 0.8, 0.8])
```

subplot   Breaks the figure window into a grid of smaller plots.

```
subplot(2, 2, 1), ezplot('x^2')
subplot(2, 2, 2), ezplot('x^3')
```

```
subplot(2, 2, 3), ezplot('x^4')
subplot(2, 2, 4), ezplot('x^5')
```

surf   Draws a solid surface.

```
[X,Y] = meshgrid(-2:.1:2, -2:.1:2);
surf(X, Y, sin(pi*X).*cos(pi*Y))
```

text   Annotates a figure, by placing text at specified coordinates.

```
text(x, y, 'string')
```

title   Assigns a title to the current figure window.

```
title 'Nice Picture'
```

xlabel   Assigns a label to the horizontal coordinate axis.

```
xlabel('Year')
```

ylabel   Assigns a label to the vertical coordinate axis.

```
ylabel('Population')
```

view   Specifies a point from which to view a 3D graph.

```
ezsurf('(x^2 + y^2)*exp(-(x^2 + y^2))'); view([0 0 1])
syms x y; ezmesh(x*y); view([1 0 0])
```

zoom   Rescales a figure by a specified factor; **zoom** by itself enables use of the mouse for zooming in or out.

```
zoom
zoom(4)
```

MATLAB Programming

any   True if any element of an array is nonzero.

```
if any(imag(x) ~= 0); error('Inputs must be real.'); end
```

all   True if all the elements of an array are nonzero.

break   Breaks out of a **for** or **while** loop.

case   Used to delimit cases after a **switch** statement.

computer   Outputs the type of computer on which MATLAB is running.

dbclear   Clears breakpoints from a file.

```
dbclear all
```

dbcont   Returns to an M-file after stopping at a breakpoint.

dbquit   Terminates an M-file after stopping at a breakpoint.

dbstep   Executes an M-file line-by-line after stopping at a breakpoint.

dbstop   Insert a breakpoint in a file.

```
dbstop in <filename> at <linenumber>
```

dos   Runs a command from the operating system, saving the result in a variable. Similar to **unix**.

end   Terminates an **if**, **for**, **while**, or **switch** statement.

else   Alternative in a conditional statement. See **if**.

elseif   Nested alternative in a conditional statement. See the online help for **if**.

error   Displays an error message and aborts execution of an M-file.

find   Reports indices of nonzero elements of an array.

```
n = find(isspace(mystring));
if ~isempty(n)
    firstword = mystring(1:n(1)-1);
    restofstring = mystring(n(1)+1:end);
end
```

for   Repeats a block of commands a specified number of times. Must be terminated by **end**.

```
close; axes; hold on
t = -1:0.05:1;
for k = 0:10
    plot(t, t.^k)
end
```

function   Used on the first line of an M-file to make it a function M-file.

```
function y = myfunction(x)
```

if   Allows conditional execution of MATLAB statements. Must be terminated by **end**.

```
if (x >= 0)
sqrt(x)
else
error('Invalid input.')
end
```

input   Prompts for user input.

```
answer = input('Please enter [x, y] coordinates: ')
```

isa   Checks whether an object is of a given class (**double**, **sym**, etc.).

```
isa(x, 'sym')
```

ischar   True if an array is a character string.

isempty   True if an array is empty.

isfinite   Checks whether elements of an array are finite.

```
isfinite(1./[-1 0 1])
```

ishold   True if **hold on** is in effect.

isinf   Checks whether elements of an array are infinite.

isletter   Checks whether elements of a string are letters of the alphabet.

```
str = 'remove my spaces'; str(isletter(str))
```

isnan   Checks whether elements of an array are "not-a-number" (which results from indeterminate forms such as 0/0).

```
isnan([-1 0 1]/0)
```

isnumeric   True if an object is of a numeric class.

ispc   True if MATLAB is running on a Windows computer.

isreal   True if an array consists only of real numbers.

isspace   Checks whether elements of a string are spaces, tabs, etc.

isunix   True if MATLAB is running on a UNIX computer.

keyboard   Returns control from an M-file to the keyboard. Useful for debugging M-files.

mex   Compiles a MEX program.

nargin   Returns the number of input arguments passed to a function M-file.

```
if (nargin < 2); error('Wrong number of arguments'); end
```

nargout   Returns the number of output arguments requested from a function M-file.

otherwise   Used to delimit an alternative case after a **switch** statement.

pause   Suspends execution of an M-file until the user presses a key.

return   Terminates execution of an M-file early or returns to an M-file after a **keyboard** command.

```
if abs(err) < tol; return; end
```

switch   Alternative to **if** that allows branching to more than two cases. Must be terminated by **end**.

```
switch num
case 1
    disp('Yes.')
case 0
```

```
        disp('No.')
    otherwise
        disp('Maybe.')
    end
```

unix   Runs a command from the operating system, saving the result in a variable. Similar to **dos**.

varargin   Used in a function M-file to handle a variable number of inputs.

varargout   Used in a function M-file to allow a variable number of outputs.

warning   Displays a warning message.

```
warning('Taking the square root of negative number.')
```

while   Repeats a block of commands until a condition fails to be met. Must be terminated by **end**.

```
mysum = 0;
x = 1;
while x > eps
    mysum = mysum + x;
    x = x/2;
end
mysum
```

Index

The index uses the same conventions for fonts that are used throughout the book. MATLAB commands, such as **dsolve**, are printed in a boldface typewriter font. Menu options, such as **File**, are printed in boldface. Names of keys, such as ENTER, are printed in small caps. Everything else is printed in a standard font.